The exact date of the composition of Beowulf is not known. T[...] around 1000 AD. The death of Hygelac, Beowulf's lord, is recorded in [...] e most probable date of Beowulf's composition, then, is thought to be [...] epic poem, not a novel. This distinction should be understood, because the qualities that make this a piece of great poetry will probably seem irksome if you are trying to read it as prose. The translation I have chosen to use is that of Francis Gummere, from The Harvard Classics vol. 49, ©1910 P.F. Collier & Son; copyright expired. The E-text conversion is by Robin Katsuya-Corbet; released into the public domain July, 1993. I chose this version because I like the way it preserves the essential feeling of Old English verse, particularly in its meter and alliteration. One side-effect, however, is that you will find a good many terms in the script which are no longer in colloquial use. Here, then, is a glossary of the ones I judge most likely to confuse the modern reader:

Atheling : a prince

Bairn : offspring ('Beanstan's Bairn' refers to Breca)

Bale (of battle) : woe, sorrow

Battle-sark braided : a shirt of woven armor (i.e., chain mail)

Beseems : befits, is seemly or suitable

(flooding) **Billow** : wave

(breastplate and) **Board** : shield

Brand : sword

Breaker-of-rings : one who produces (breaks out) or divides (breaks up) the ring-shaped armbands, necklaces, rings, and brooches prized by the vikings

Breast-hoard : (poetic description for) unexpressed feelings

Burgstead : town environs

(far) **Descried** : seen (from afar)

Dole : grief

Erewhile - heretofore; from a while ago until now

Erst : previously

Fain : Glad, gladly

Falchions : swords

(the) Flood : the Ocean

Frank : member of a West German people who occupied much of Gaul (France) and the Netherlands

Frisian : inhabitant of the Frisian islands, in the North Sea

Front : confront

Geat : a member of the clan of the Geats Beowulf's tribe), inhabiting Geatland (now Southern Sweden)

Glee-wood : wooden musical instruments

Gripe : grip, hand, arm

Hale (from the hero-play): healthy

Hale (to his home) : haul, carry

Hart : male deer, stag

Healfdene's son : Hrothgar

Heardred : Hygelac's son

Hides : Old English units of land measurement

Hoary - ancient

Hrones Headland : a sea-cliff somewhere in Sweden. (Chickering translates it as "Whale's Cliff").

Hurly : mighty

Hygelac : Beowulf's lord and kinsman

Main : strength

(The) **Main** : the high sea

March-riever : borderland robber, bandit

Meet : proper, fitting

Nicors : sea serpents

Or lief or loath : gladly or reluctantly

Recks : has regard for

Reft - stolen

Ring-dight : ring-dressed; decorated with circular motifs

Rounds and rings : coins and jewelry

Scyldings : Sons of Scyld (a Danish chieftain)

Scylfings : a Swedish clan

Sennight : seven nights

Sovran : sovereign, lord

Stay (in council) : a support

Thanes : retainers, henchmen

Vaunt : boast

Waegmunding : another name for Beowulf's clan/ family line

Wan : pallid, sickly

"Warriors'-friends" : false friendship

Weder-folk, Weders : yet another name for the Geats, Beowulf's clansmen

Weeds (of war) : clothing (armor)

Ween : predict

Welkin : the clouds, sky, or heavens

Welter (of waters) : turmoil

Weohstan's bairn : Wiglaf (son of Weohstan, a Geatish noble)

Whelmed : overcome

Wight : creature, person

Winsome : happy, cheerful

Wise (of thee) : with regard to

Wont : to be used to, or to strive for

Oft Scyld the Scefing from squadroned foes,
from many a tribe, the mead-bench tore,
awing the earls. Since erst he lay
friendless, a foundling, fate repaid him:
for he waxed under welkin, in wealth he throve,
till before him the folk, both far and near,
who house by the whalepath, heard his mandate,
gave him gifts: a good king he!

To him an heir was afterward born,
a son in his halls, with world's renown.
Famed was this Beow: far flew the boast of him,
son of Scyld, in the Scandian lands.

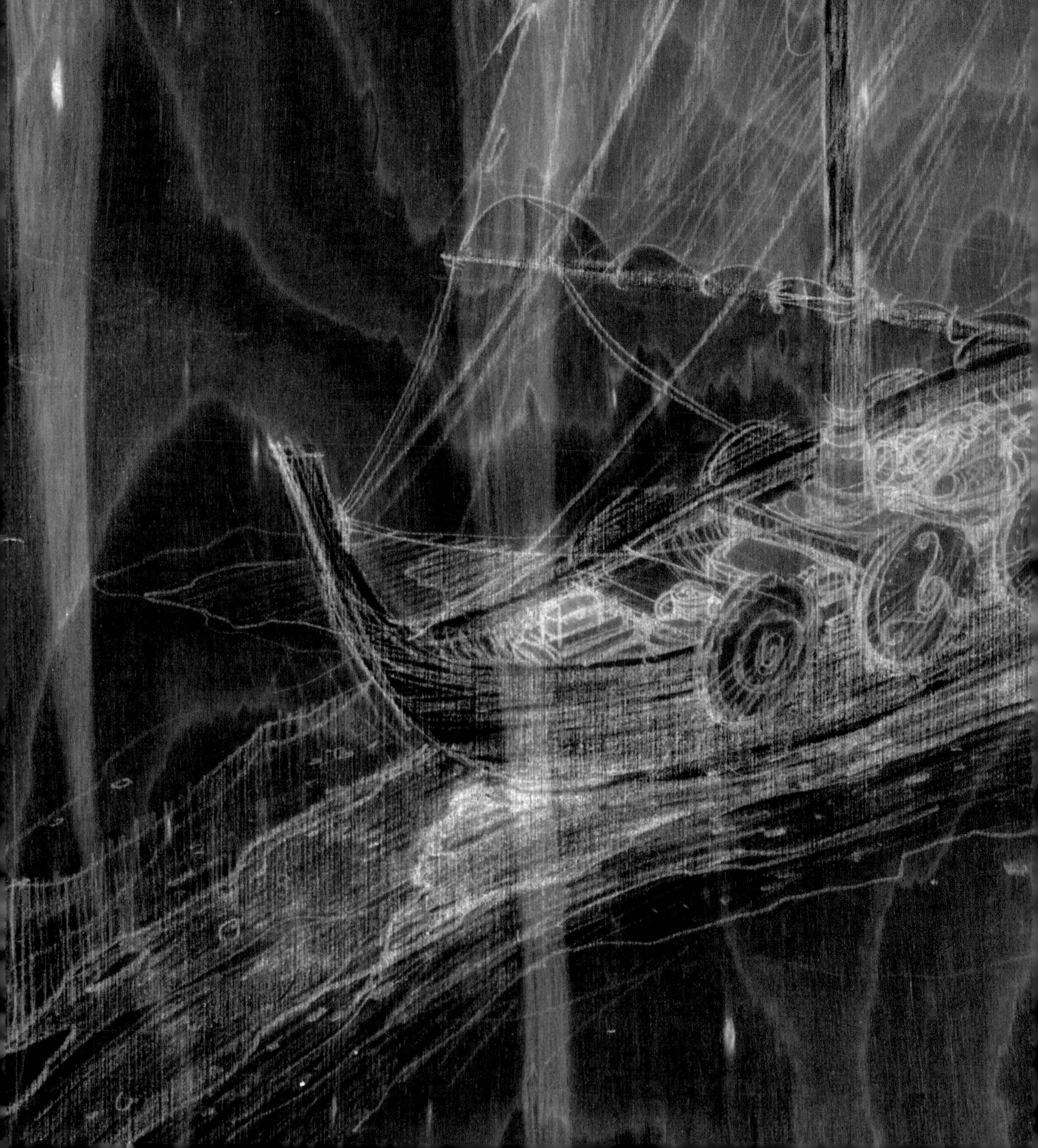

Then forth did fare, at the fated moment,
sturdy Scyld, into the shelter of God.
In the roadstead rocked a ring-dight vessel,
ice-flecked, outbound, atheling's barge:
there laid they down their darling lord
on the breast of the boat, the breaker-of-rings,
by the mast the mighty one. Many a treasure
fetched from afar was freighted with him.
No ship have I known so nobly decked
with weapons of war and weeds of battle,
with breastplate and blade: on his bosom lay
a heaped hoard that hence should go
far o'er the flood with him floating away.

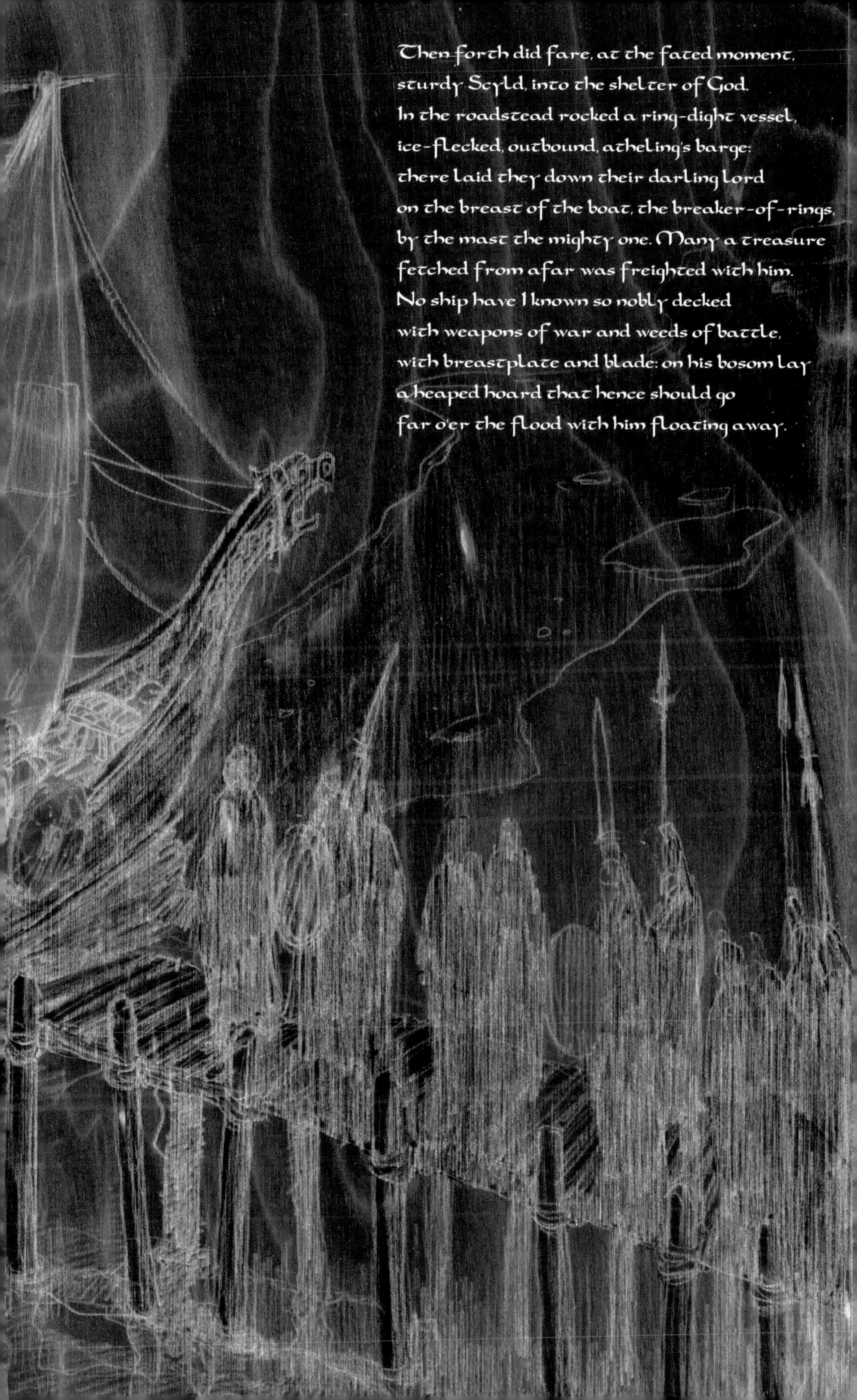

Now Beow bode in the burg of the Scyldings,
leader beloved, and long he ruled
in fame with all folk, since his father had gone
away from the world, till awoke an heir,
haughty Healfdene, who held through life,
sage and sturdy, the Scyldings glad.
Then, one after one, there woke to him,
to the chieftain of clansmen, children four:

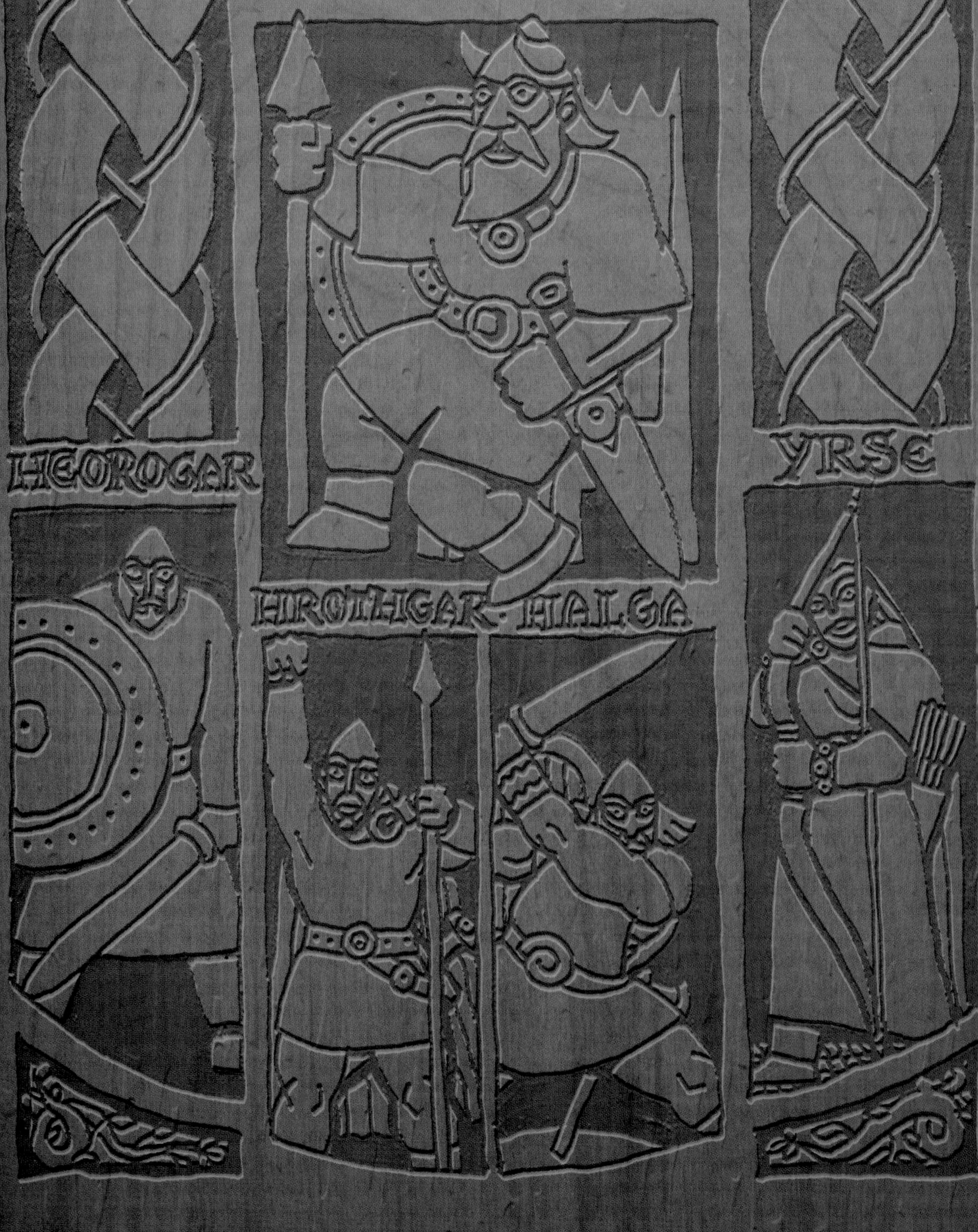
HEOROGAR
YRSE
HROTHGAR · HALGA

BOOK 1

To Hrothgar was given such glory of war,
such honor of combat, that all his kin
obeyed him gladly till great grew his band
of youthful comrades. It came in his mind
to bid his henchmen a hall uprear,
a master mead-house, mightier far
than ever was seen by the sons of earth,
and within it then, to old and young
he would all allot that the Lord had sent him,
save only the land and the lives of his men.

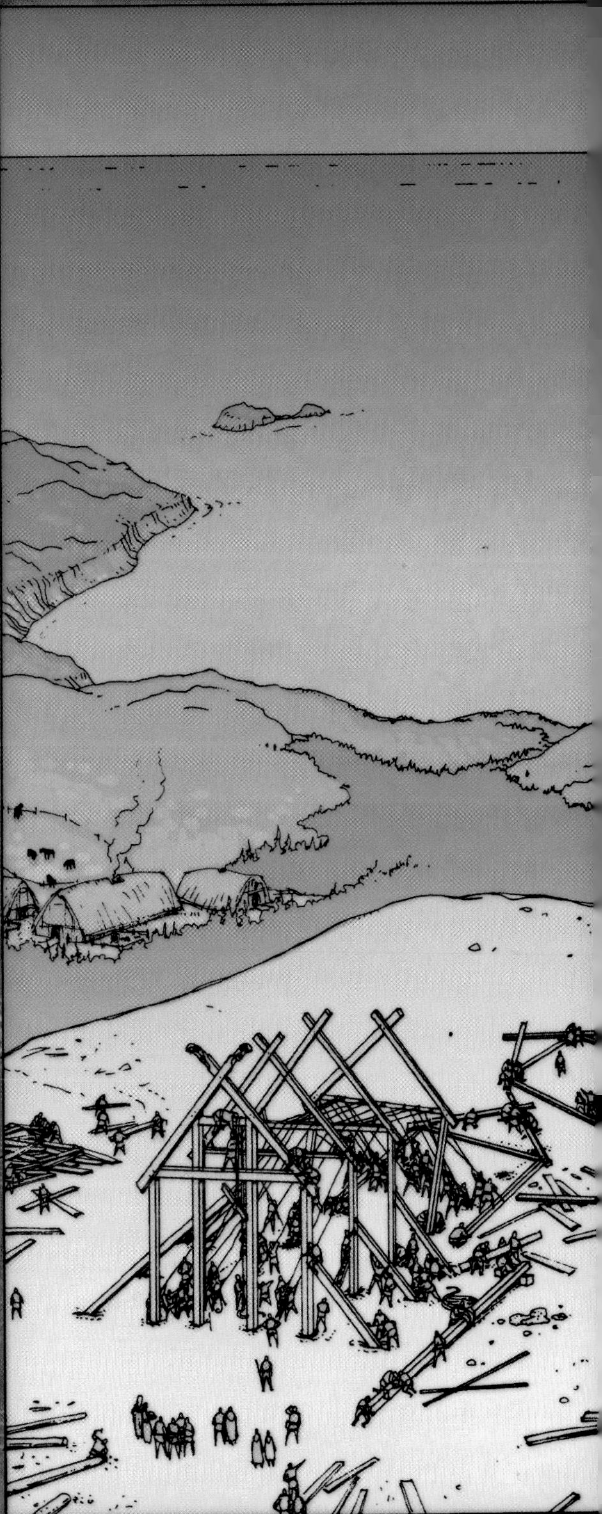

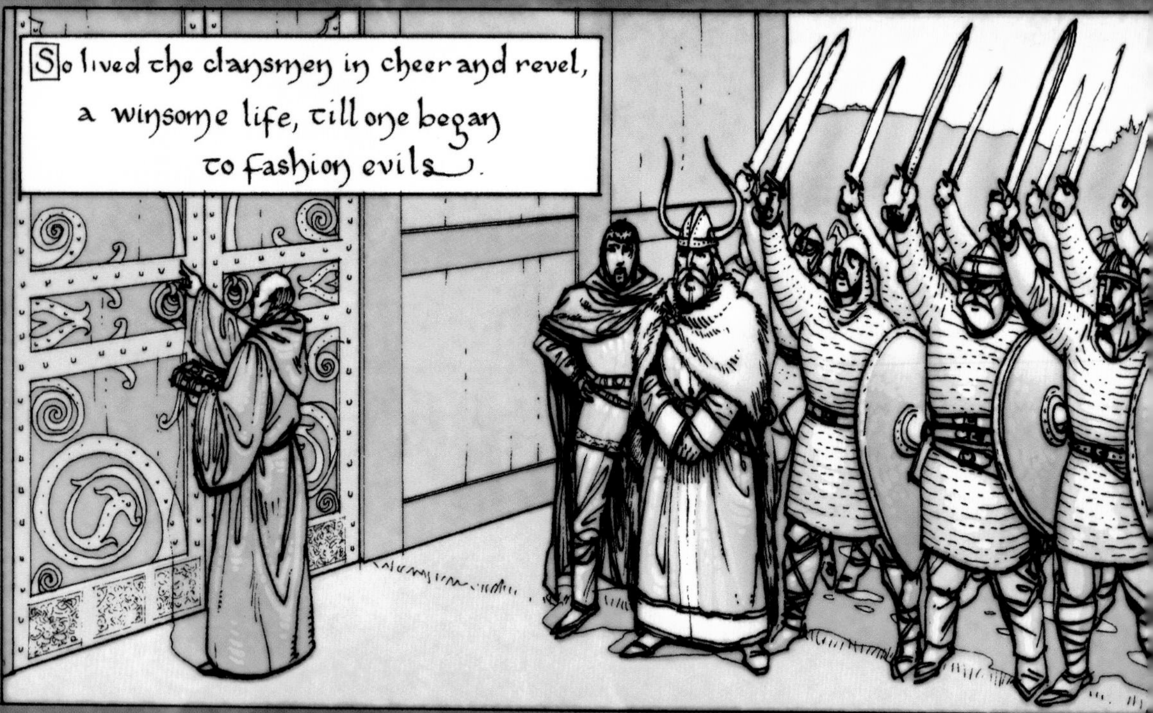
So lived the clansmen in cheer and revel,
a winsome life, till one began
to fashion evils.

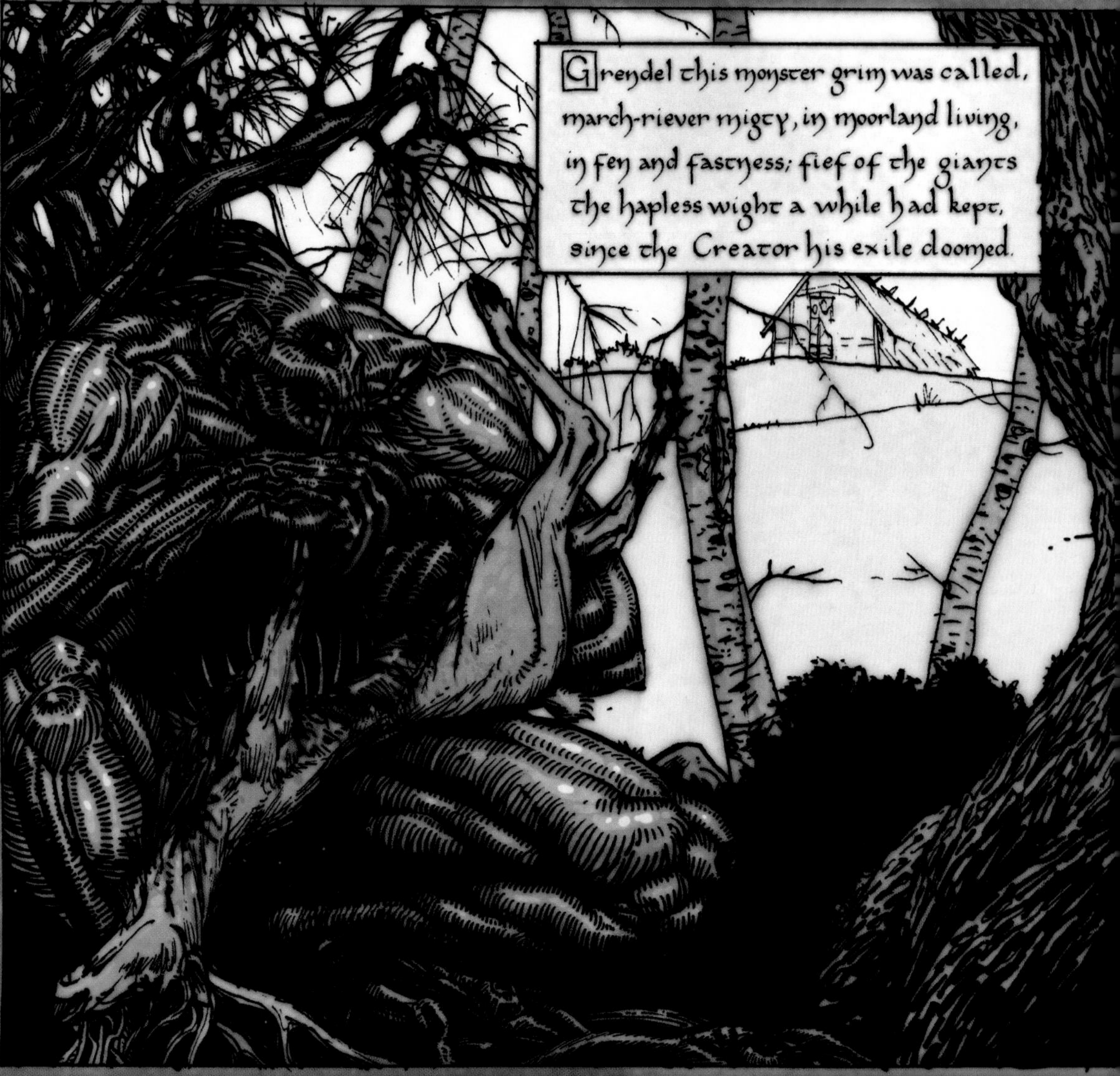
Grendel this monster grim was called,
march-riever migty, in moorland living,
in fen and fastness; fief of the giants
the hapless wight a while had kept,
since the Creator his exile doomed.

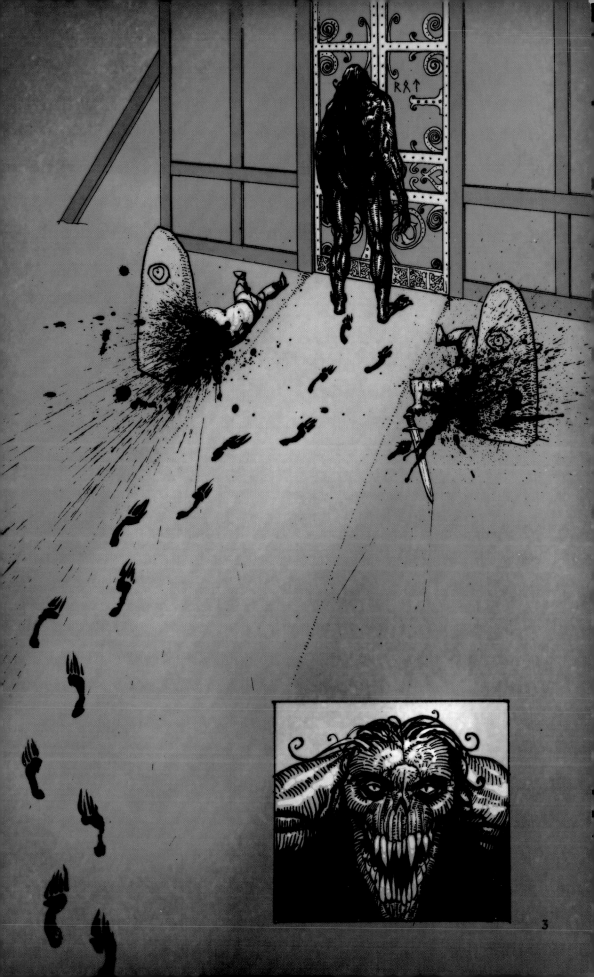

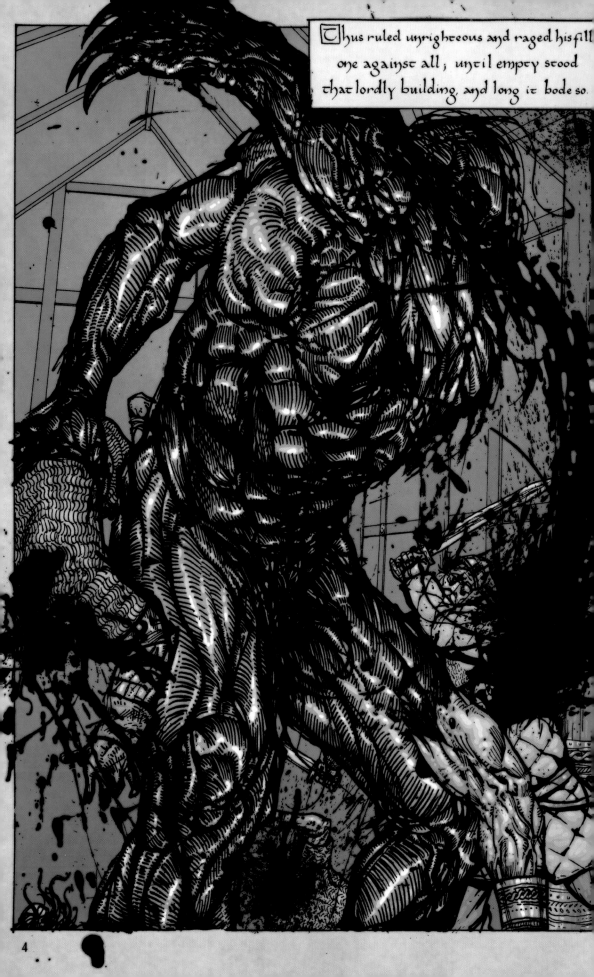

Thus ruled unrighteous and raged his fill one against all; until empty stood that lordly building, and long it bode so.

4

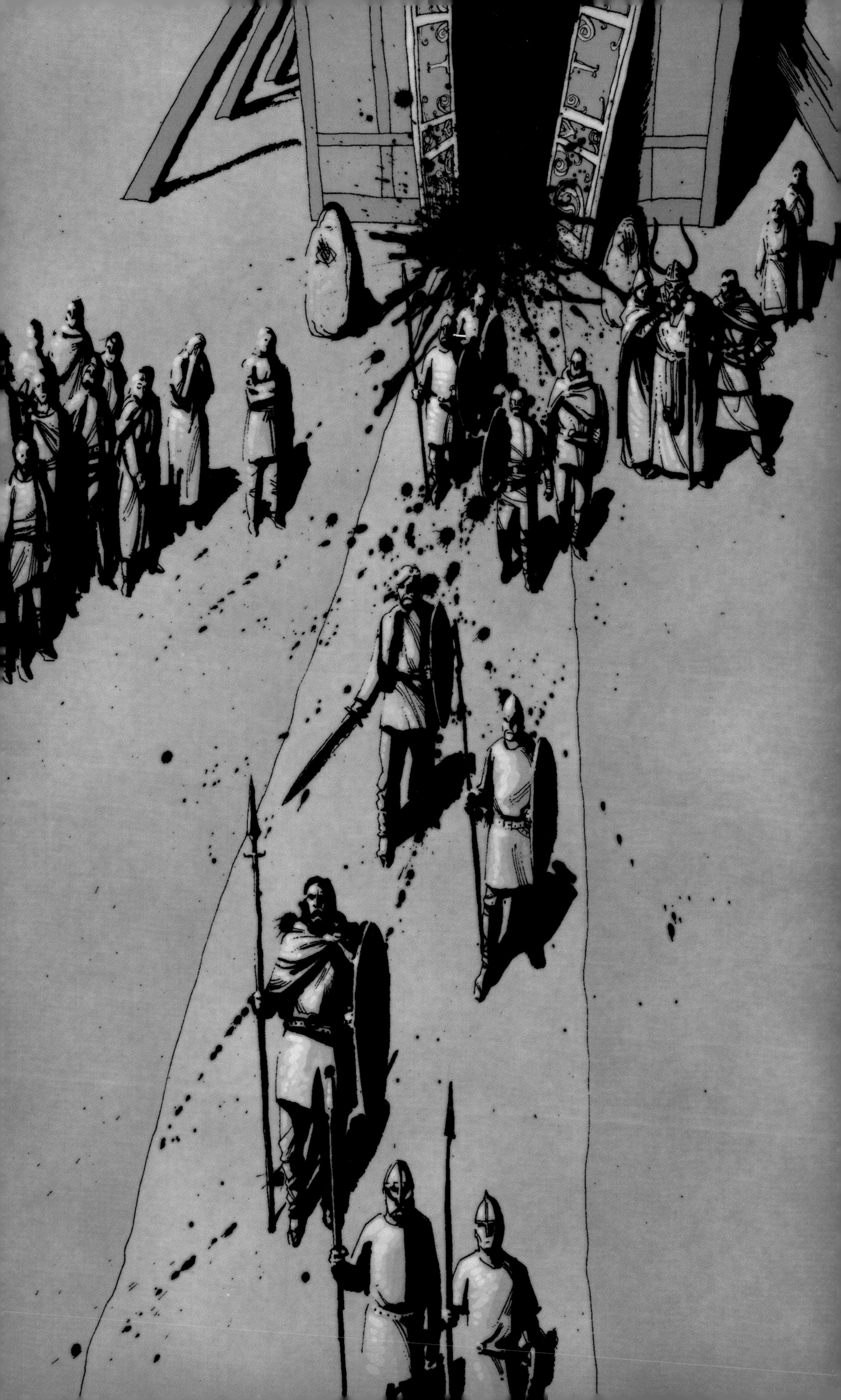

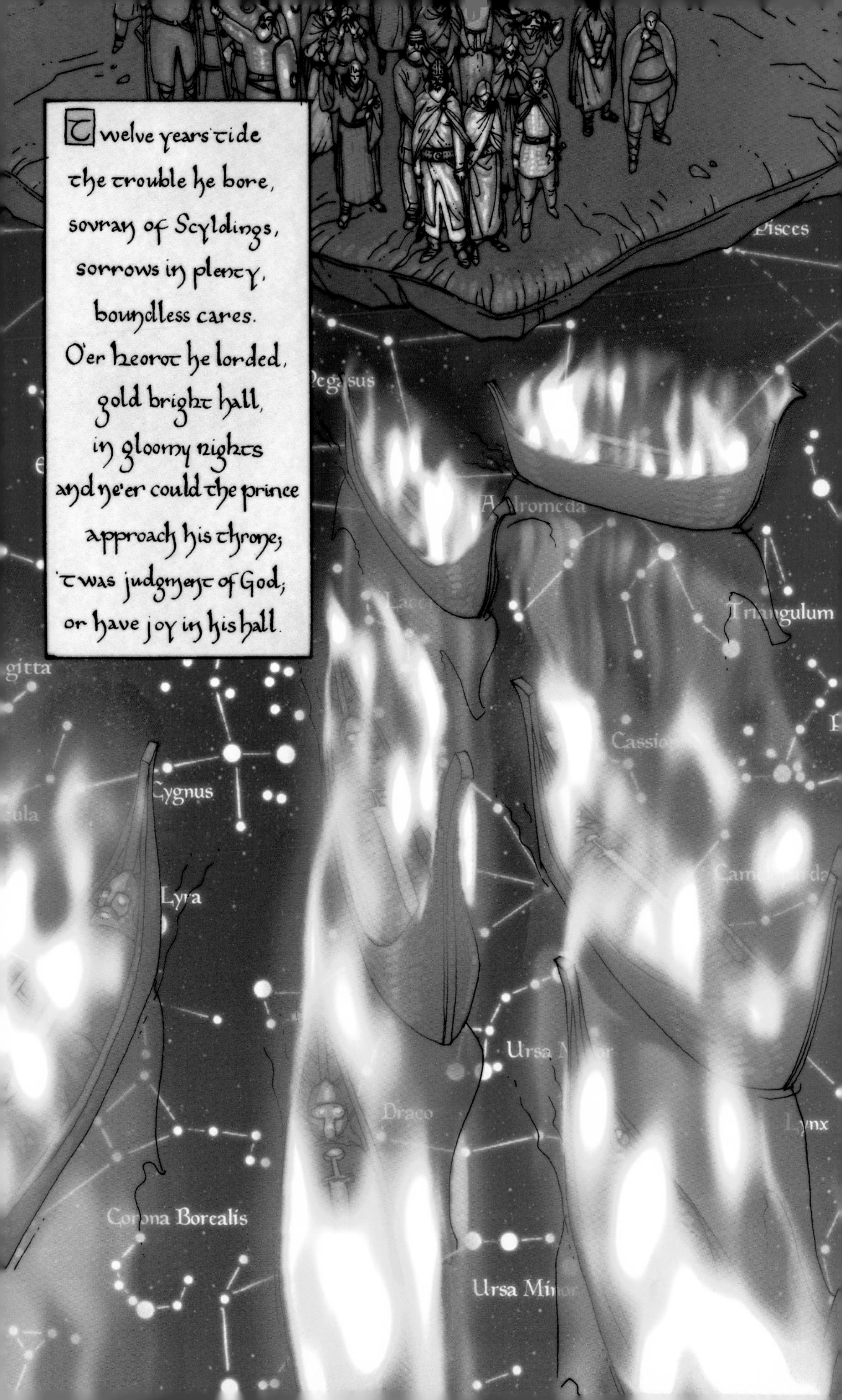

Twelve years' tide
the trouble he bore,
sovran of Scyldings,
sorrows in plenty,
boundless cares.
O'er Heorot he lorded,
gold bright hall,
in gloomy nights
and ne'er could the prince
approach his throne;
'twas judgment of God;
or have joy in his hall.
Pisces
Pegasus
Triangulum
Cygnus
Lyra
Draco
Lynx
Corona Borealis
Ursa Minor

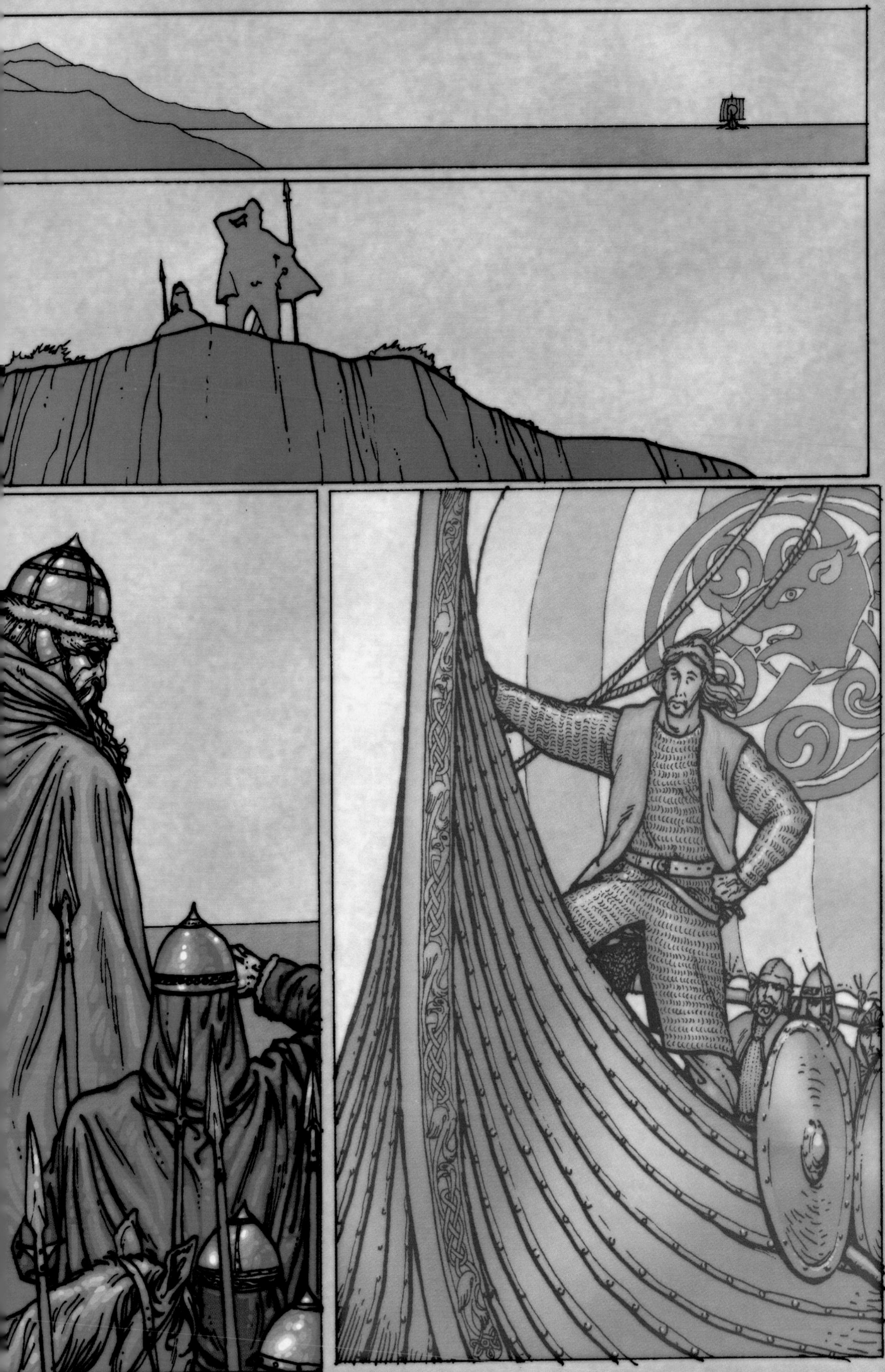

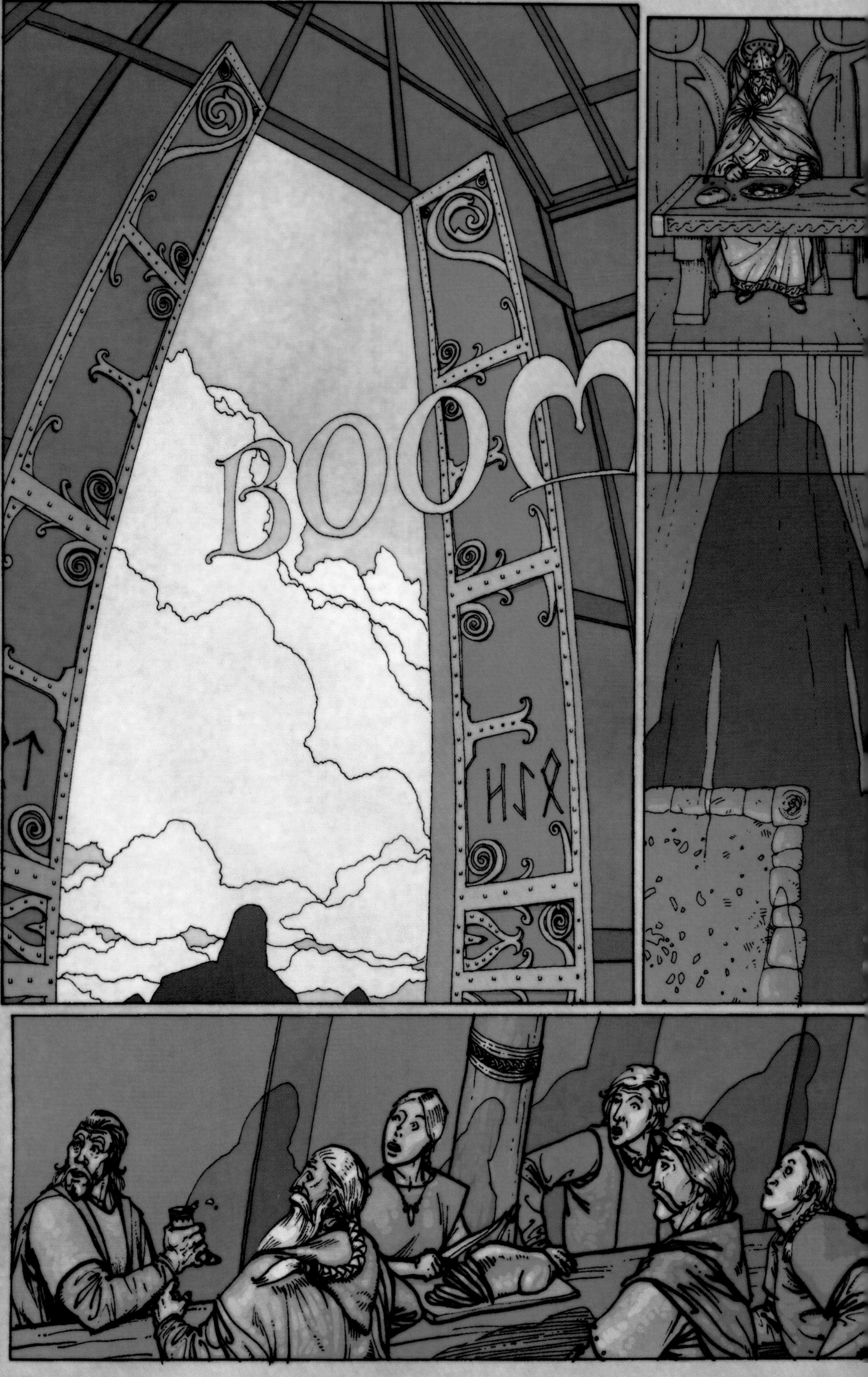
BOOM

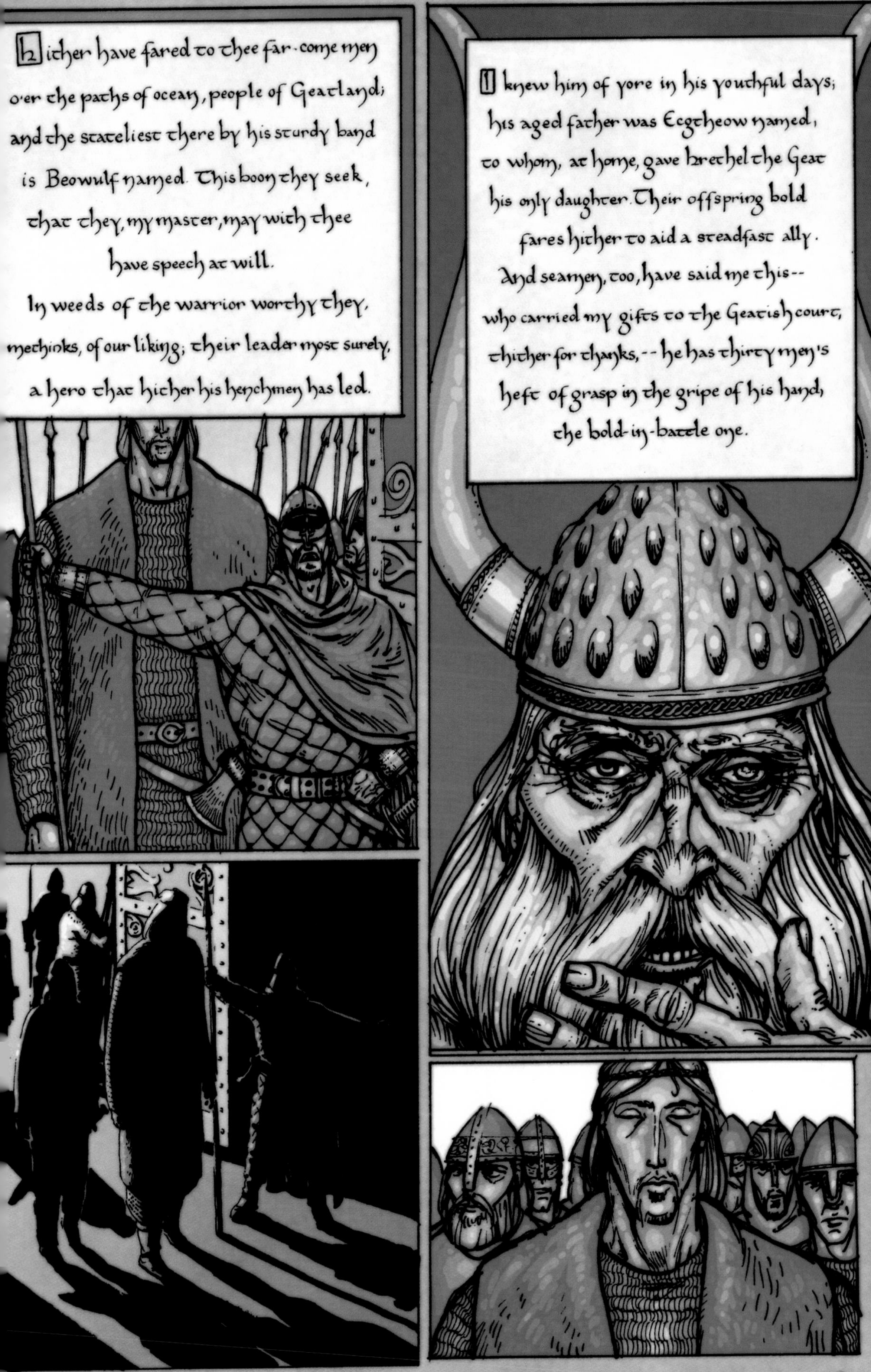
Hither have fared to thee far-come men
o'er the paths of ocean, people of Geatland;
and the stateliest there by his sturdy band
is Beowulf named. This boon they seek,
that they, my master, may with thee
have speech at will.
In weeds of the warrior worthy they,
methinks, of our liking; their leader most surely,
a hero that hither his henchmen has led.
I knew him of yore in his youthful days;
his aged father was Ecgtheow named,
to whom, at home, gave Hrethel the Geat
his only daughter. Their offspring bold
fares hither to aid a steadfast ally.
And seamen, too, have said me this--
who carried my gifts to the Geatish court,
thither for thanks, -- he has thirty men's
heft of grasp in the gripe of his hand,
the bold-in-battle one.

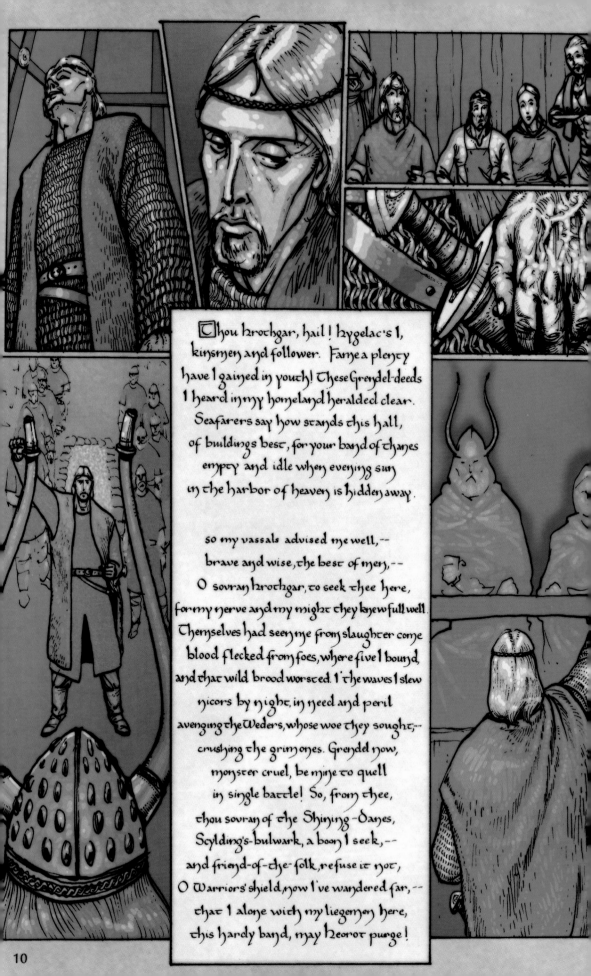

Thou Hrothgar, hail! Hygelac's I,
kinsmen and follower. Fame a plenty
have I gained in youth! These Grendel-deeds
I heard in my homeland heralded clear.
Seafarers say how stands this hall,
of buildings best, for your band of thanes
empty and idle when evening sun
in the harbor of heaven is hidden away.

So my vassals advised me well,--
brave and wise, the best of men,--
O sovran Hrothgar, to seek thee here,
for my nerve and my might they knew full well.
Themselves had seen me from slaughter come
blood flecked from foes, where five I bound,
and that wild brood worsted. I' the waves I slew
nicors by night, in need and peril
avenging the Weders, whose woe they sought,--
crushing the grim ones. Grendel now,
monster cruel, be mine to quell
in single battle! So, from thee,
thou sovran of the Shining-Danes,
Scylding's-bulwark, a boon I seek,--
and friend-of-the-folk, refuse it not,
O Warriors' shield, now I've wandered far,--
that I alone with my liegemen here,
this hardy band, may Heorot purge!

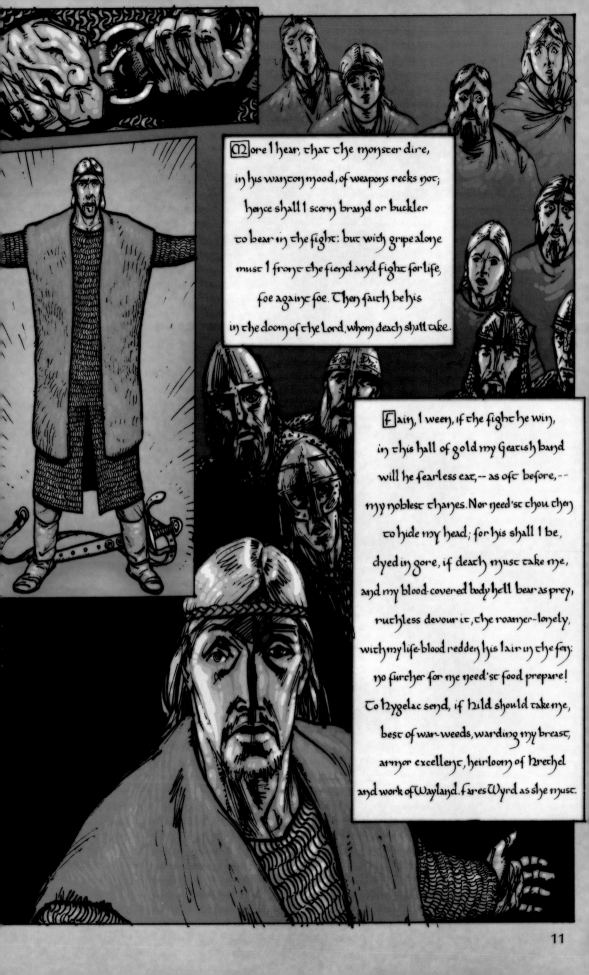

More I hear, that the monster dire,
in his wanton mood, of weapons recks not;
hence shall I scorn brand or buckler
to bear in the fight: but with gripe alone
must I front the fiend and fight for life,
foe against foe. Then faith be his
in the doom of the Lord, whom death shall take.

Fain, I ween, if the fight he win,
in this hall of gold my Geatish band
will he fearless eat, -- as oft before, --
my noblest thanes. Nor need'st thou then
to hide my head; for his shall I be,
dyed in gore, if death must take me,
and my blood-covered body he'll bear as prey,
ruthless devour it, the roamer-lonely,
with my life-blood redden his lair in the fen:
no further for me need'st food prepare!
To Hygelac send, if Hild should take me,
best of war-weeds, warding my breast,
armor excellent, heirloom of Hrethel
and work of Wayland. Fares Wyrd as she must.

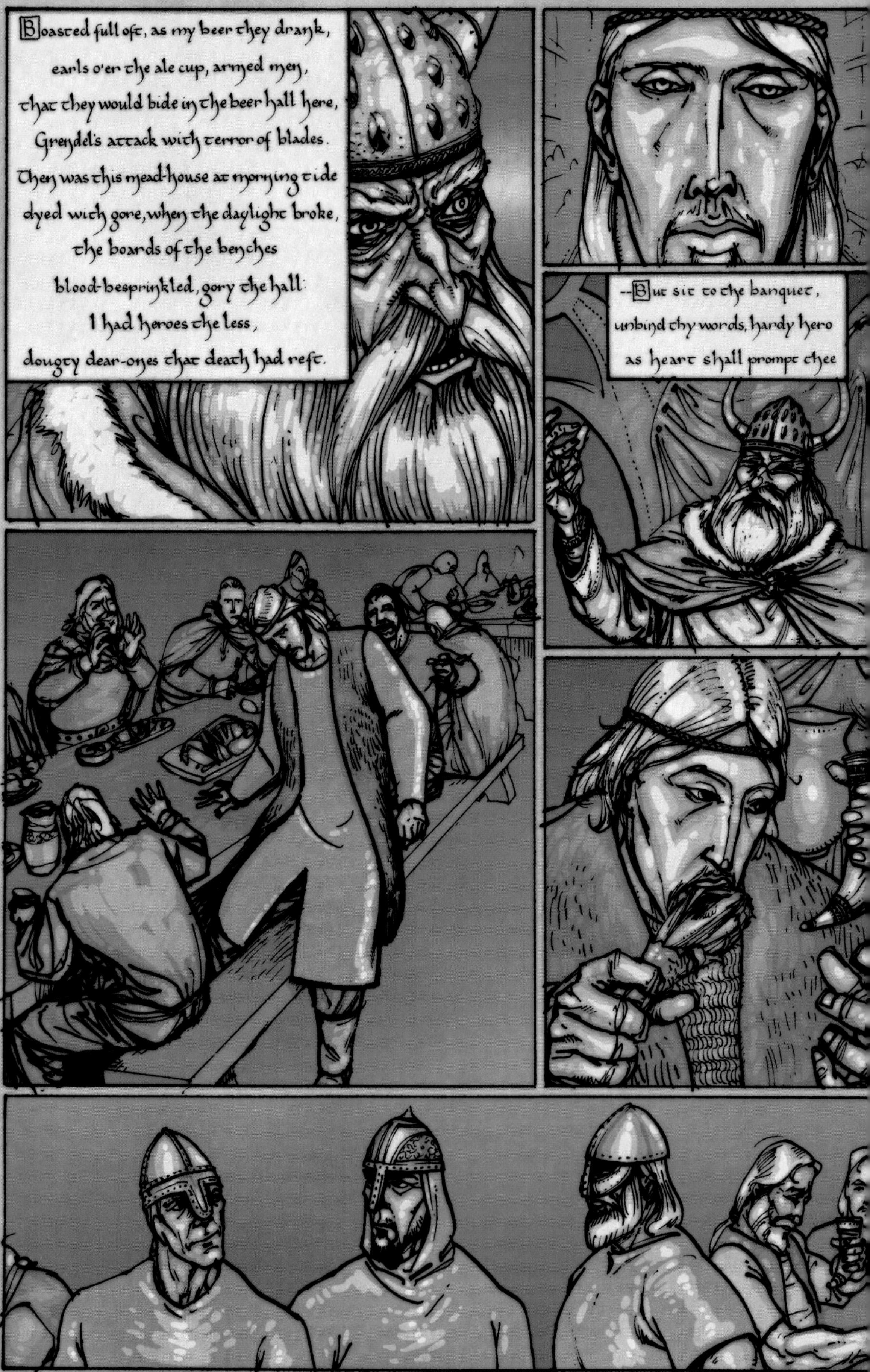
Boasted full oft, as my beer they drank,
earls o'er the ale cup, armed men,
that they would bide in the beer hall here,
Grendel's attack with terror of blades.
Then was this mead-house at morning tide
dyed with gore, when the daylight broke,
the boards of the benches
blood-besprinkled, gory the hall:
I had heroes the less,
dougty dear-ones that death had reft.
--But sit to the banquet,
unbind thy words, hardy hero
as heart shall prompt thee

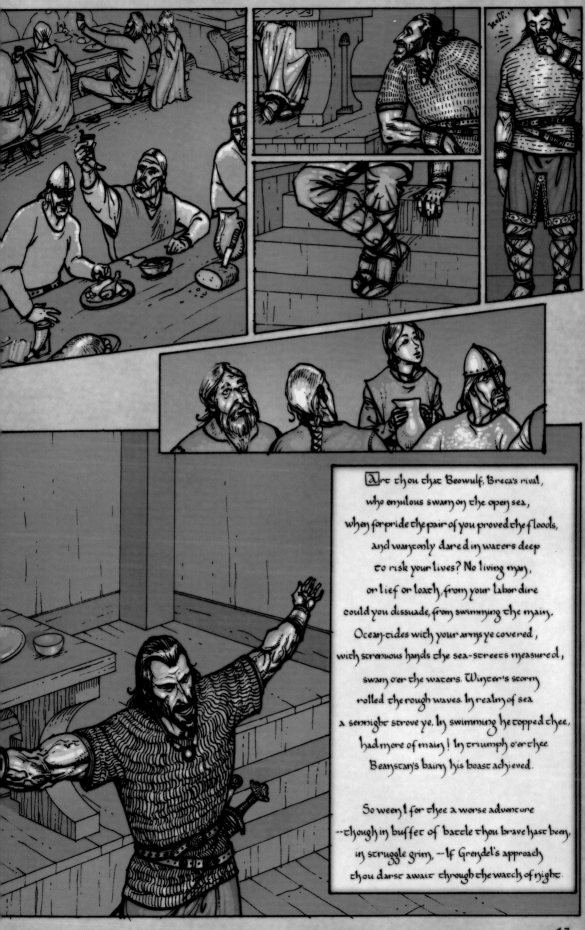

Art thou that Beowulf, Breca's rival,
who emulous swam on the open sea,
when for pride the pair of you proved the floods,
and wantonly dared in waters deep
to risk your lives? No living man,
or lief or loath, from your labor dire
could you dissuade, from swimming the main.
Ocean-tides with your arms ye covered,
with strenuous hands the sea-streets measured,
swam o'er the waters. Winter's storm
rolled the rough waves. In realm of sea
a sennight strove ye. In swimming he topped thee,
had more of main! In triumph o'er thee
Beanstan's bairn his boast achieved.

So ween I for thee a worse adventure
--though in buffet of battle thou brave hast been,
in struggle grim, -- If Grendel's approach
thou darst await through the watch of night.

13

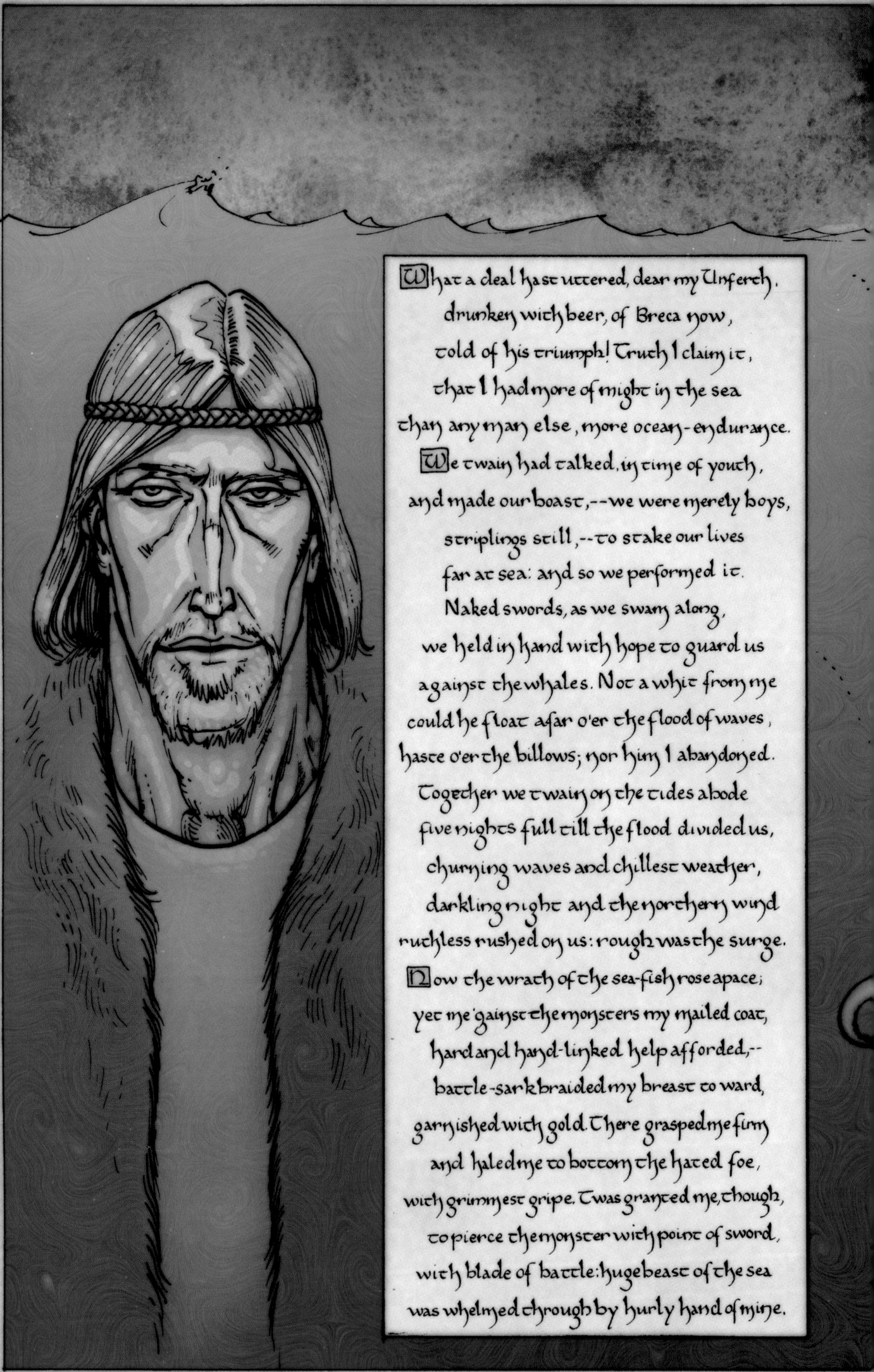

What a deal hast uttered, dear my Unferth,
drunken with beer, of Breca now,
told of his triumph! Truth I claim it,
that I had more of might in the sea
than any man else, more ocean-endurance.
We twain had talked, in time of youth,
and made our boast,--we were merely boys,
striplings still,--to stake our lives
far at sea: and so we performed it.
Naked swords, as we swam along,
we held in hand with hope to guard us
against the whales. Not a whit from me
could he float afar o'er the flood of waves,
haste o'er the billows; nor him I abandoned.
Together we twain on the tides abode
five nights full till the flood divided us,
churning waves and chillest weather,
darkling night and the northern wind
ruthless rushed on us: rough was the surge.
Now the wrath of the sea-fish rose apace;
yet me 'gainst the monsters my mailed coat,
hard and hand-linked help afforded,--
battle-sark braided my breast to ward,
garnished with gold. There grasped me firm
and haled me to bottom the hated foe,
with grimmest gripe. 'Twas granted me, though,
to pierce the monster with point of sword,
with blade of battle: huge beast of the sea
was whelmed through by hurly hand of mine.

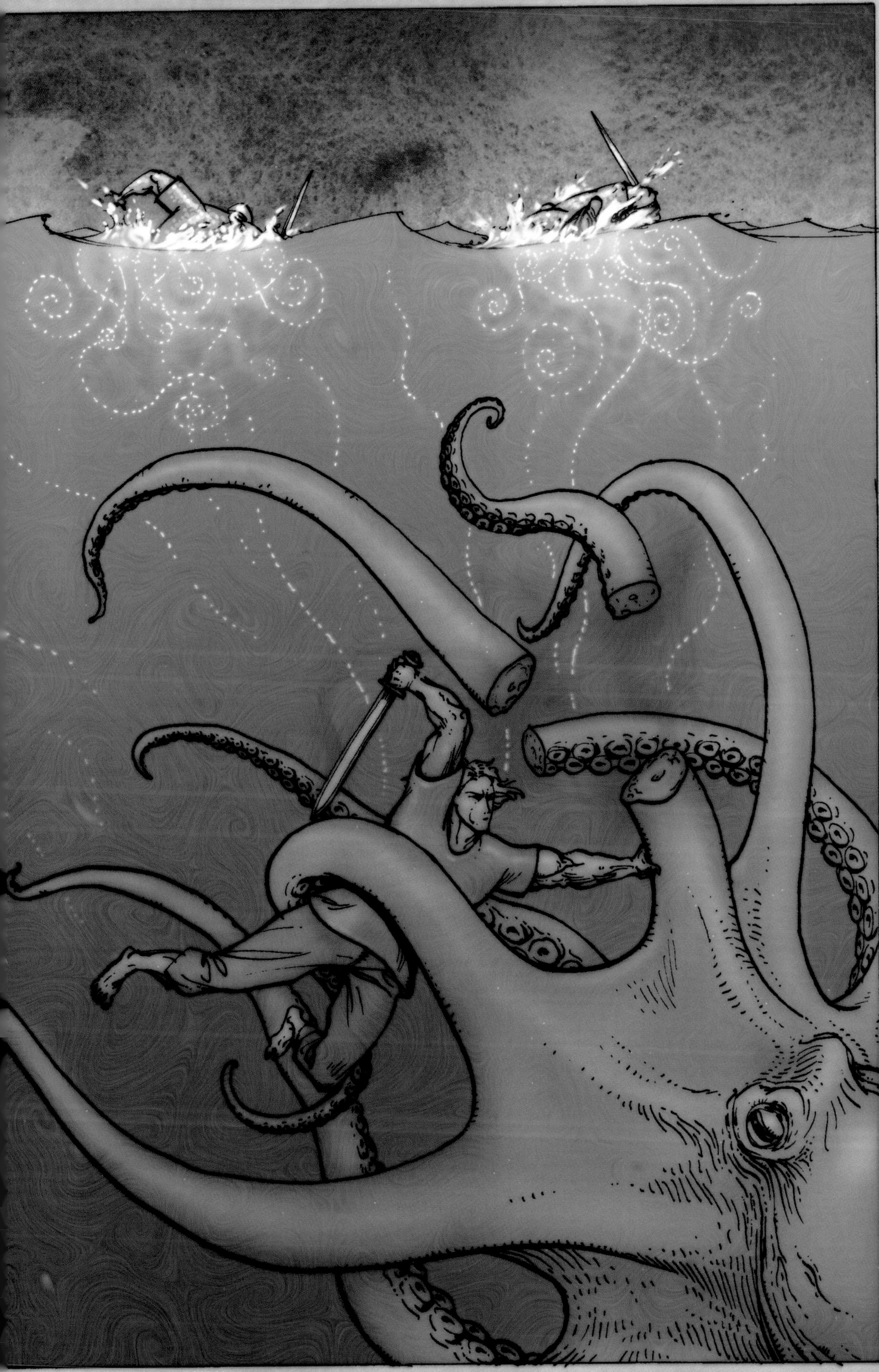

And so it came that I killed with my sword nine of the nicors. Of night fought battles ne'er heard I a harder 'neath heaven's dome, nor adrift on the deep a more desolate man! Yet I came unharmed from that hostile clutch, though spent with swimming. The sea upbore me, flood of the tide, on Finnish land, the welling waters.

No wise of thee have I heard men tell such terror of falchions, bitter battle.

THONK!

Ha Ha Ha Ha Ha Ha

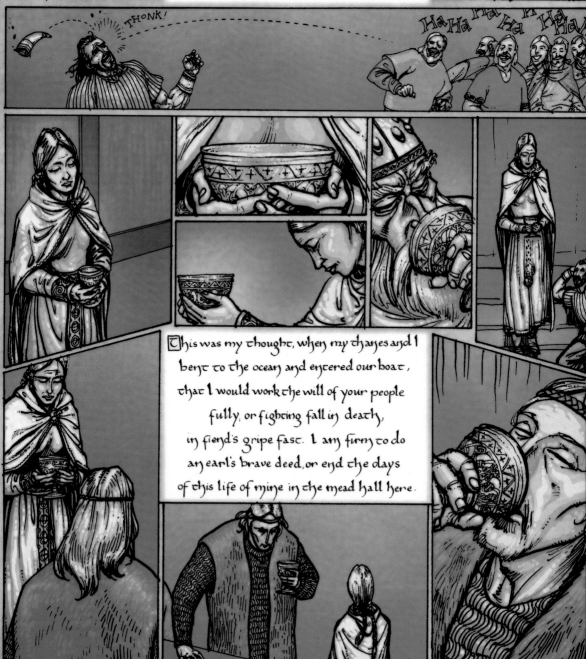

This was my thought, when my thanes and I bent to the ocean and entered our boat, that I would work the will of your people fully, or fighting fall in death, in fiend's gripe fast. I am firm to do an earl's brave deed, or end the days of this life of mine in the mead hall here.

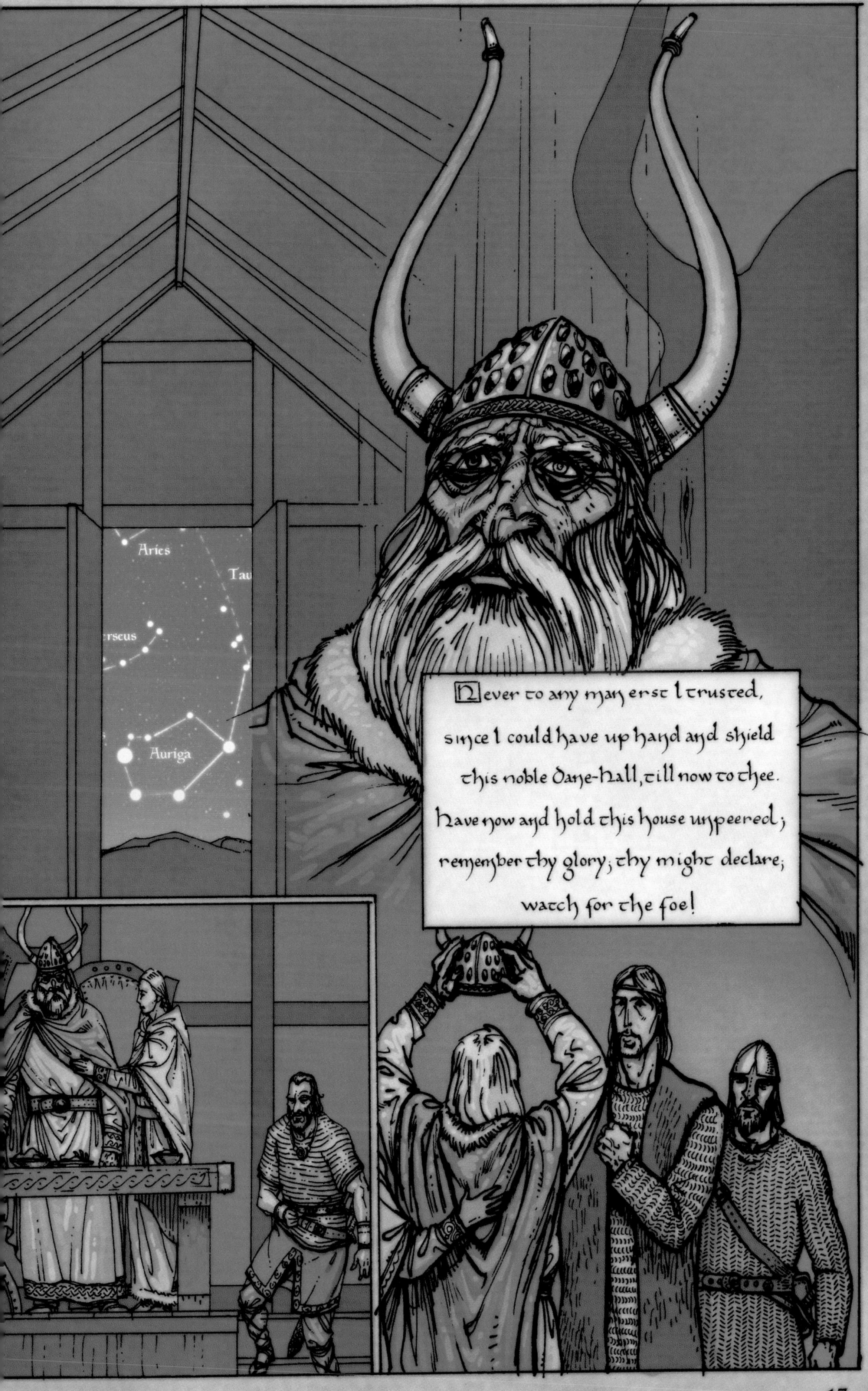
Aries
Auriga
Never to any man erst I trusted,
since I could have up hand and shield
this noble Dane-Hall, till now to thee.
Have now and hold this house unpeered;
remember thy glory; thy might declare;
watch for the foe!

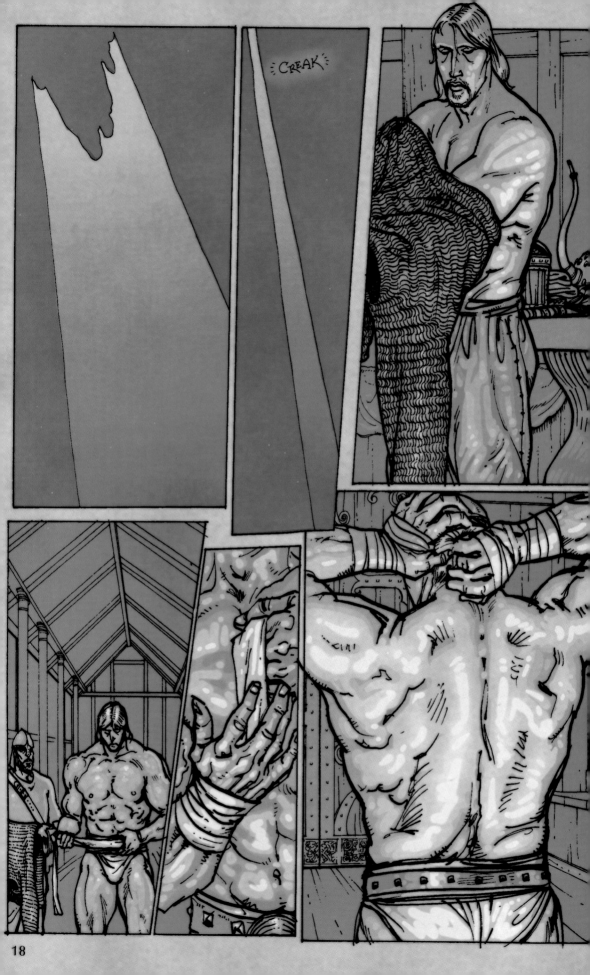

CREAK

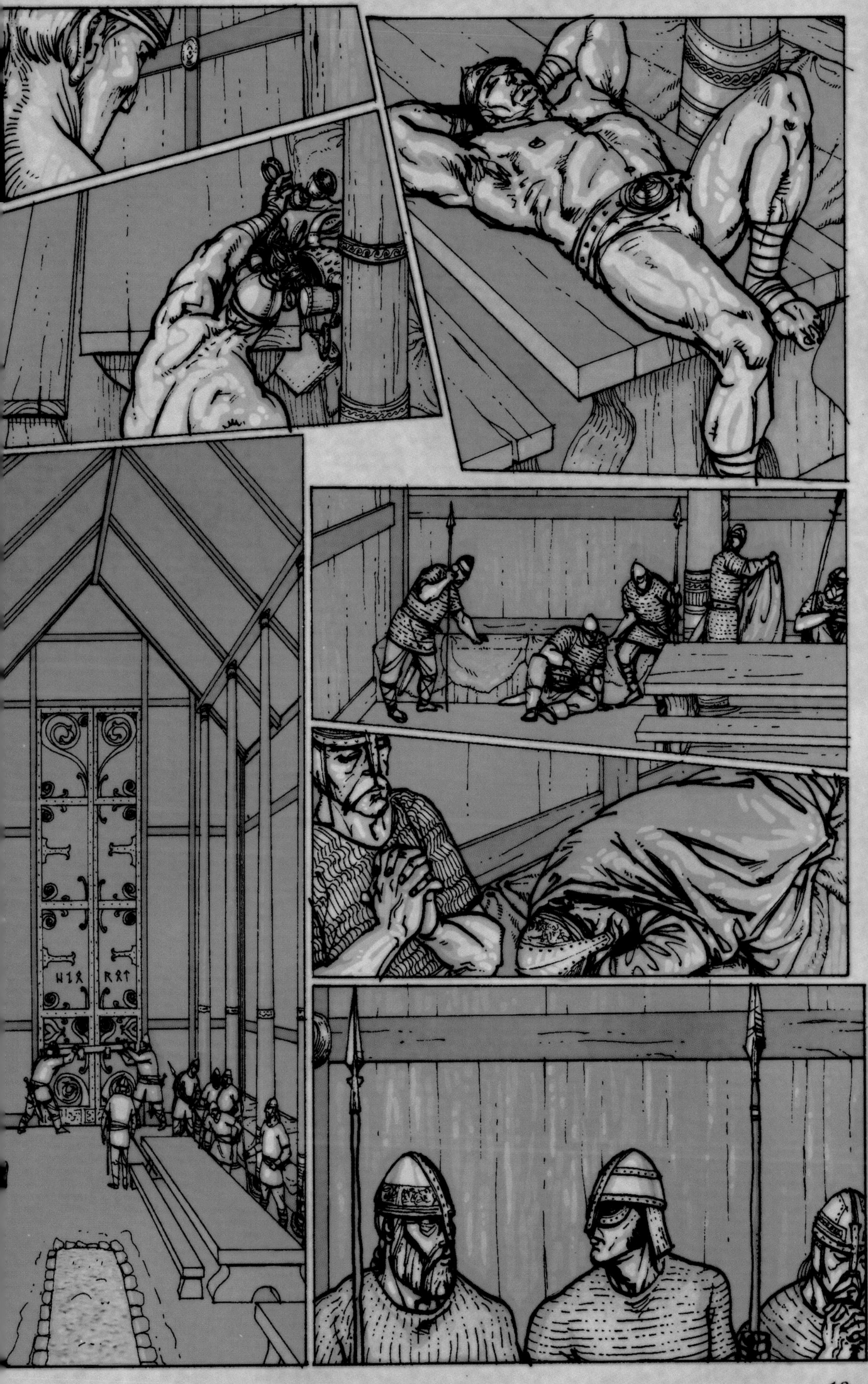

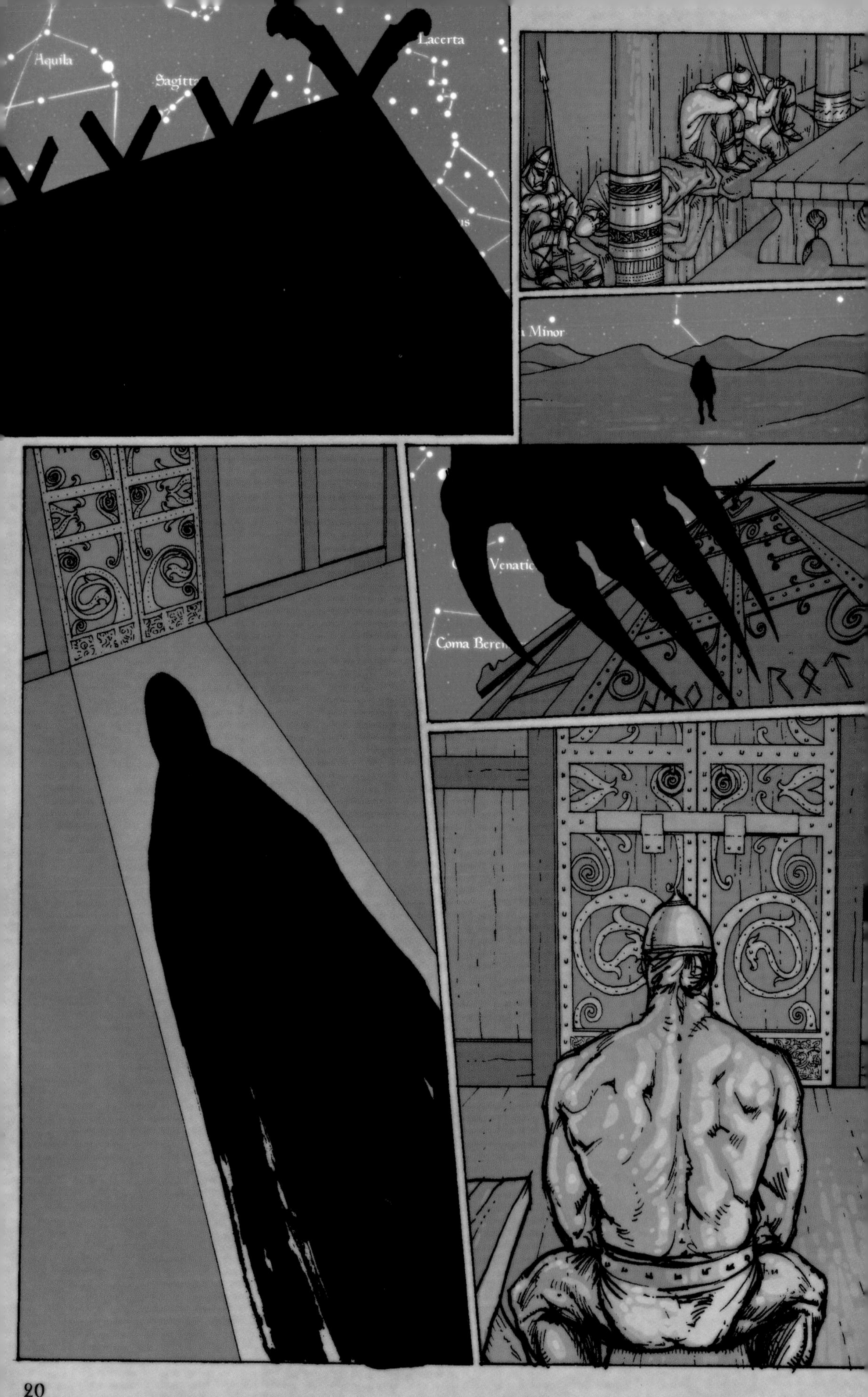
Aquila
Lacerta

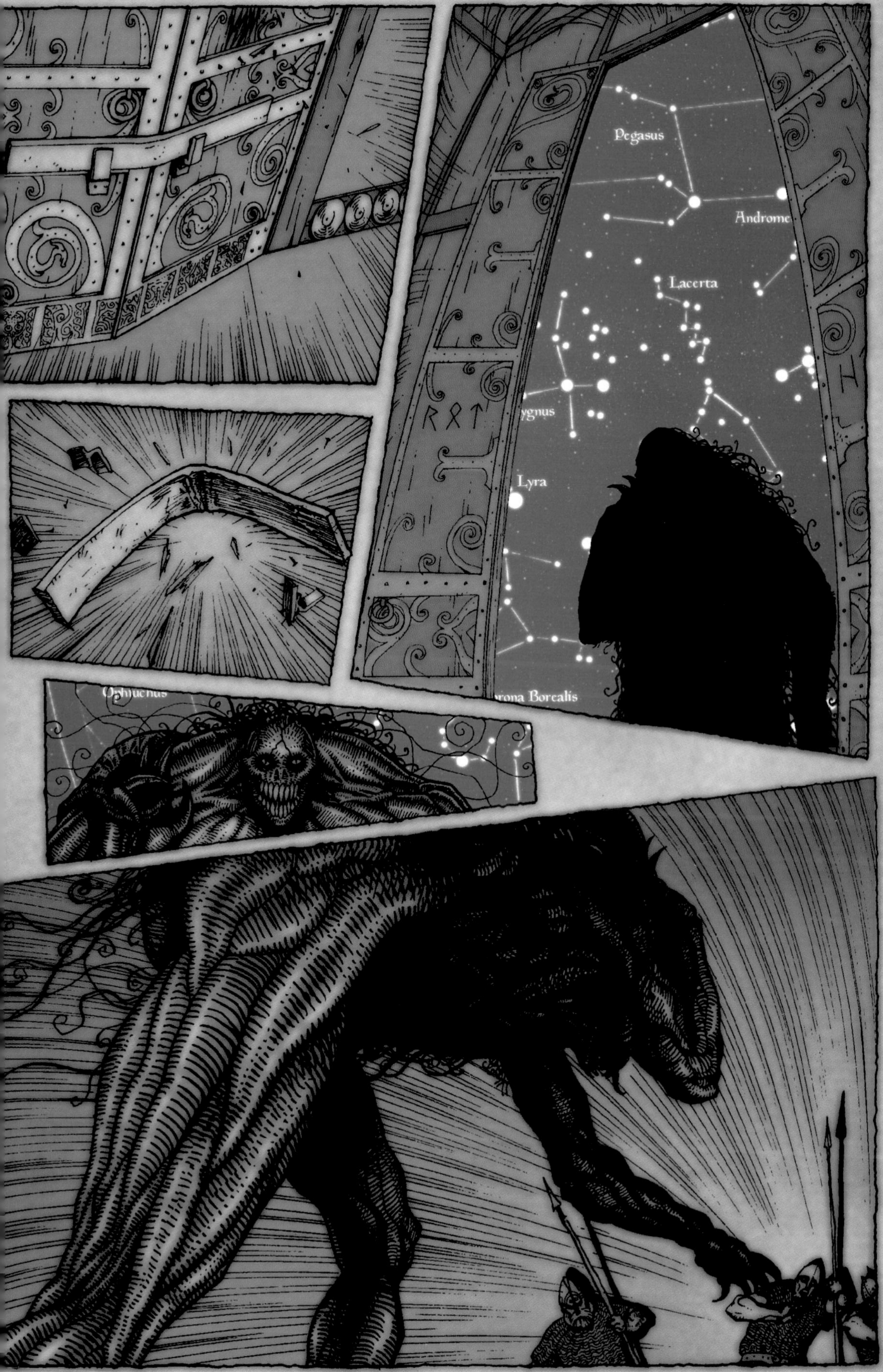
Pegasus
Androme
Lacerta
ygnus
Lyra
orona Borealis
Ophiuchus

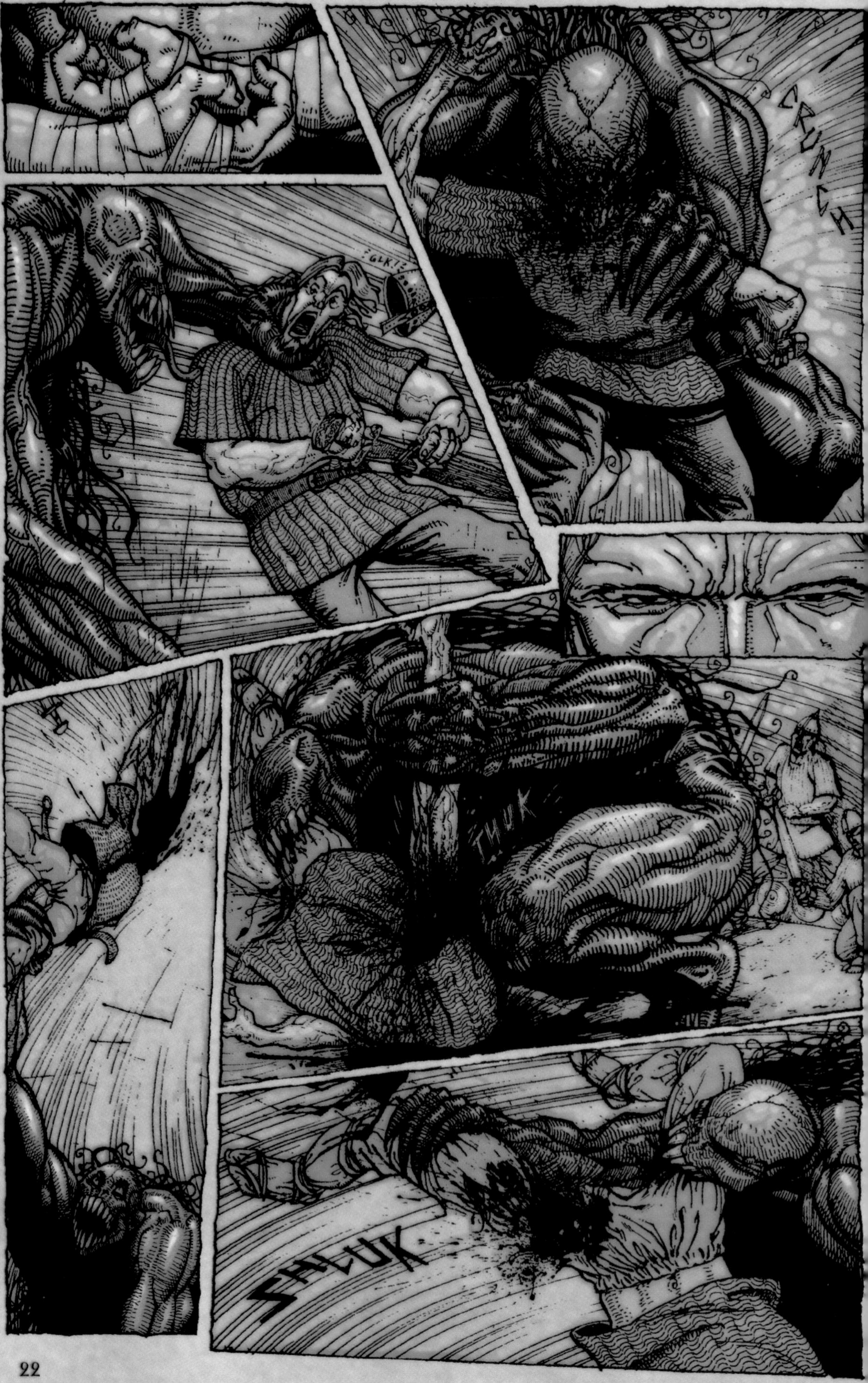
CRUNCH
GLK!
THUK
SHLUK

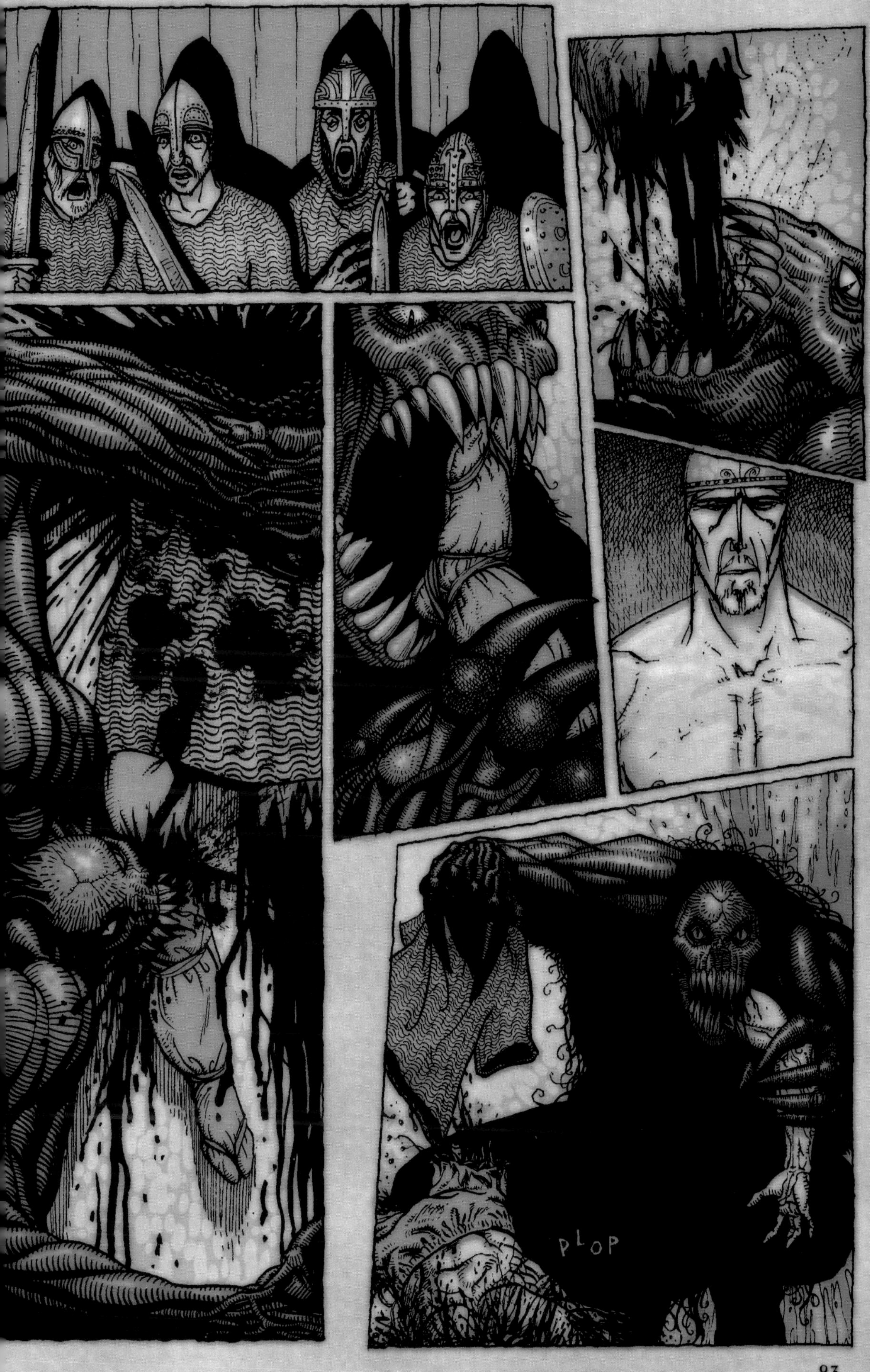
PLOP

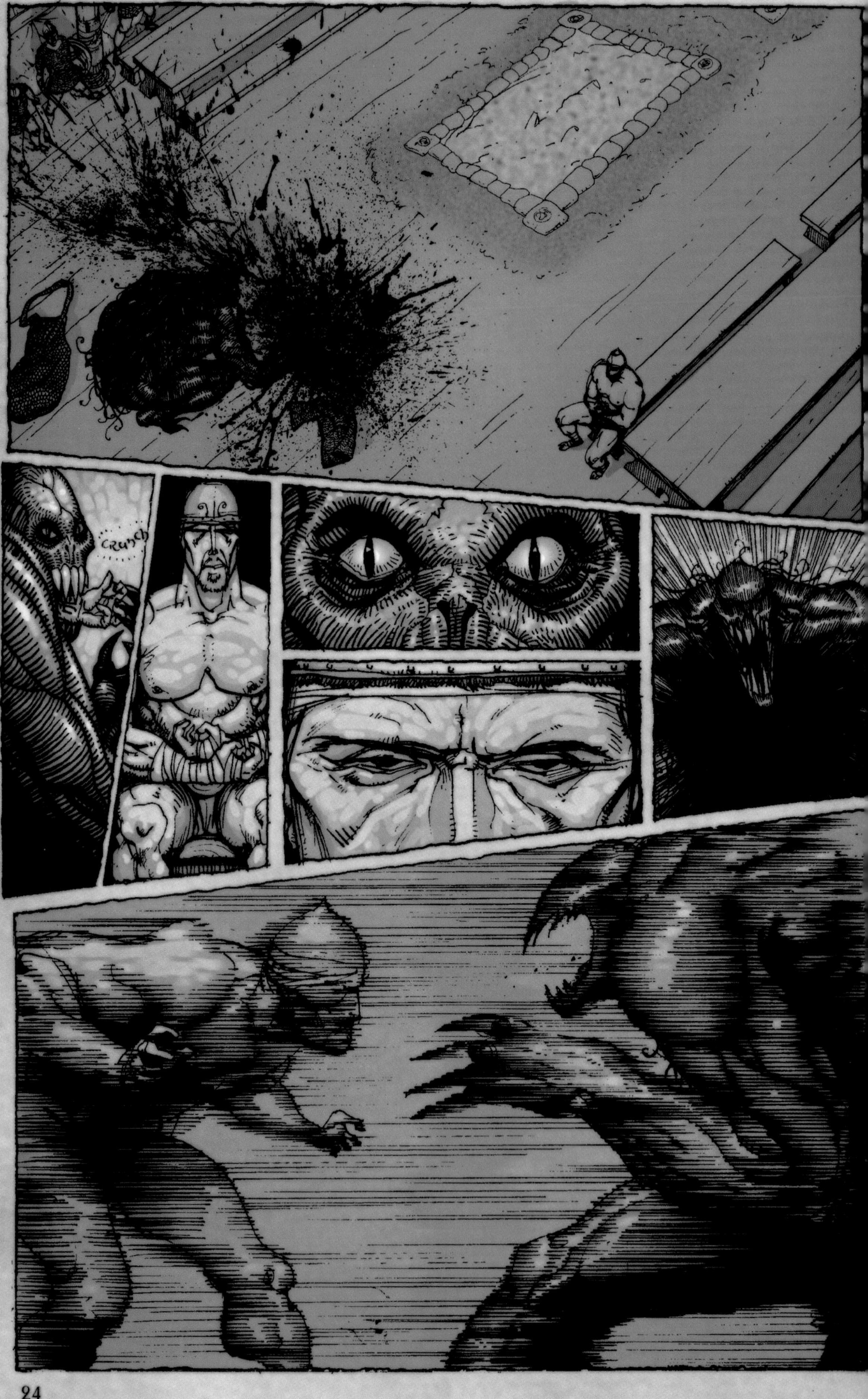
CRUNCH

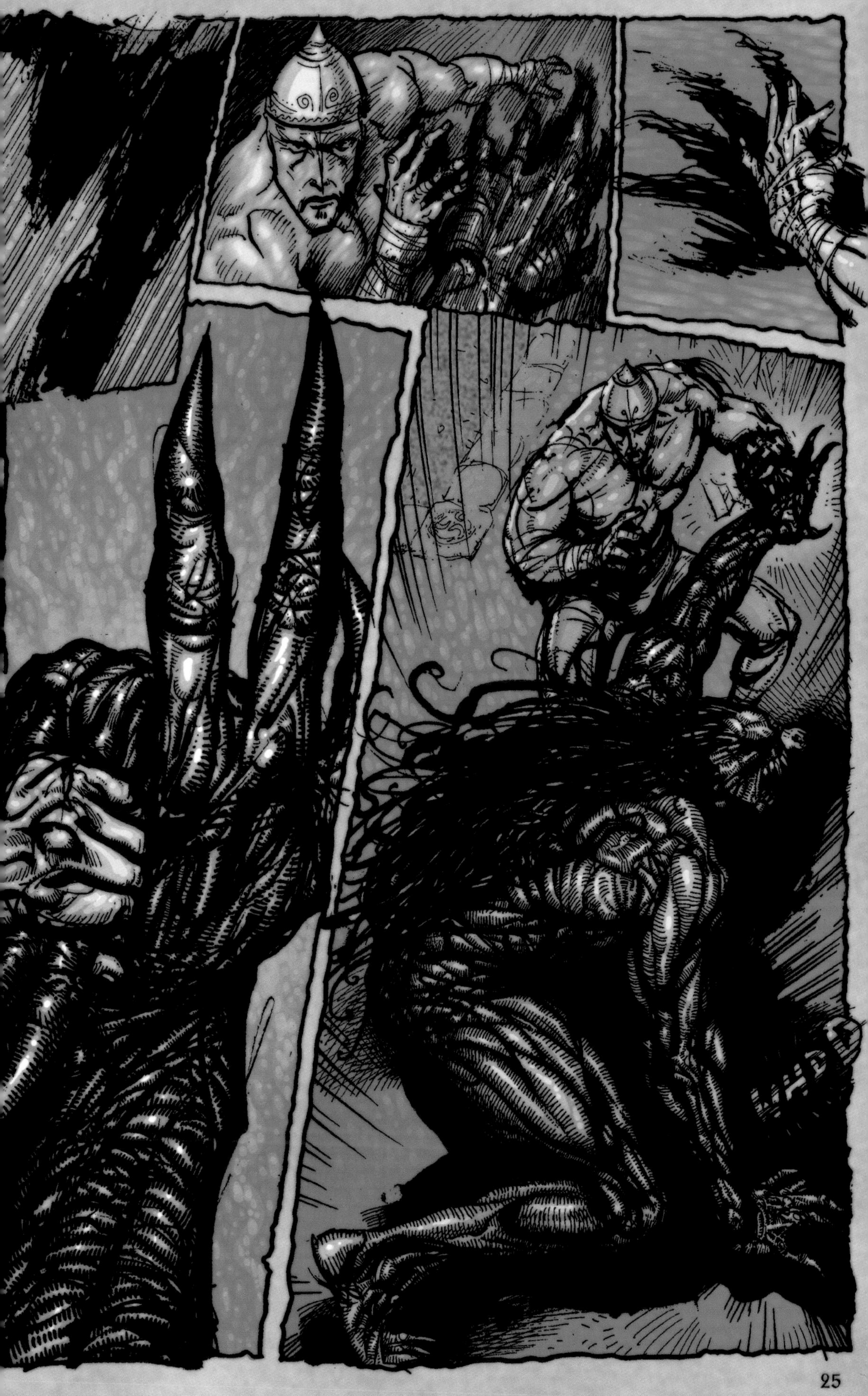

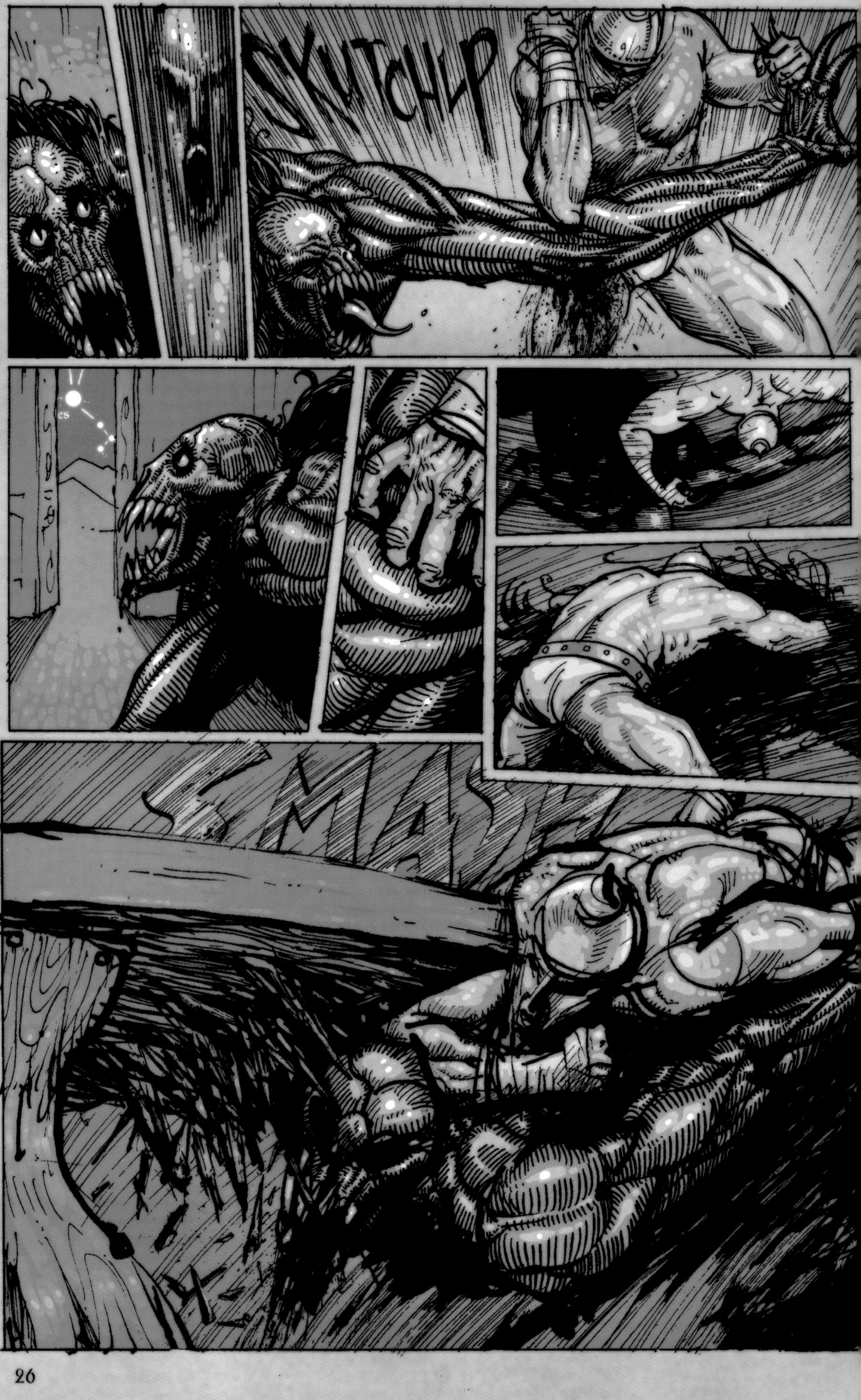
SKUTCHLP
SMASH

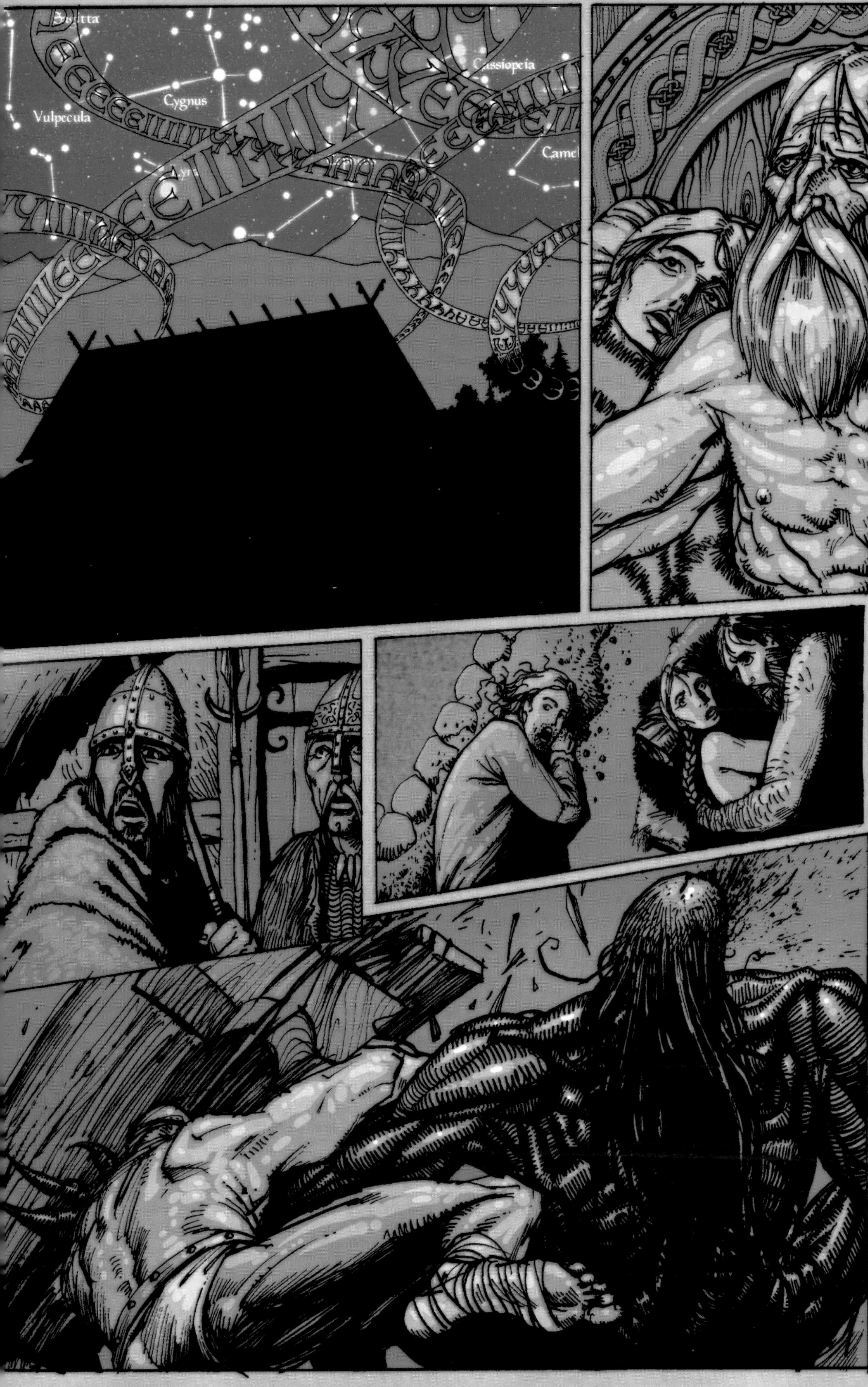
Cassiopeia
Cygnus
Vulpecula
Camel

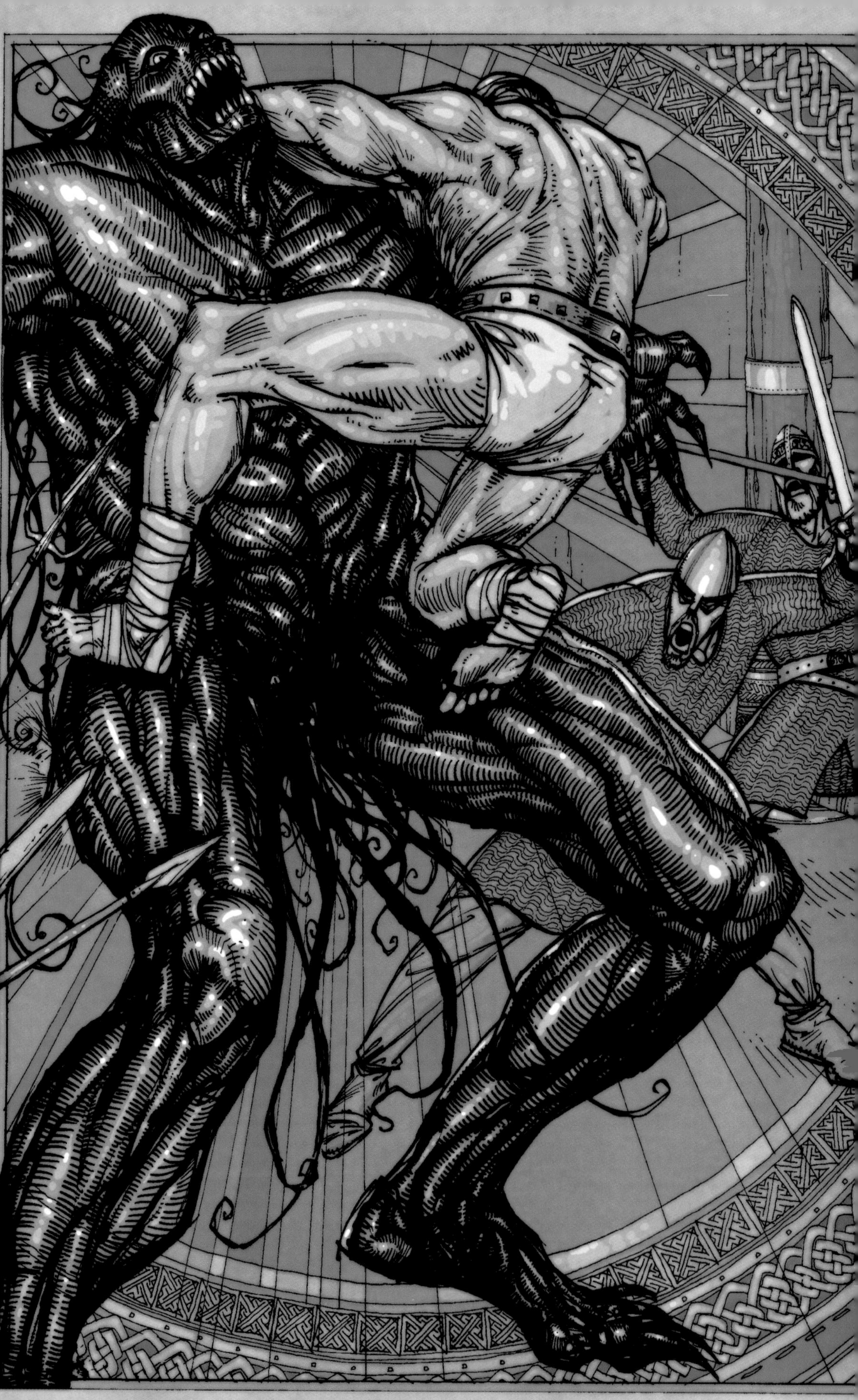

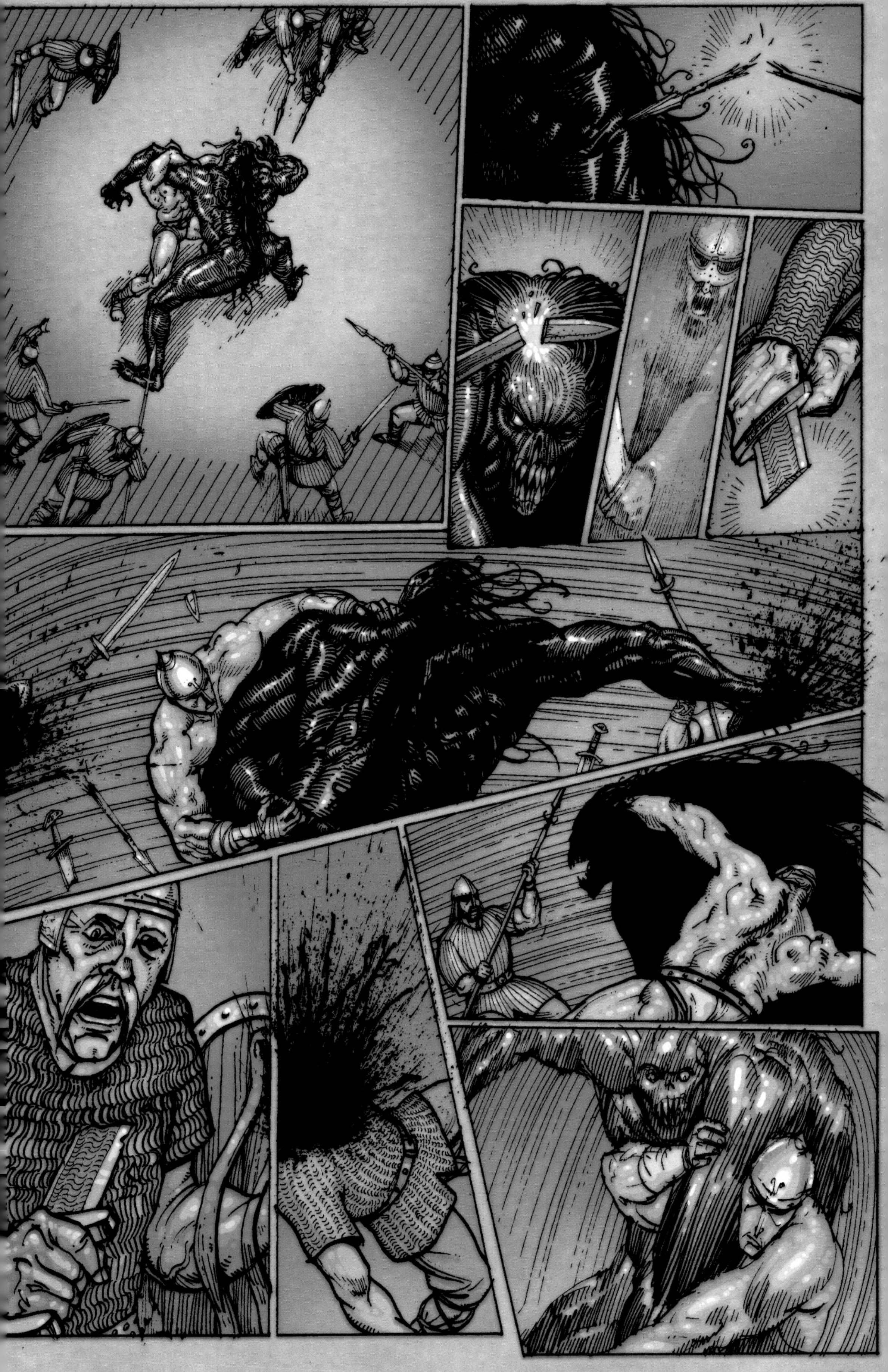

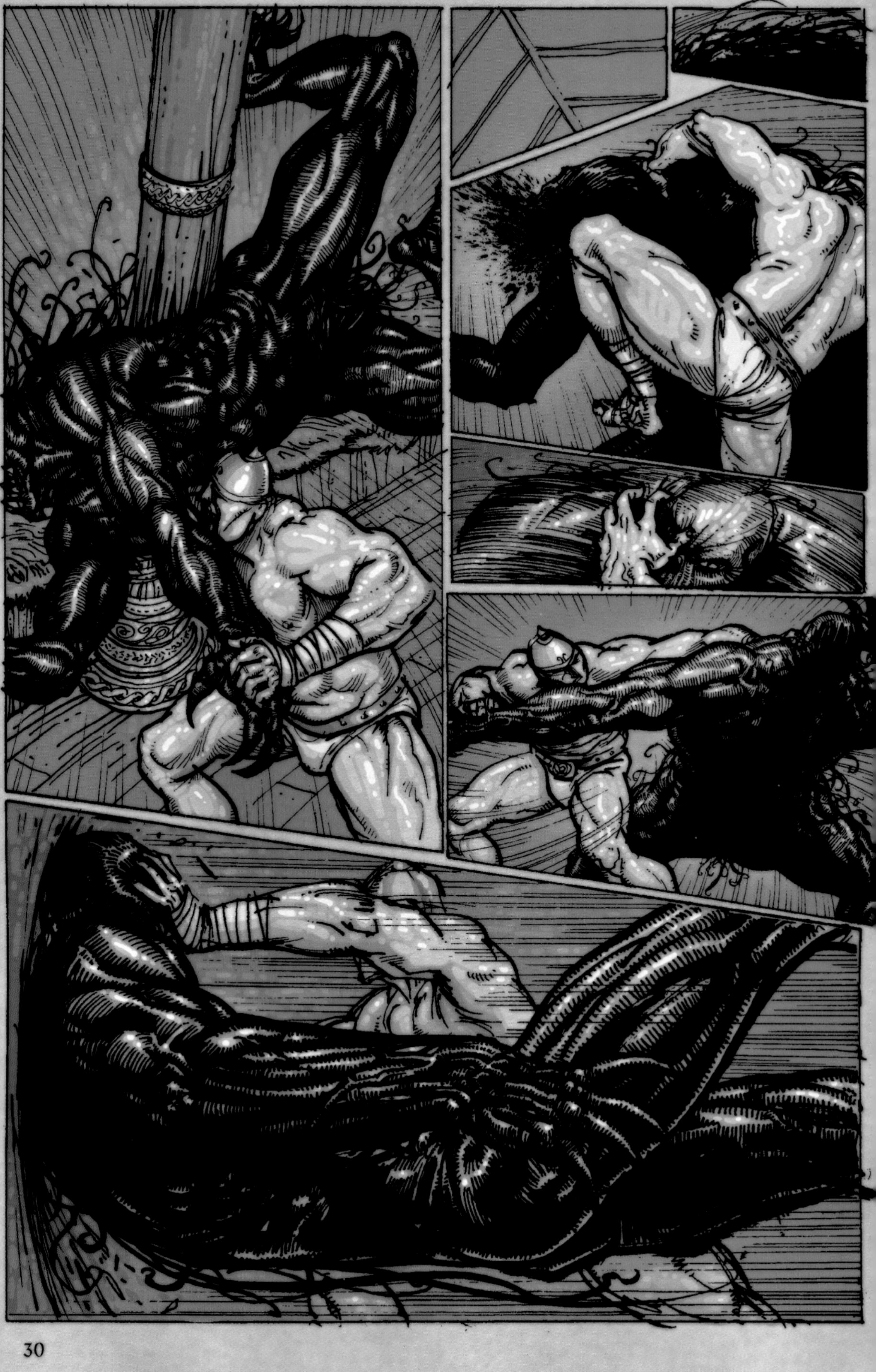

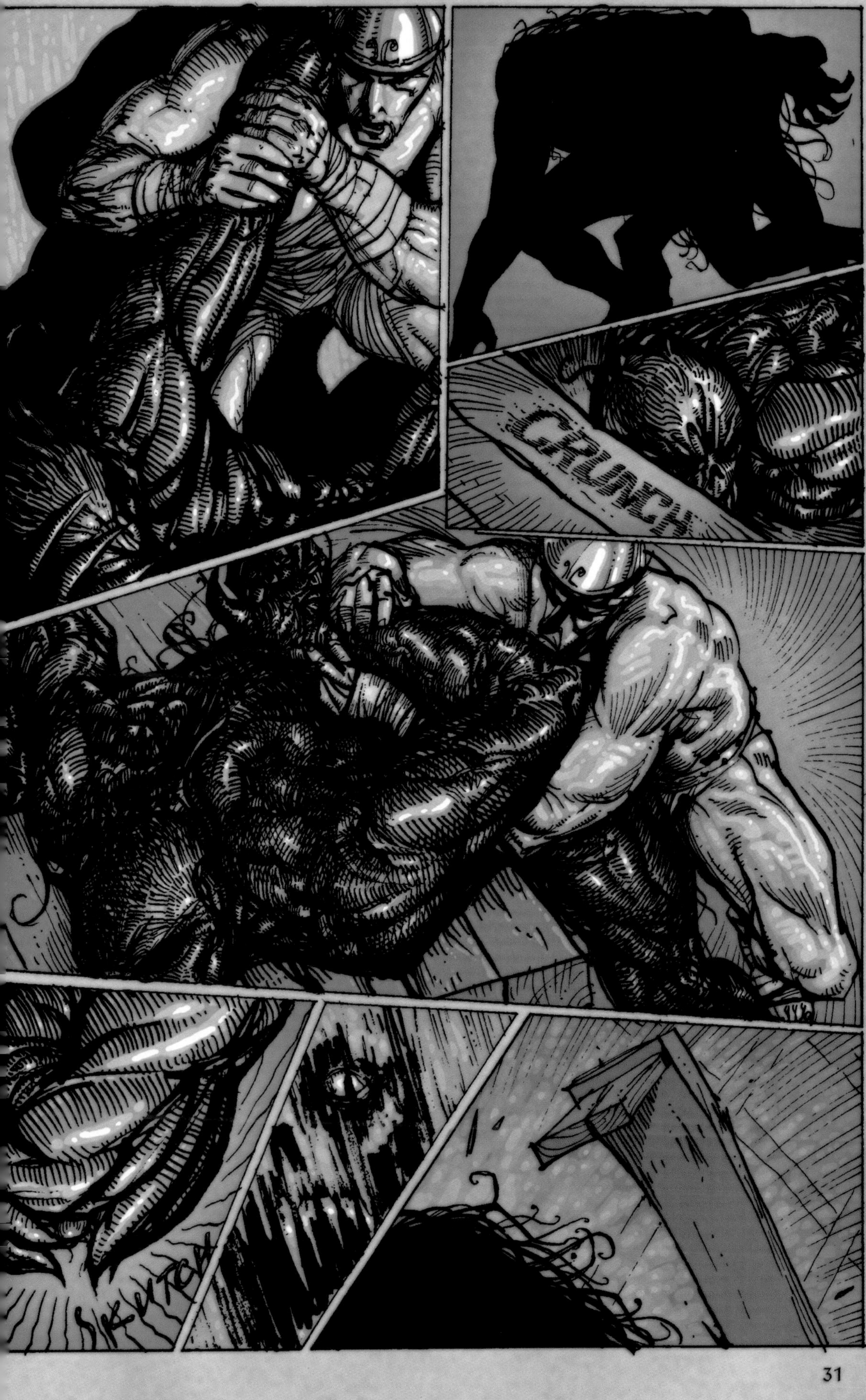
CRUNCH
SKRUTCH

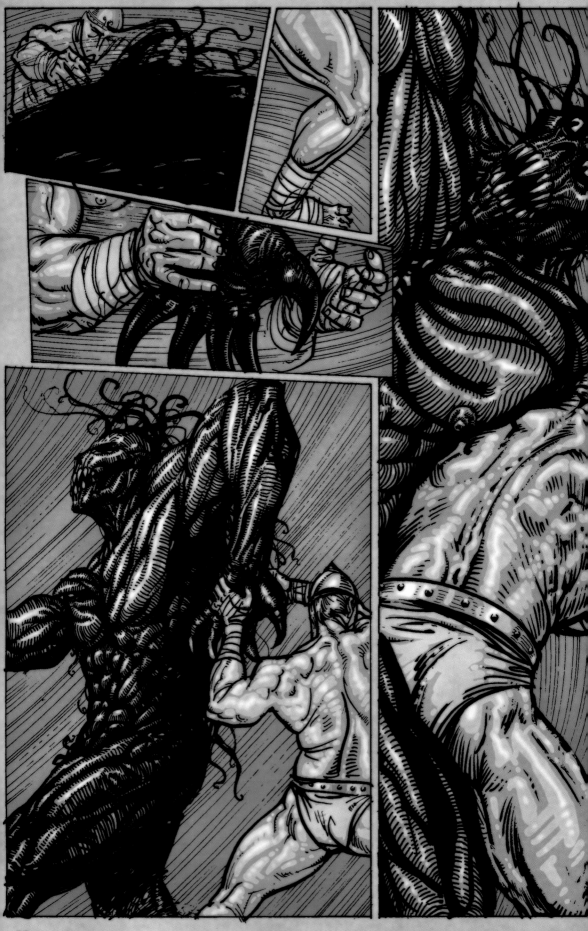

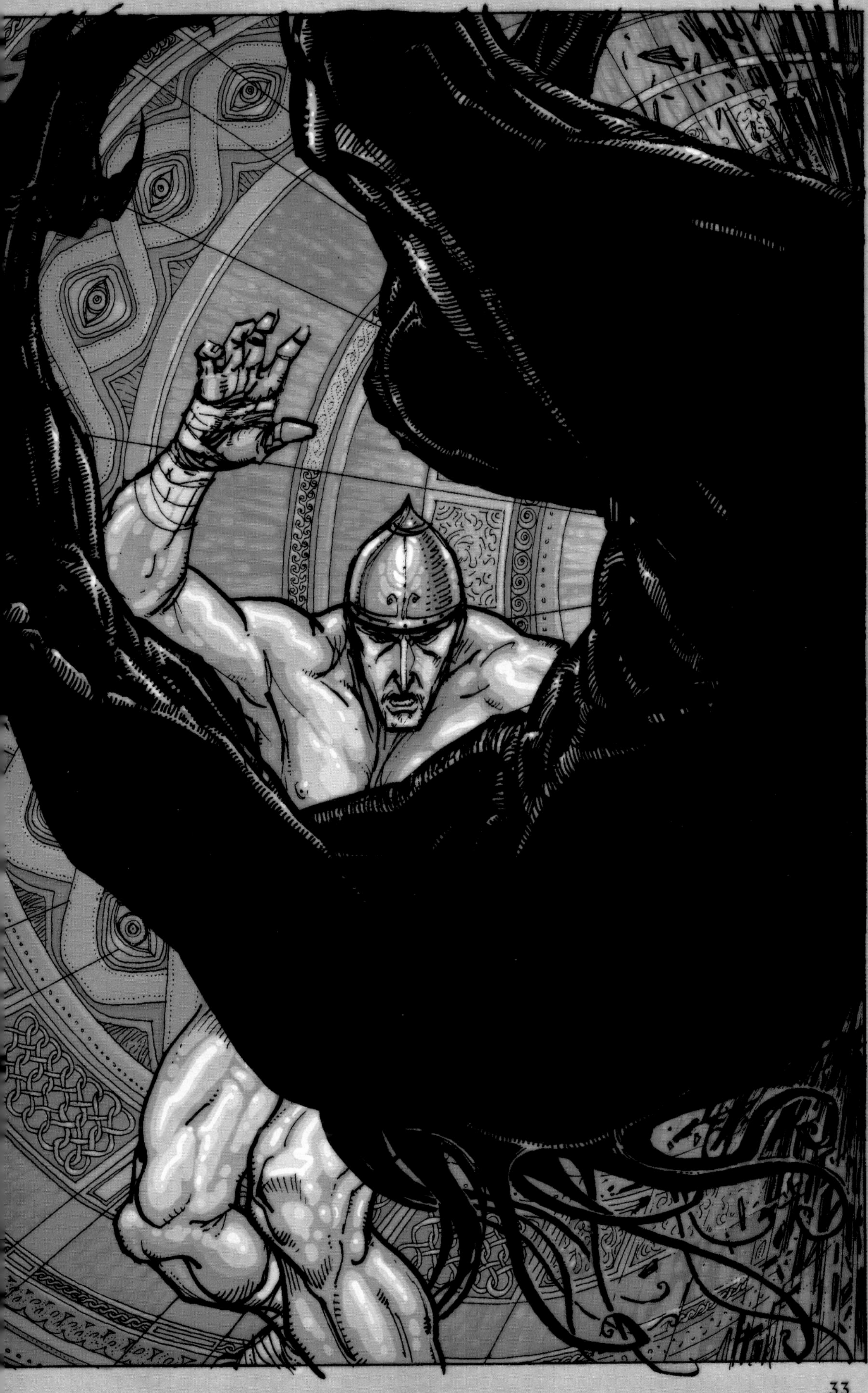

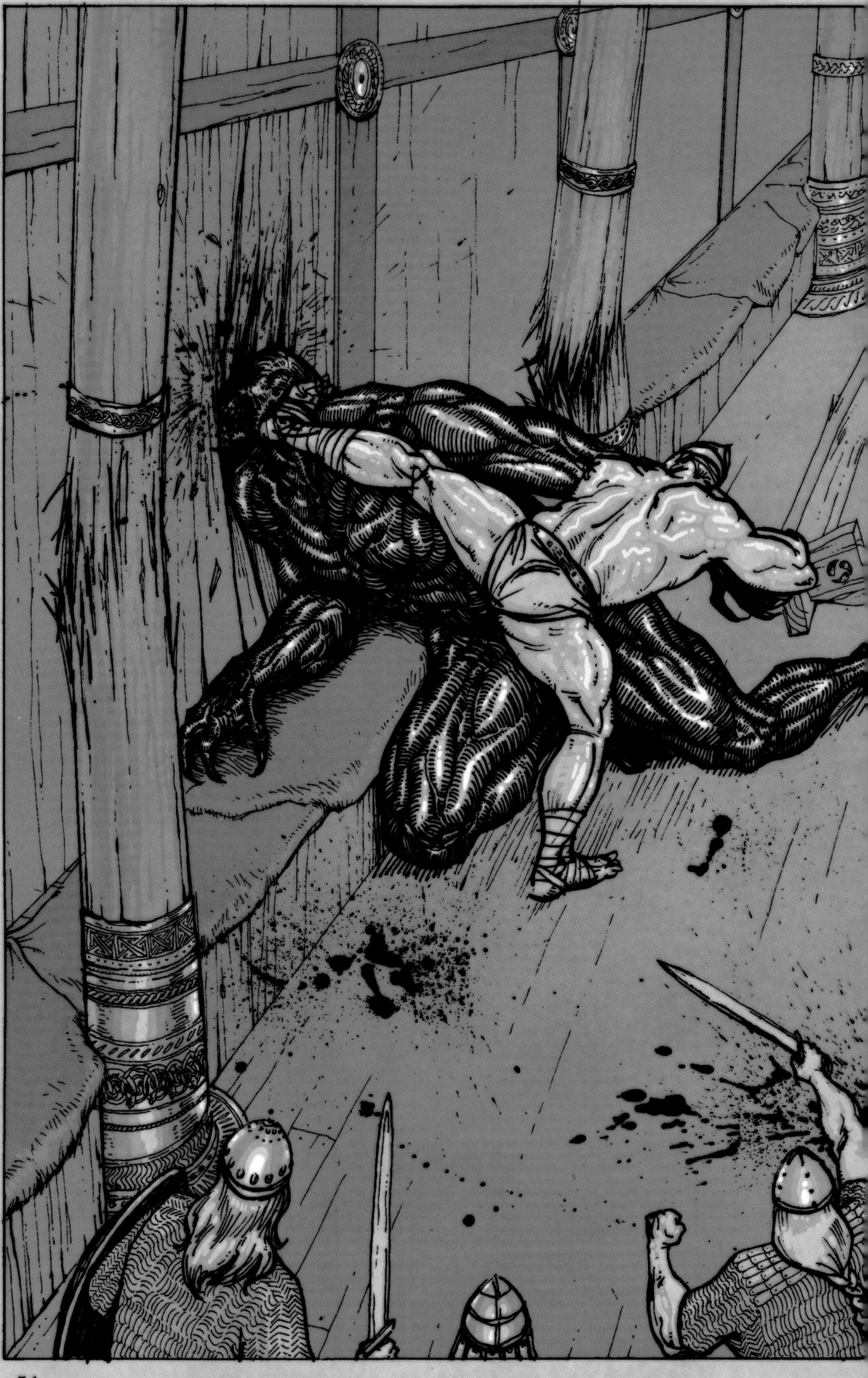

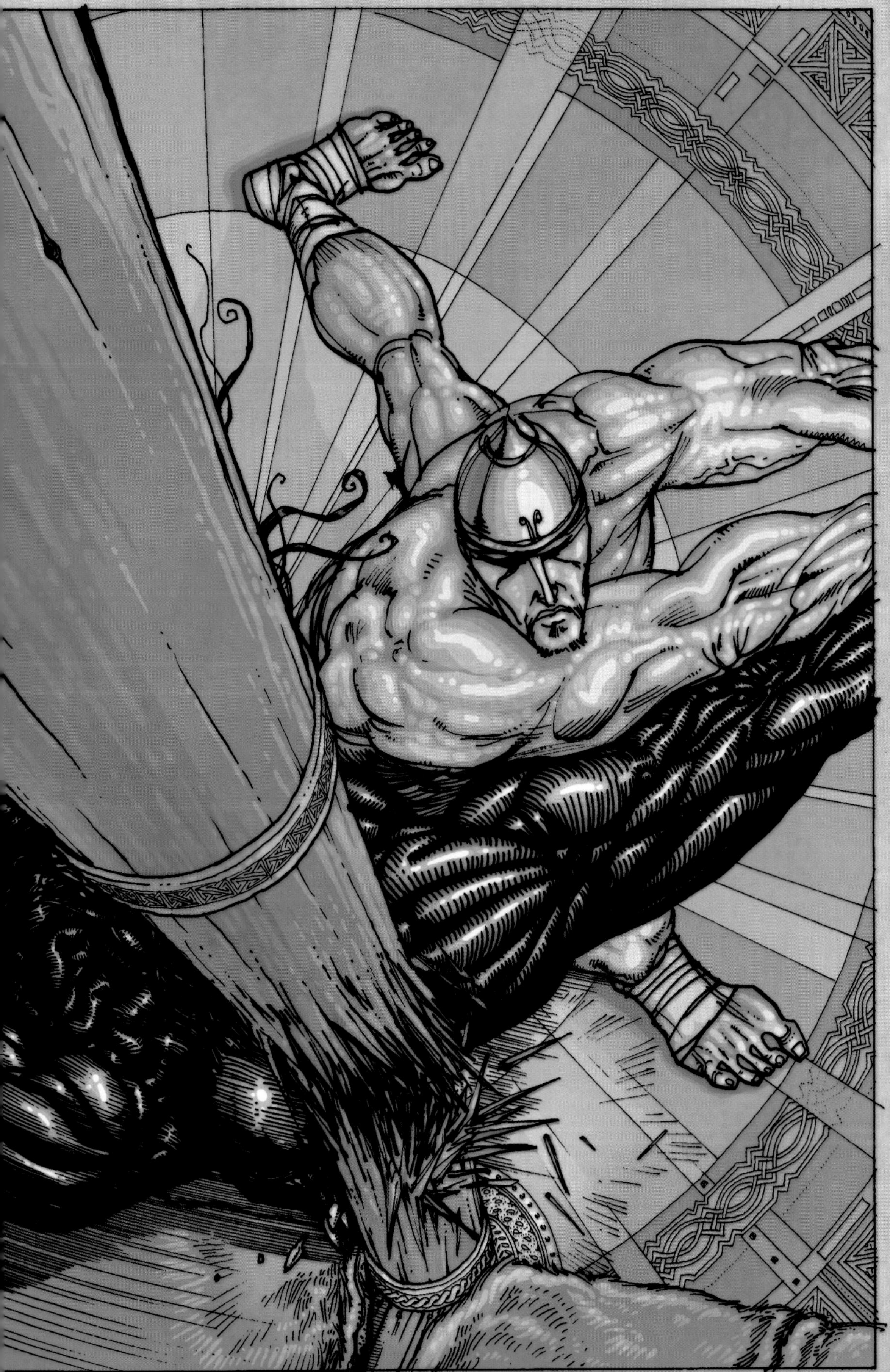

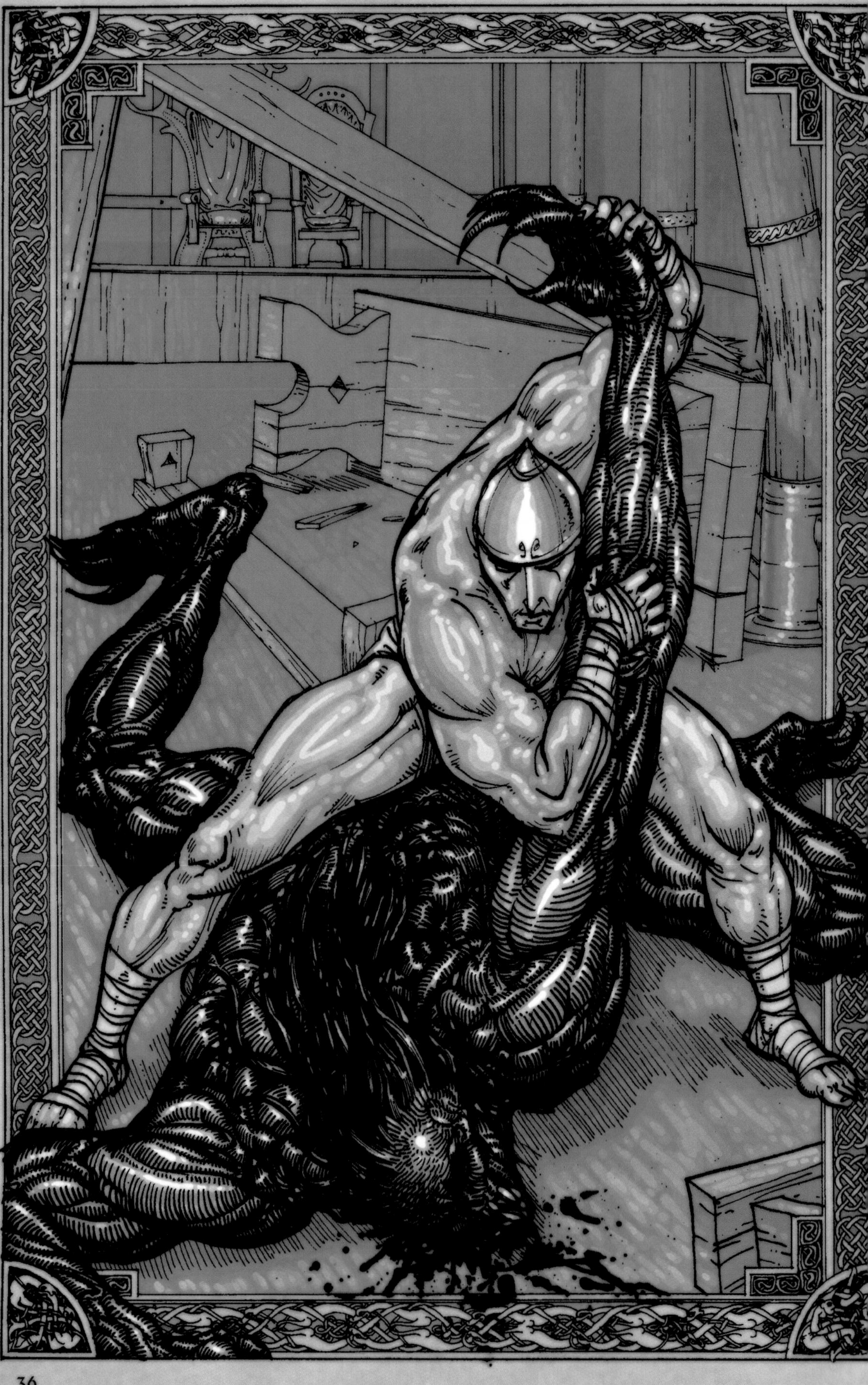

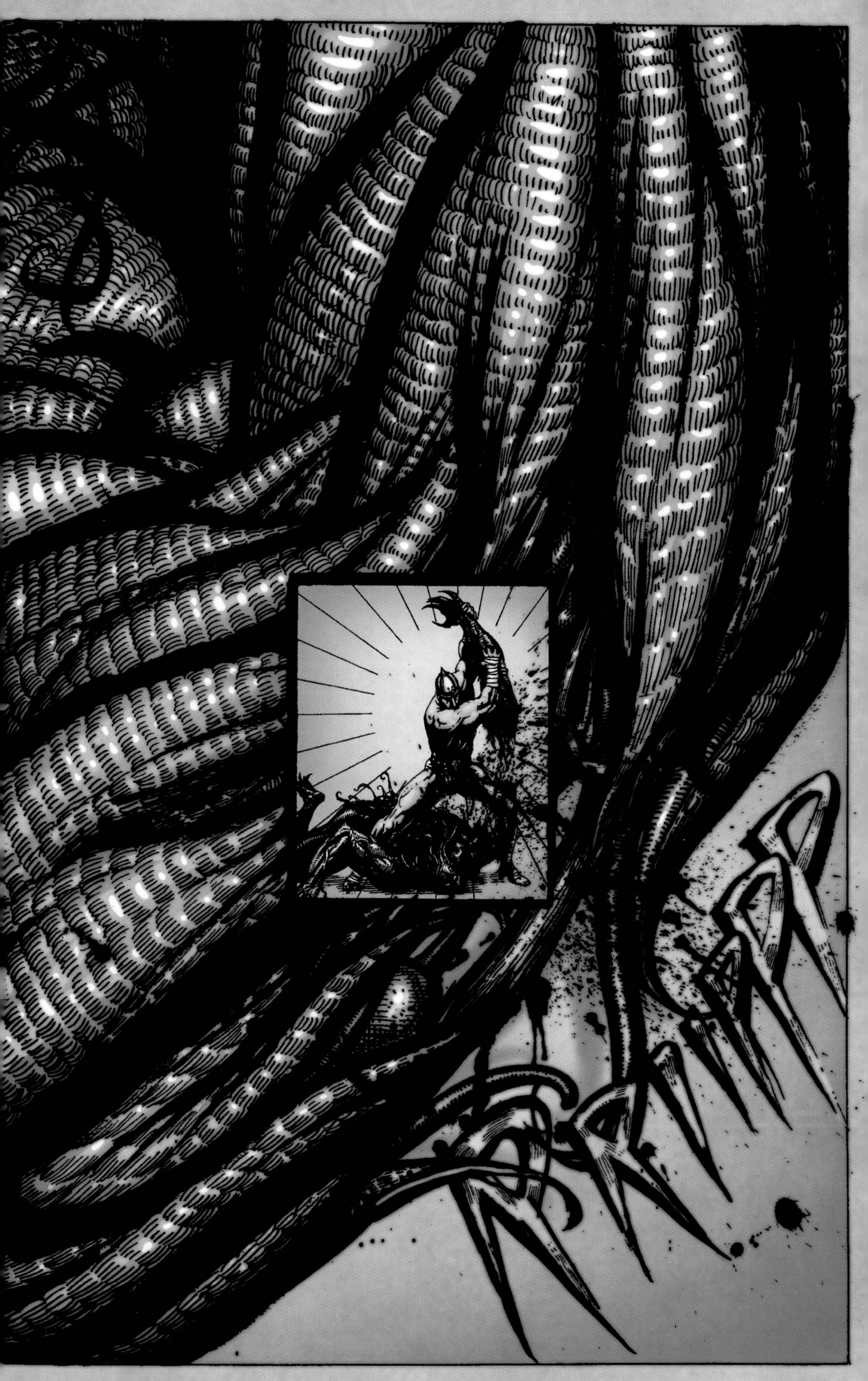

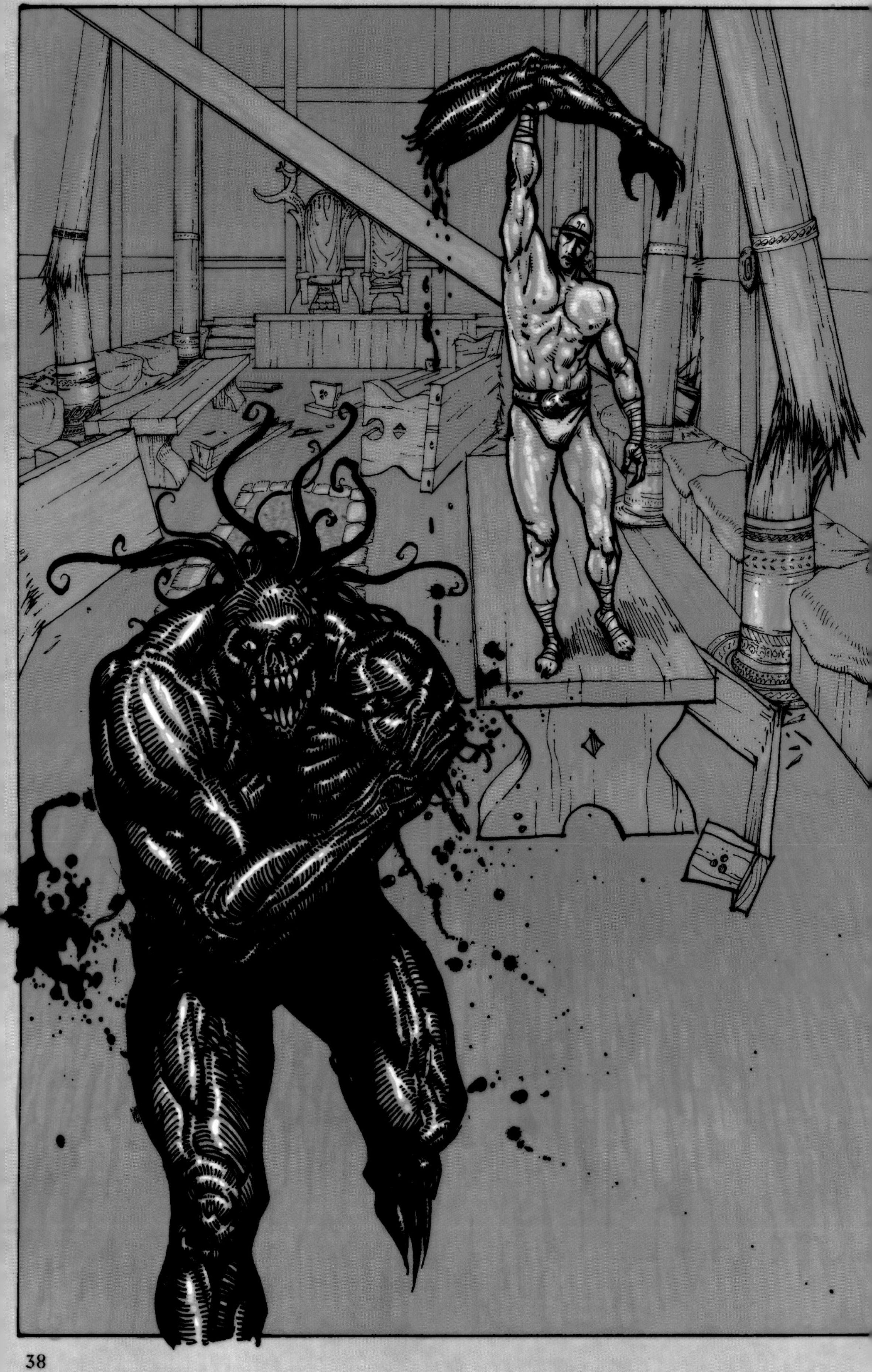

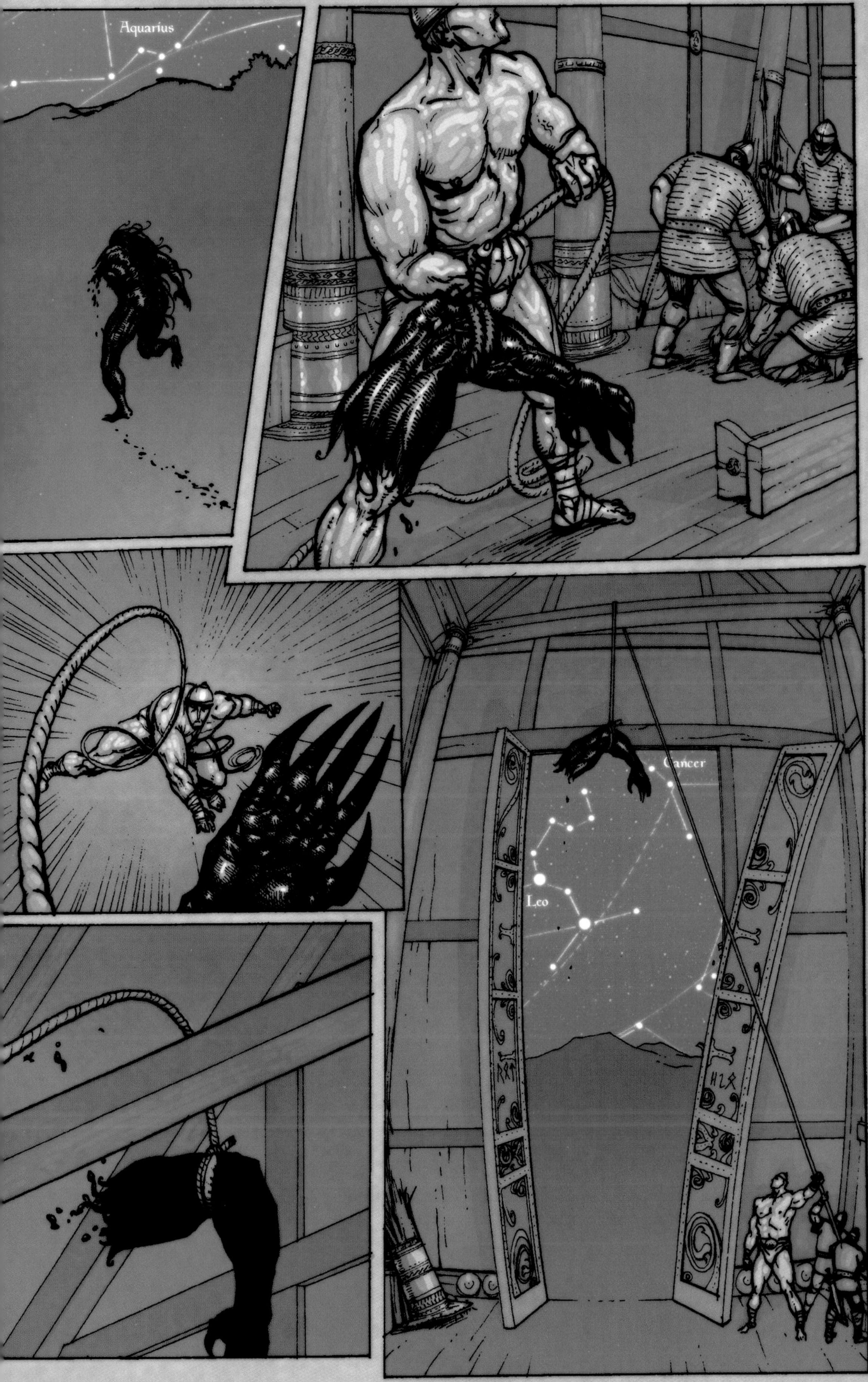
Aquarius
Cancer
Leo

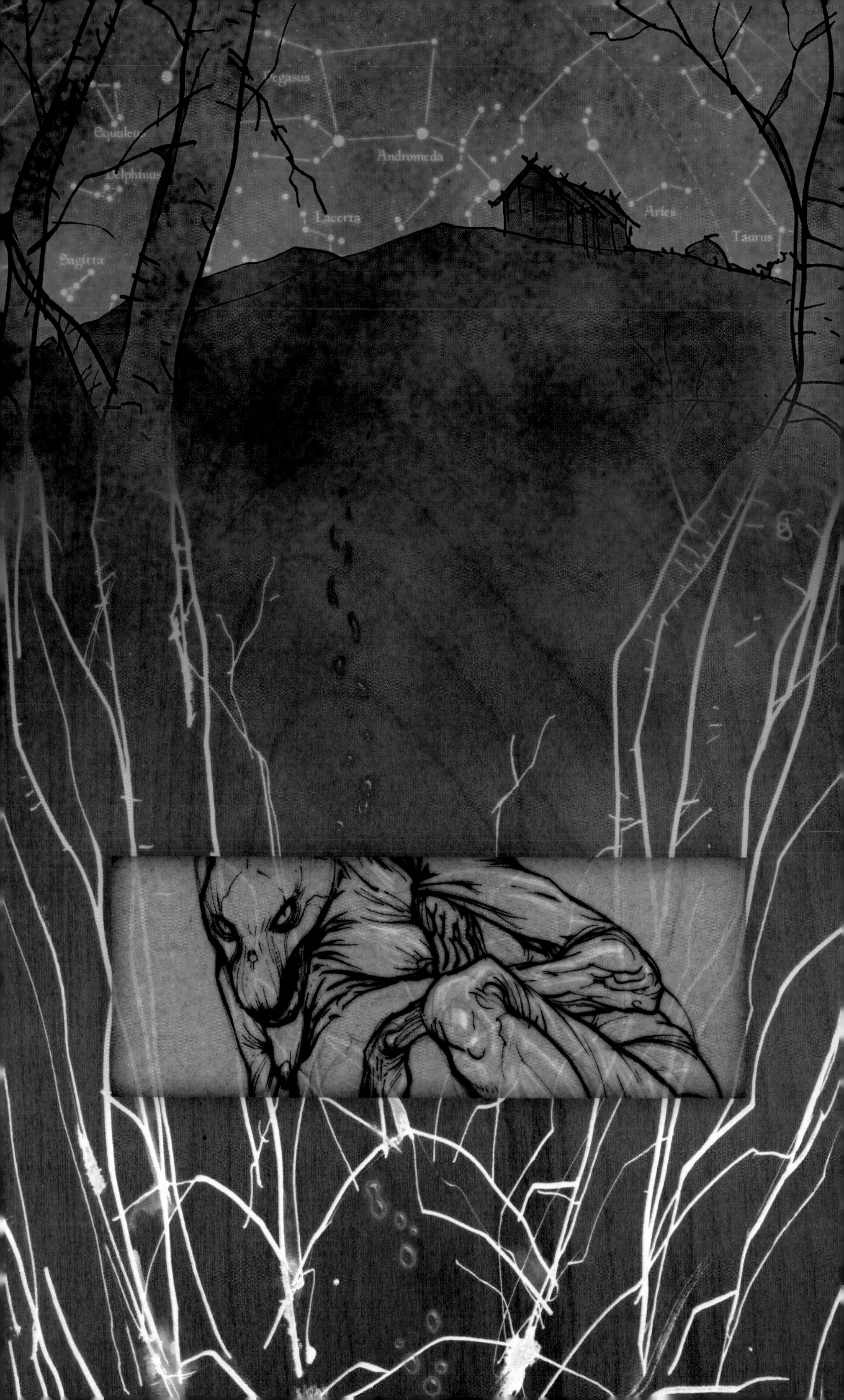

Pegasus
Equuleus
Andromeda
Delphinus
Lacerta
Aries
Sagitta
Taurus

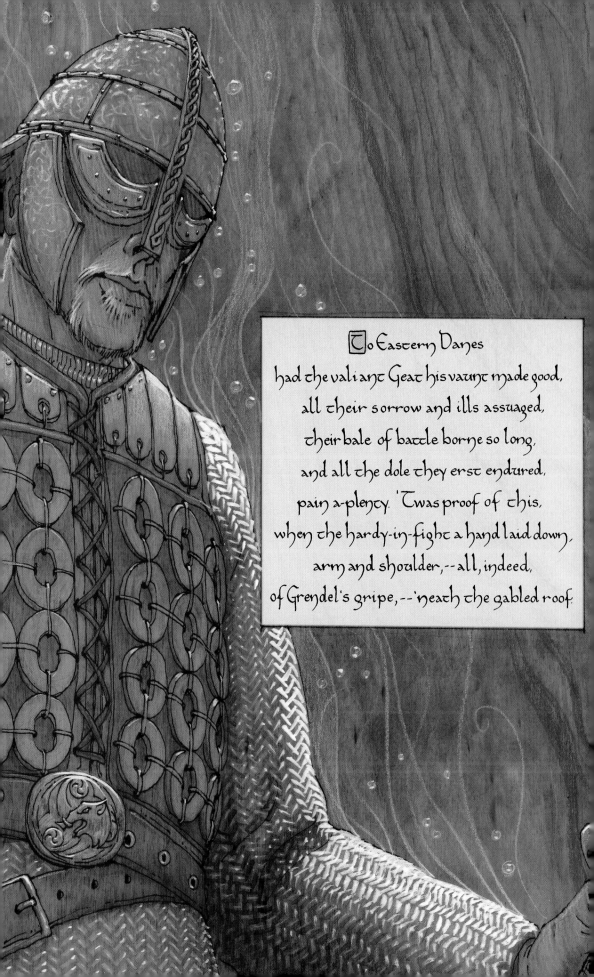

To Eastern Danes
had the valiant Geat his vaunt made good,
all their sorrow and ills assuaged,
their bale of battle borne so long,
and all the dole they erst endured,
pain a-plenty. 'Twas proof of this,
when the hardy-in-fight a hand laid down,
arm and shoulder,--all, indeed,
of Grendel's gripe,--'neath the gabled roof.

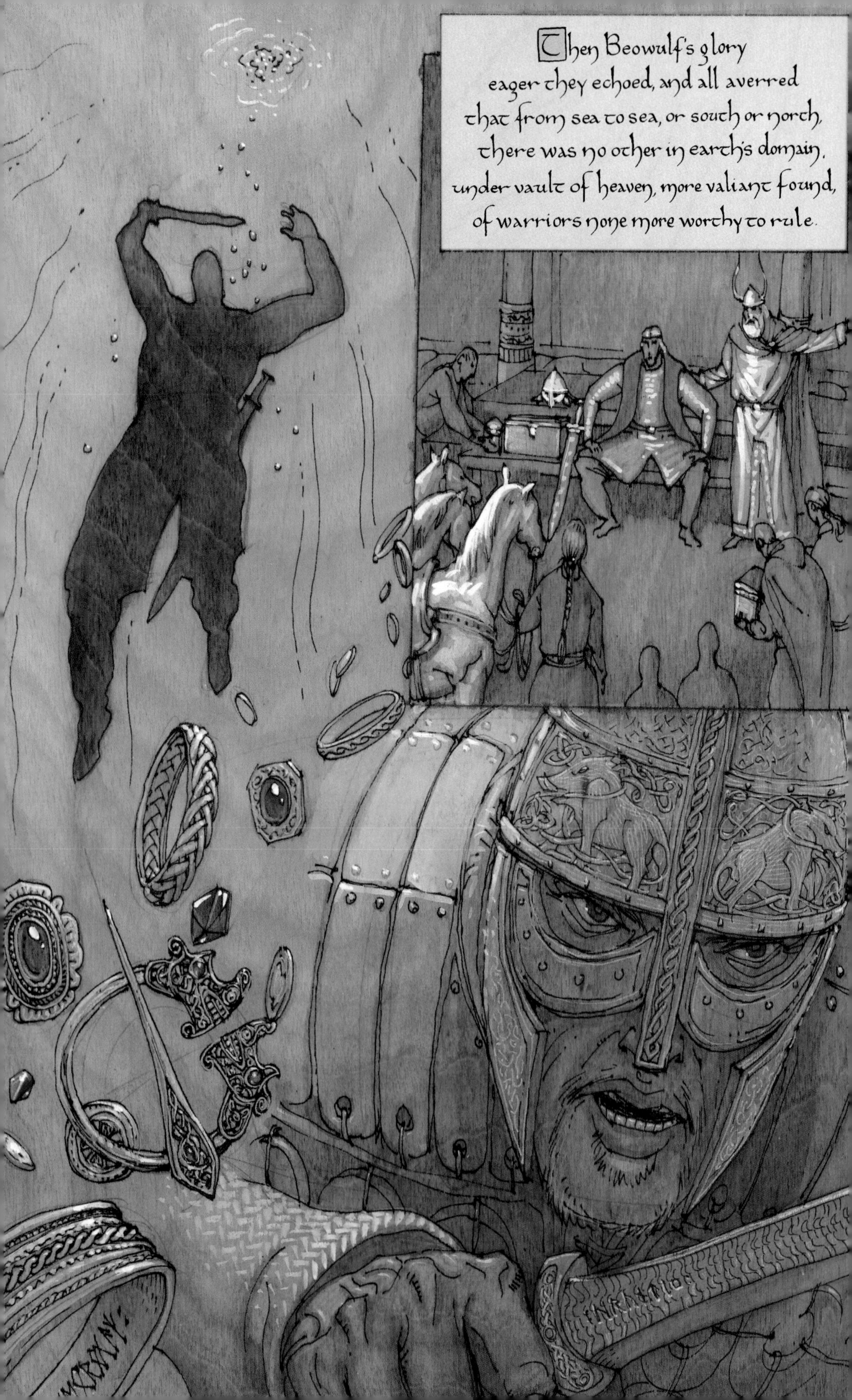
Then Beowulf's glory
eager they echoed, and all averred
that from sea to sea, or south or north,
there was no other in earth's domain,
under vault of heaven, more valiant found,
of warriors none more worthy to rule.

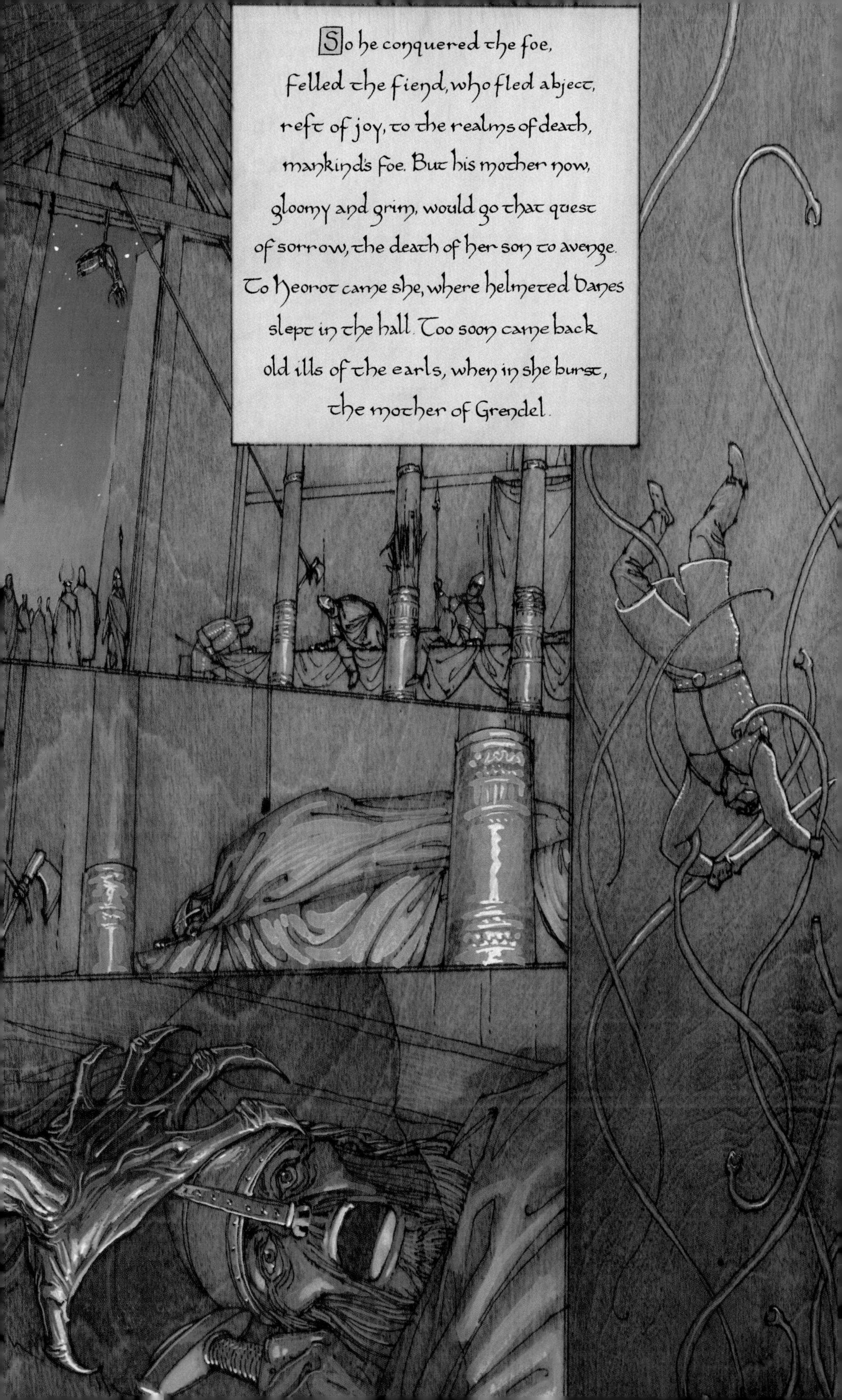
So he conquered the foe,
felled the fiend, who fled abject,
reft of joy, to the realms of death,
mankind's foe. But his mother now,
gloomy and grim, would go that quest
of sorrow, the death of her son to avenge.
To Heorot came she, where helmeted Danes
slept in the hall. Too soon came back
old ills of the earls, when in she burst,
the mother of Grendel.

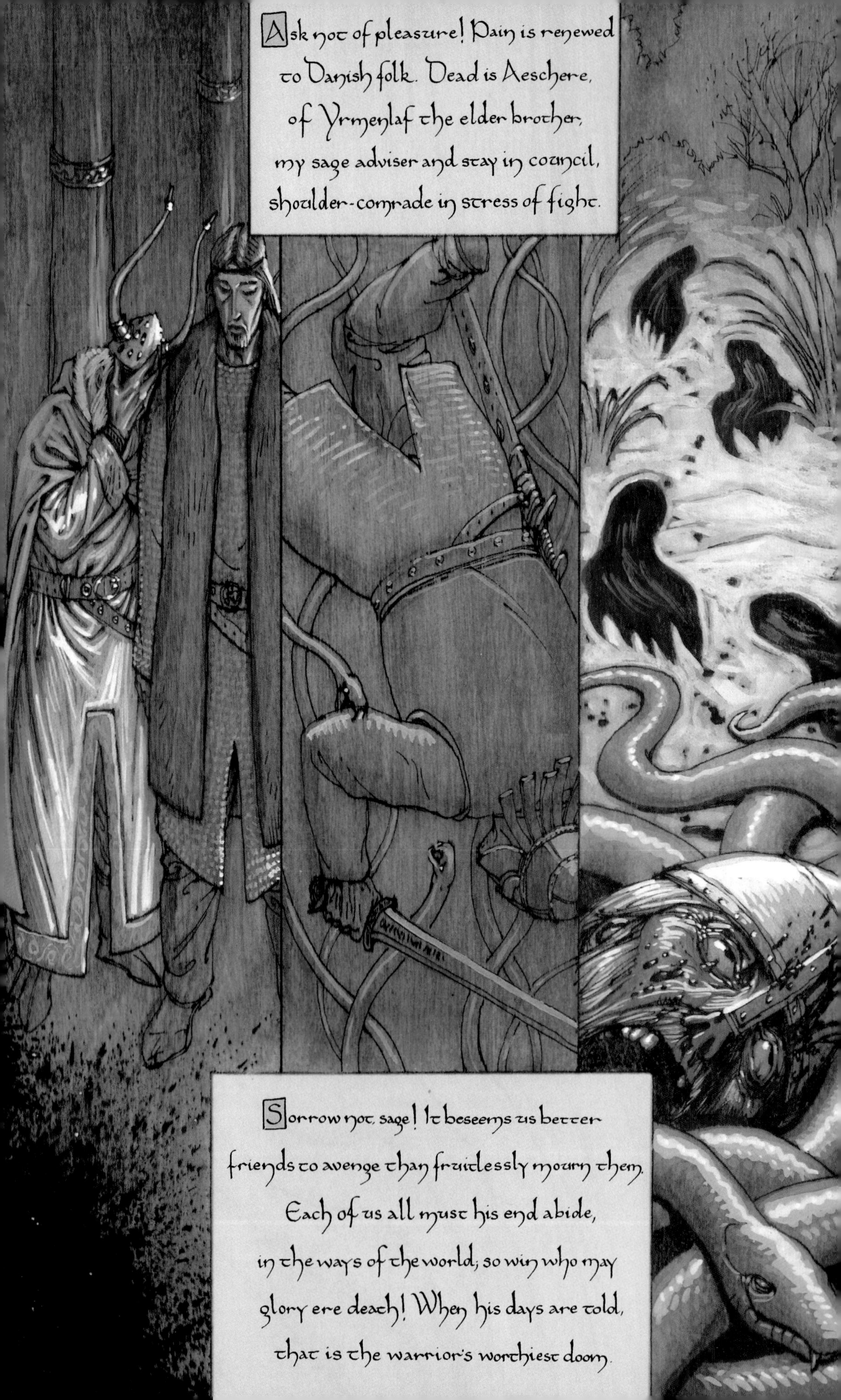
Ask not of pleasure! Pain is renewed
to Danish folk. Dead is Aeschere,
of Yrmenlaf the elder brother,
my sage adviser and stay in council,
shoulder-comrade in stress of fight.
Sorrow not, sage! It beseems us better
friends to avenge than fruitlessly mourn them.
Each of us all must his end abide,
in the ways of the world; so win who may
glory ere death! When his days are told,
that is the warrior's worthiest doom.

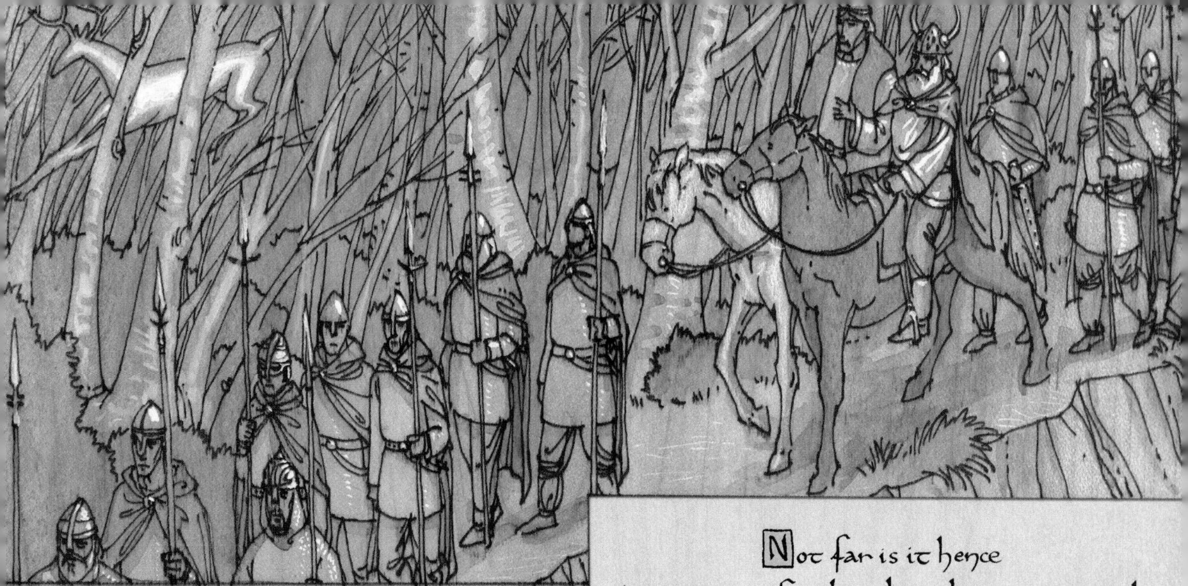

Not far is it hence
in measure of miles that the mere expands,
and o'er it the frost-bound forest hanging,
sturdily rooted, shadows the wave.
By night is a wonder weird to see,
fire on the waters.
Nay, though the heath-rover, harried by dogs,
the horn-proud hart, this holt should seek,
long distance driven, his dear life first
on the brink he yields, ere he brave the plunge
to hide his head: 'tis no happy place!

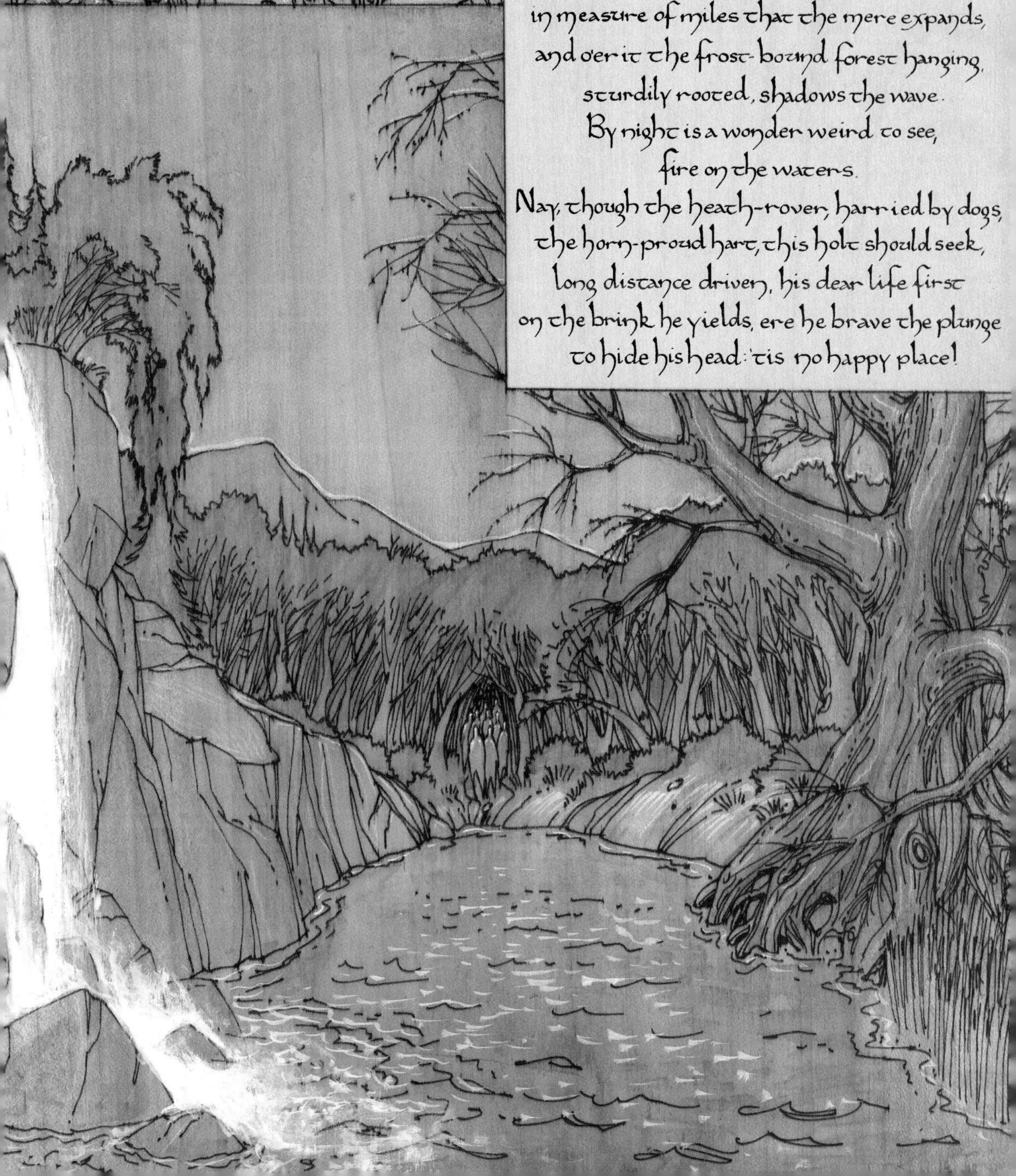

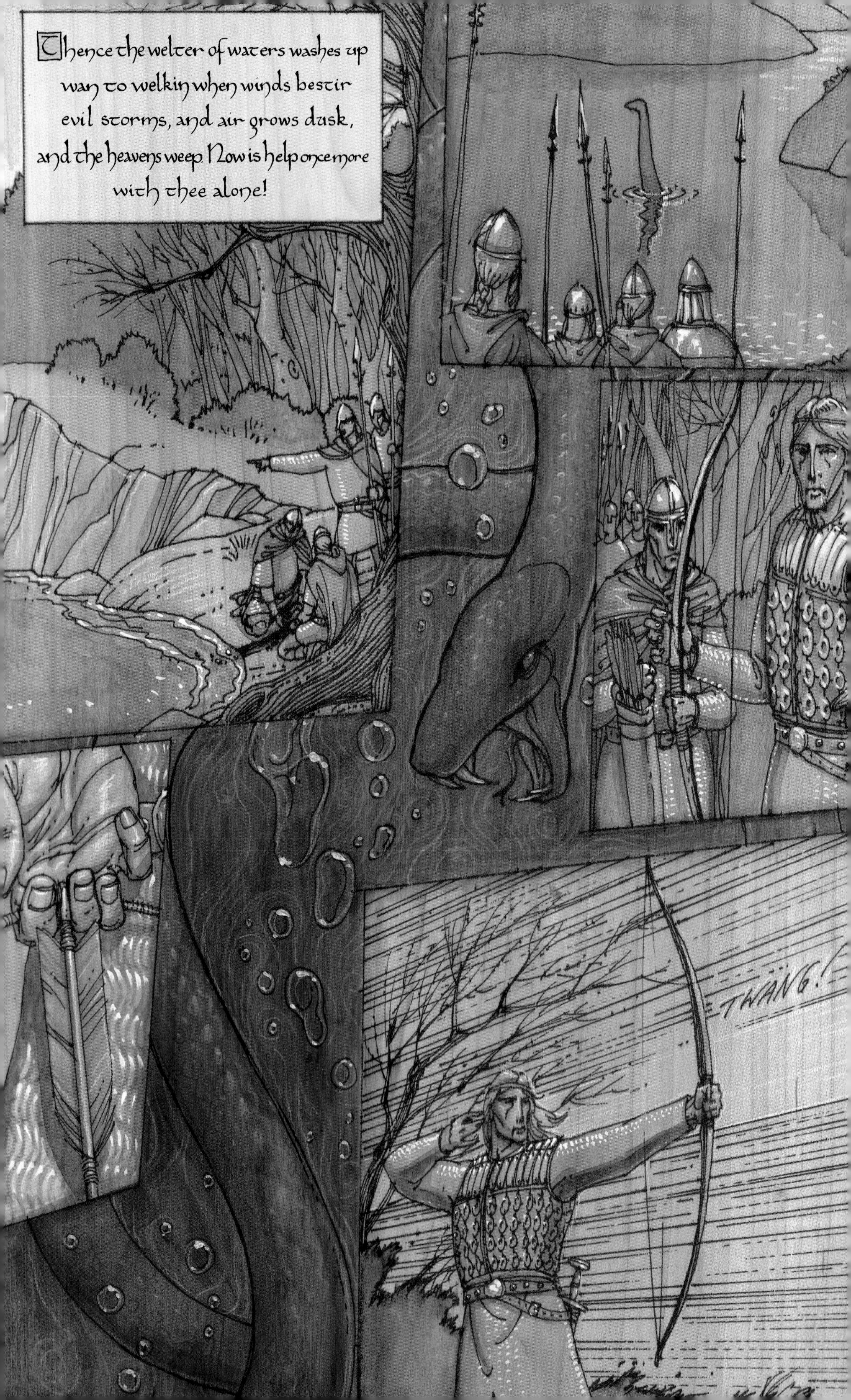
Thence the welter of waters washes up wan to welkin when winds bestir evil storms, and air grows dusk, and the heavens weep. Now is help once more with thee alone!
TWANG!

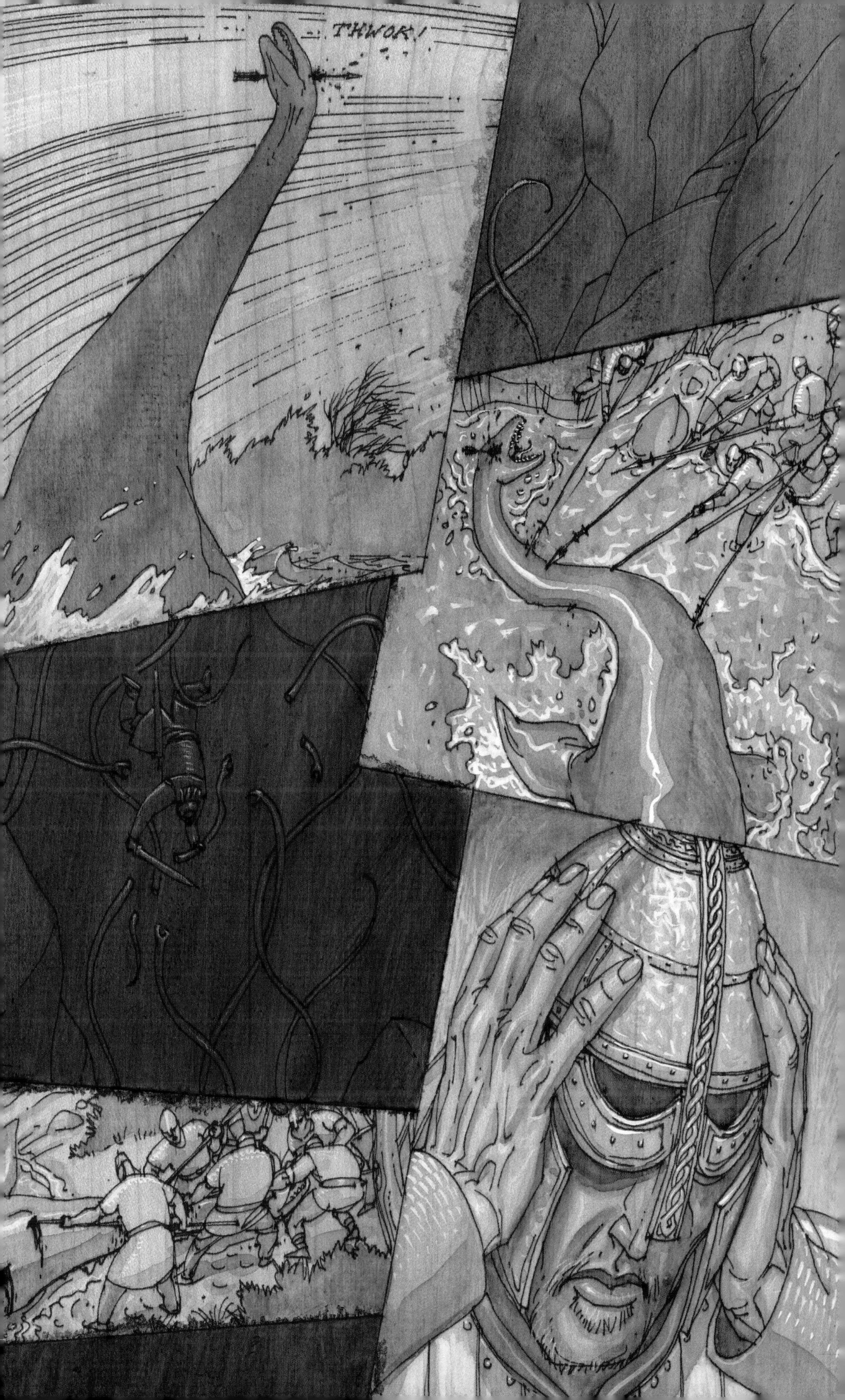
THWOK!

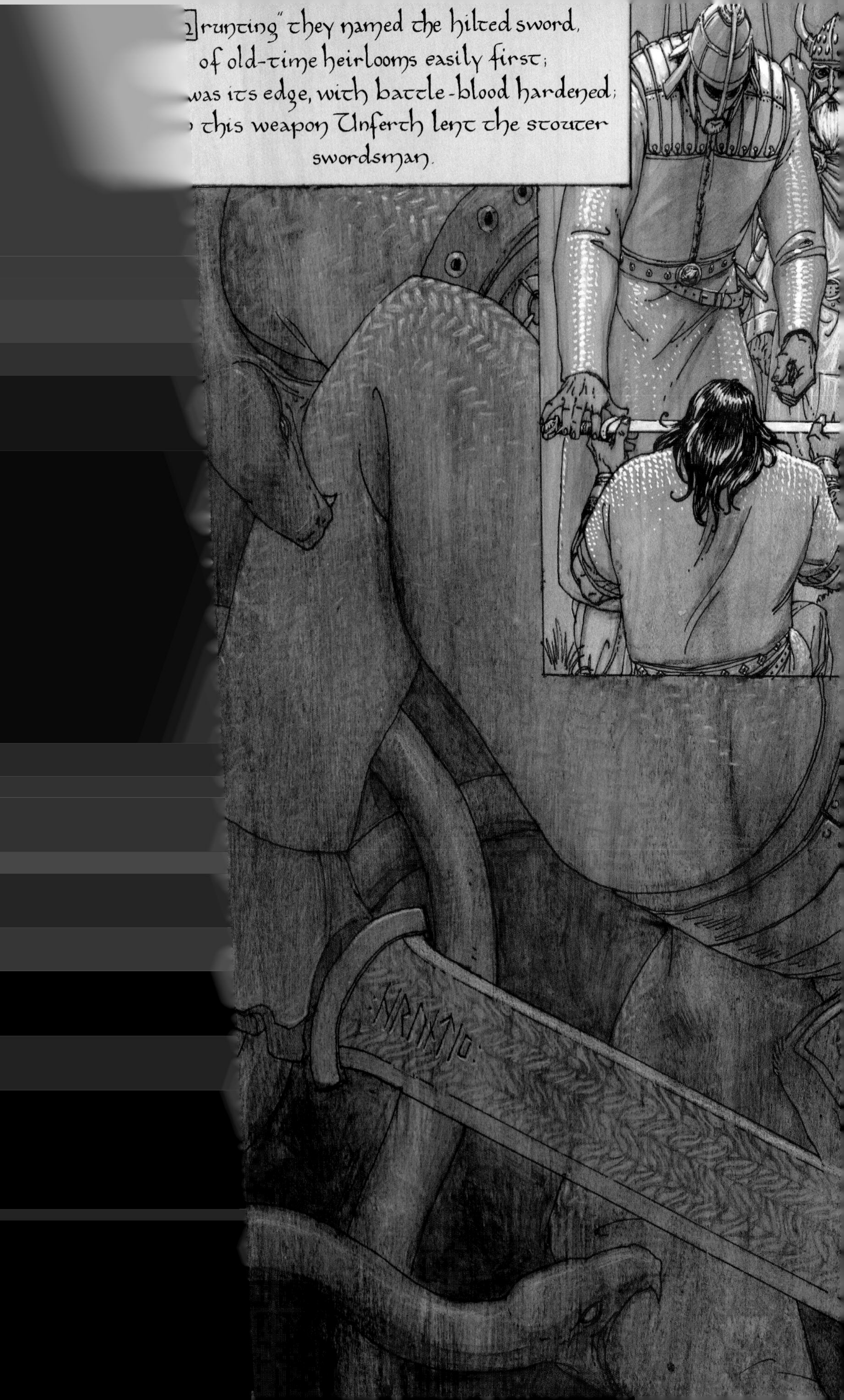
runting" they named the hilted sword,
of old-time heirlooms easily first;
was its edge, with battle-blood hardened;
this weapon Unferth lent the stouter
swordsman.

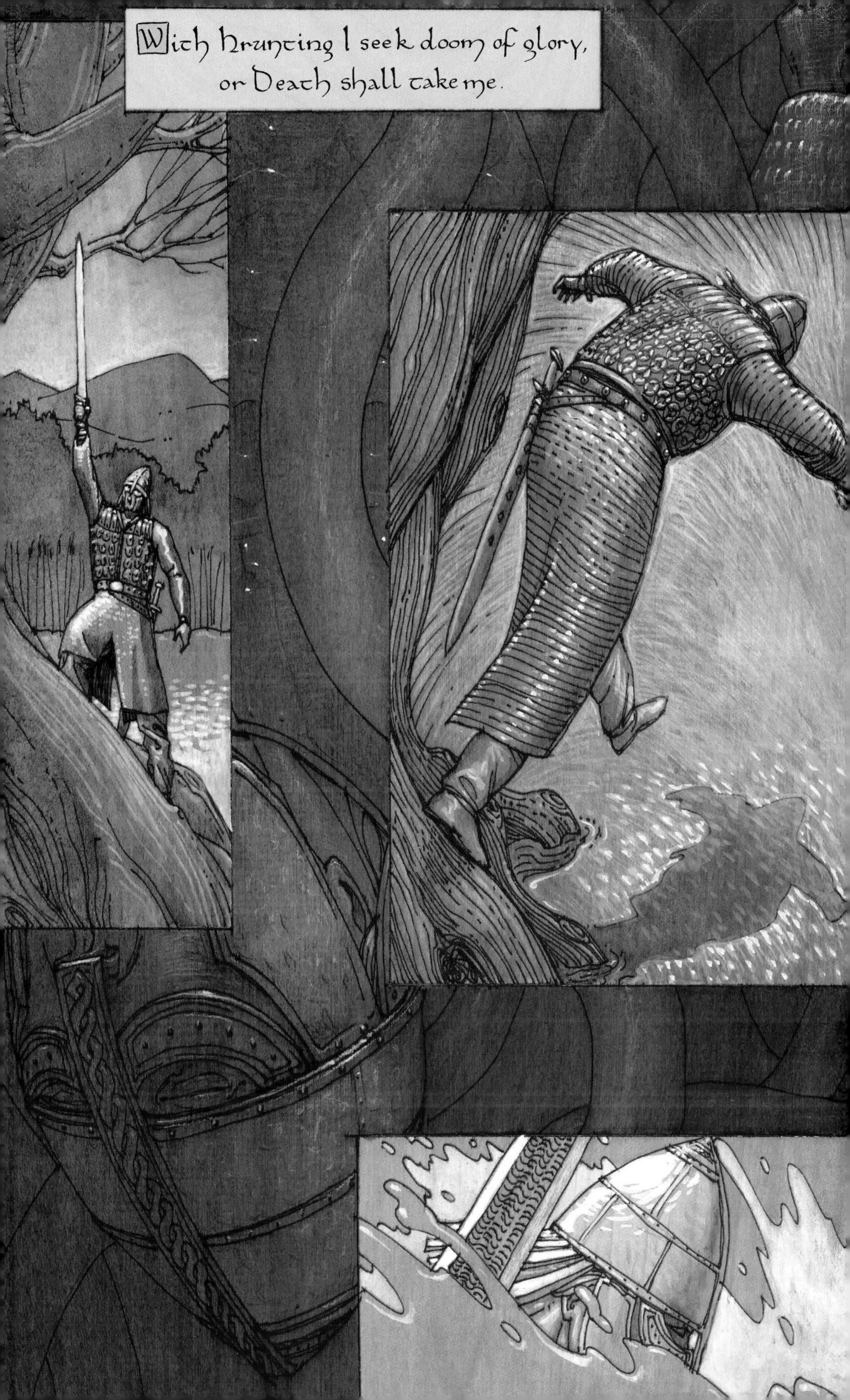
With Hrunting I seek doom of glory, or Death shall take me.

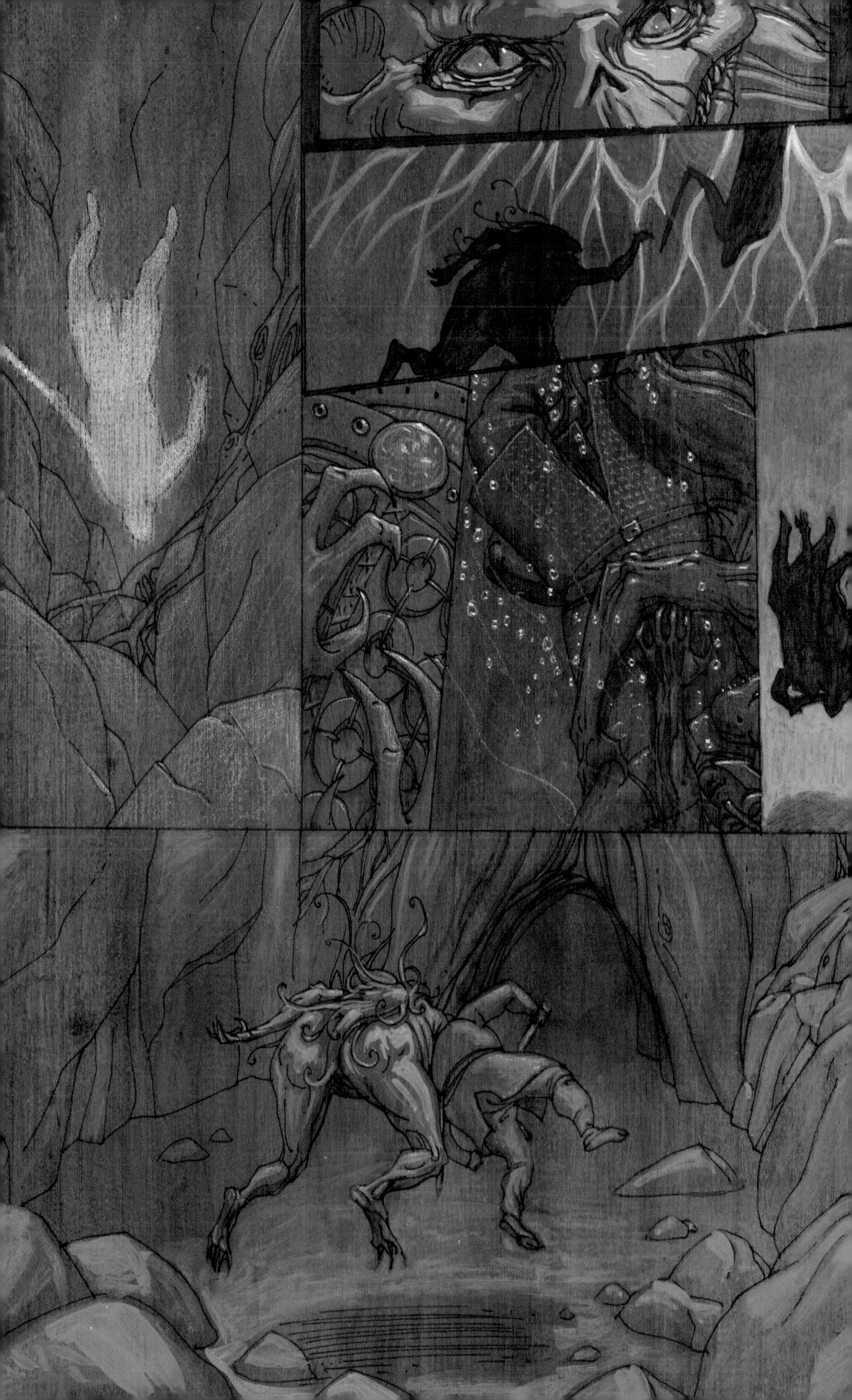

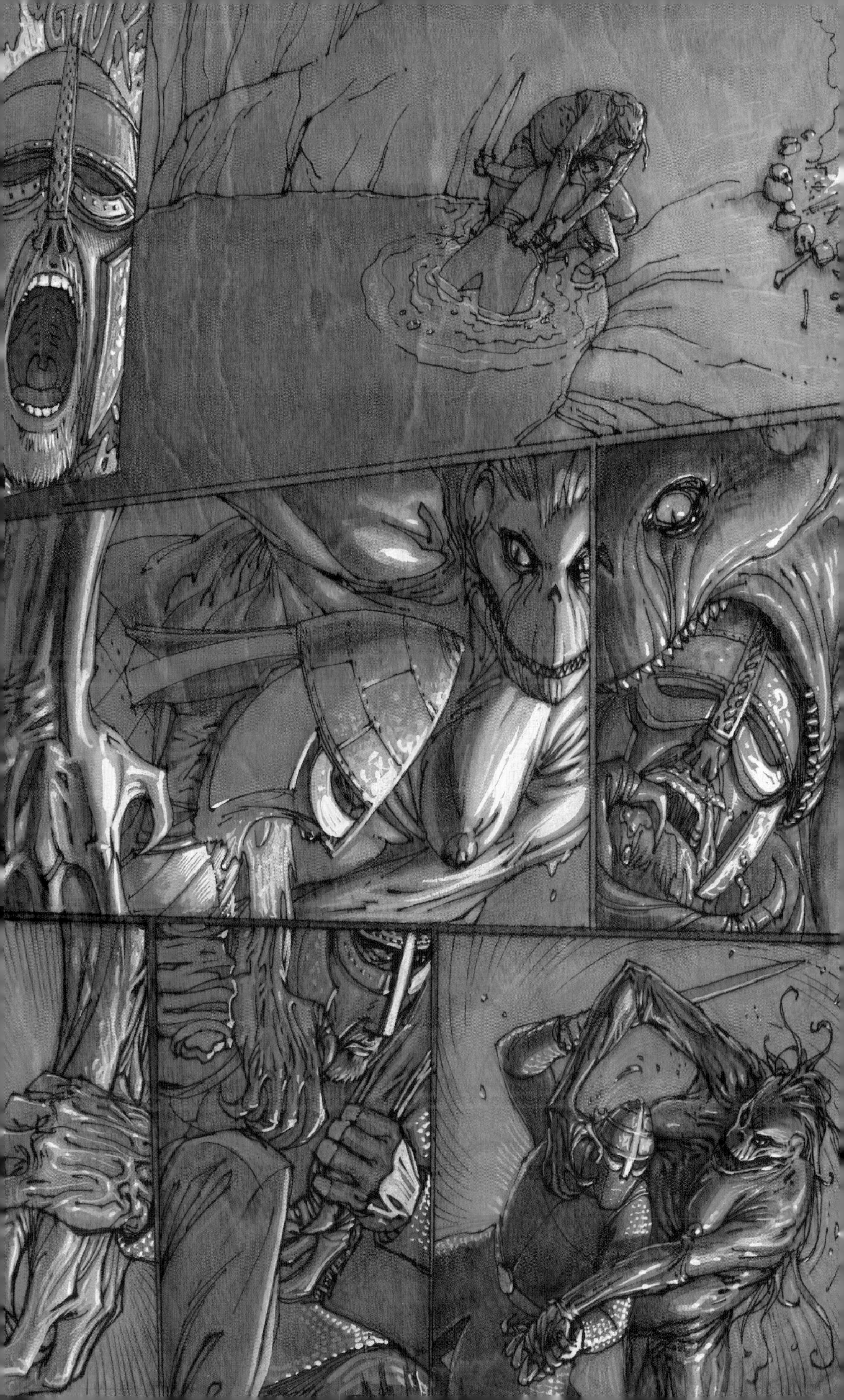
GHUK!

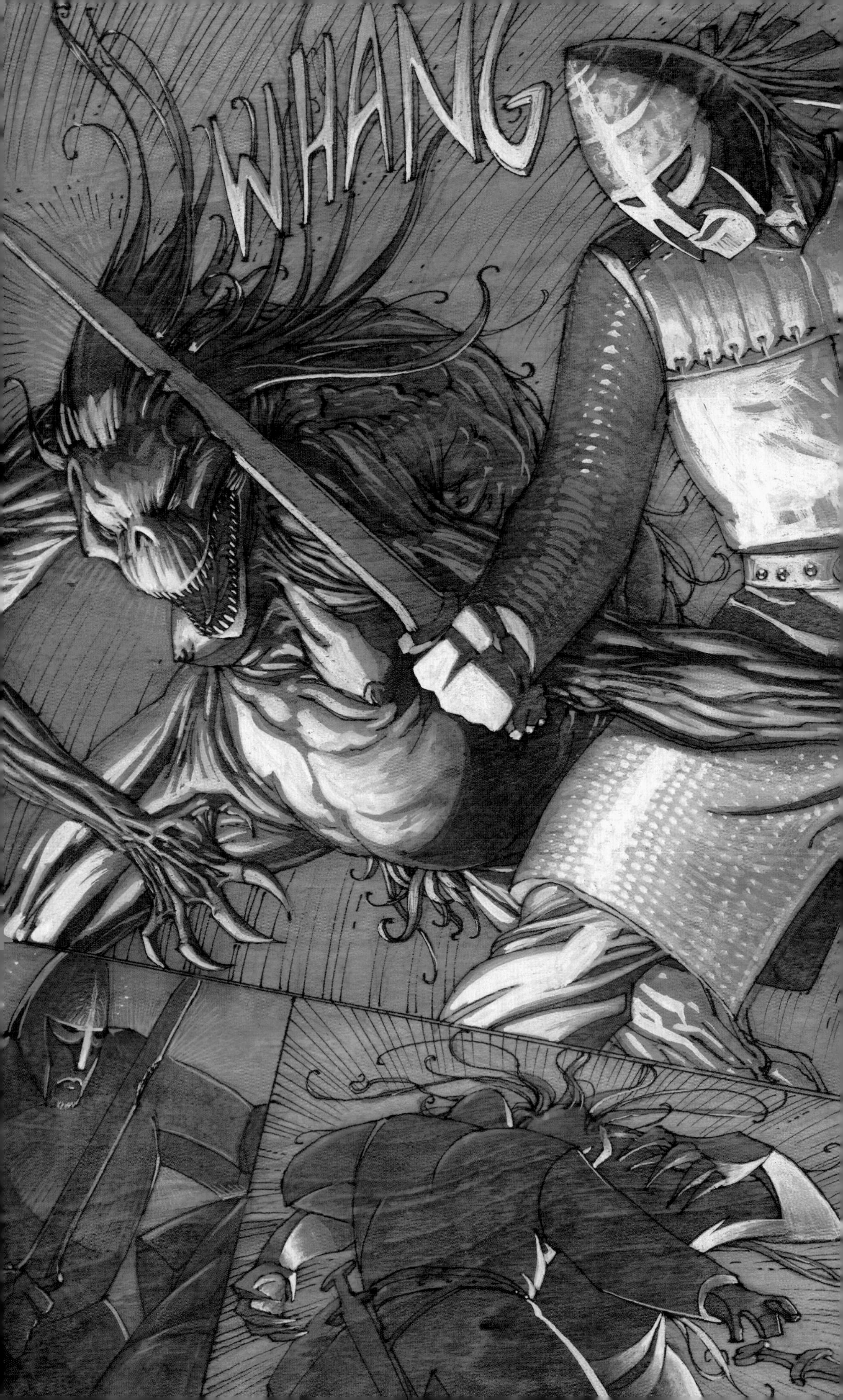
WHANG

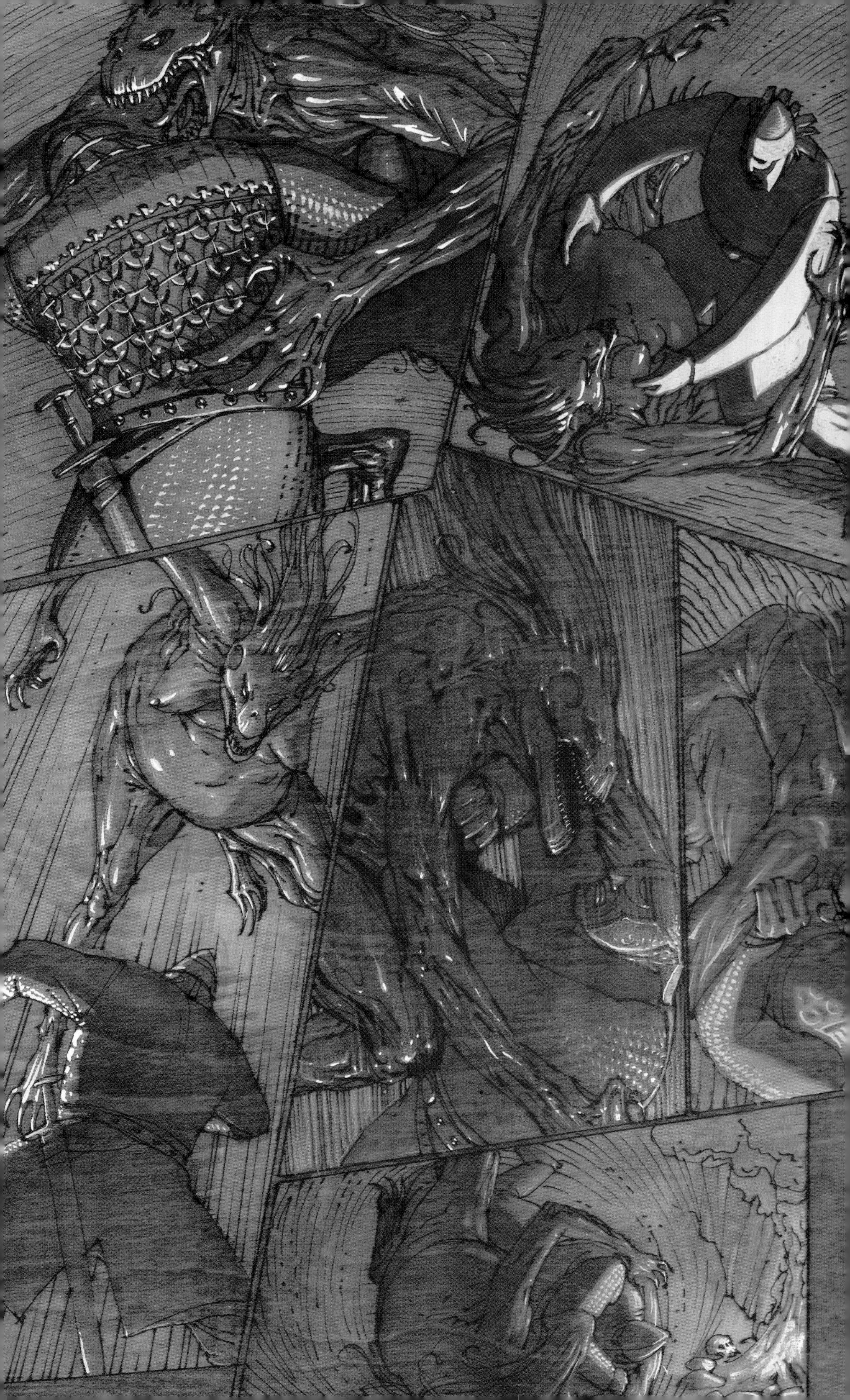

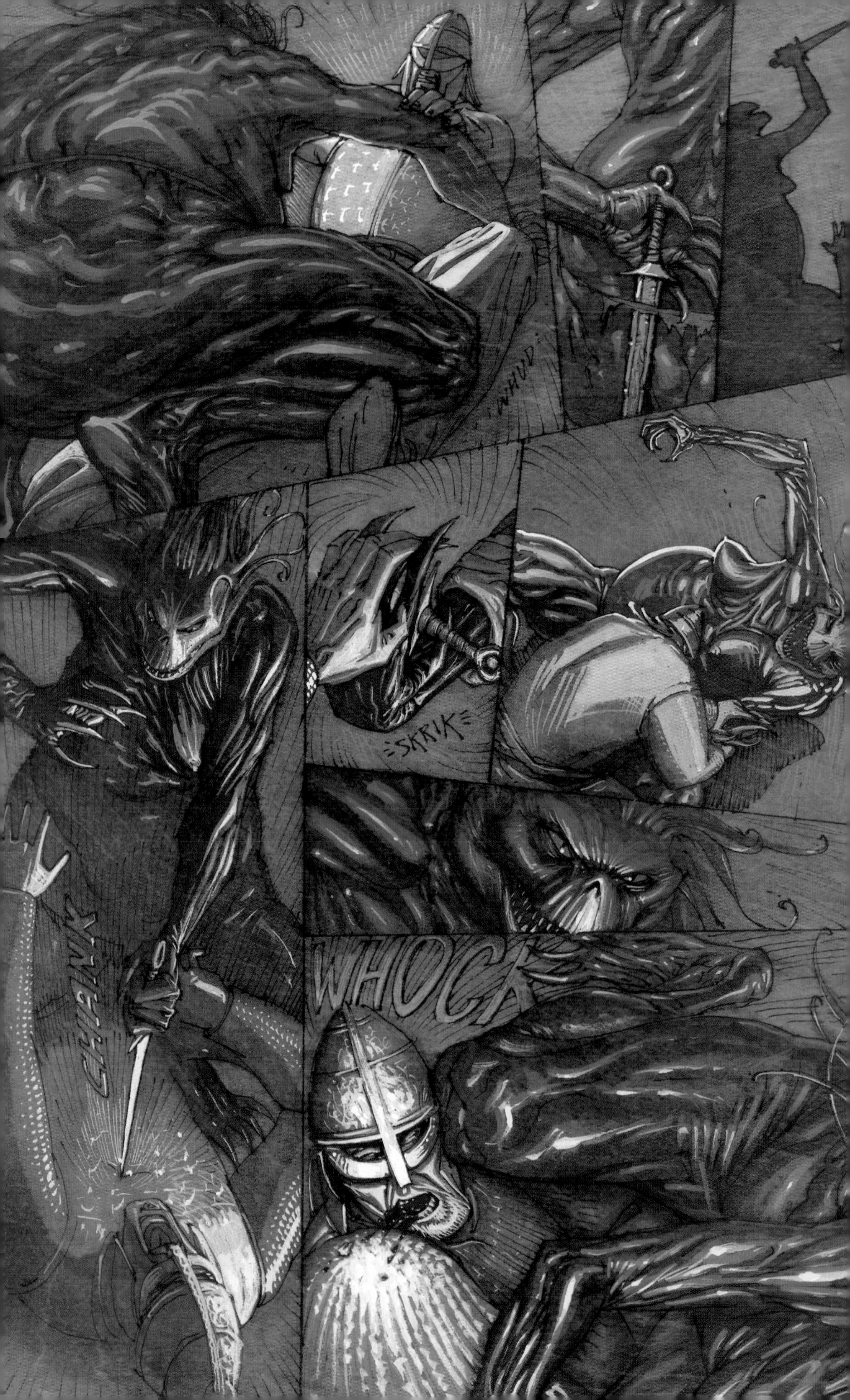
WHUD
SKRIK
WHOCK

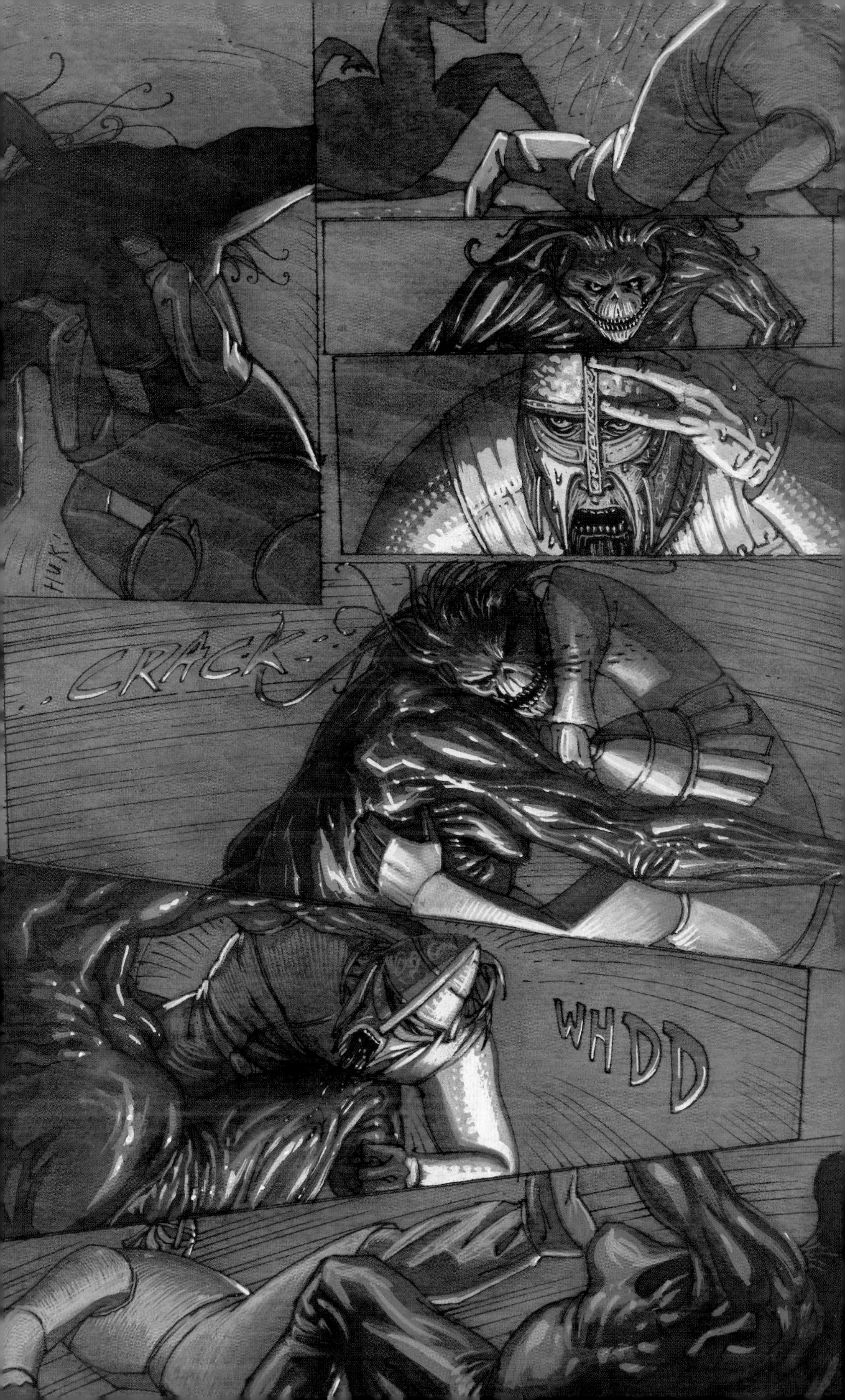
HUK
CRACK
WHDD

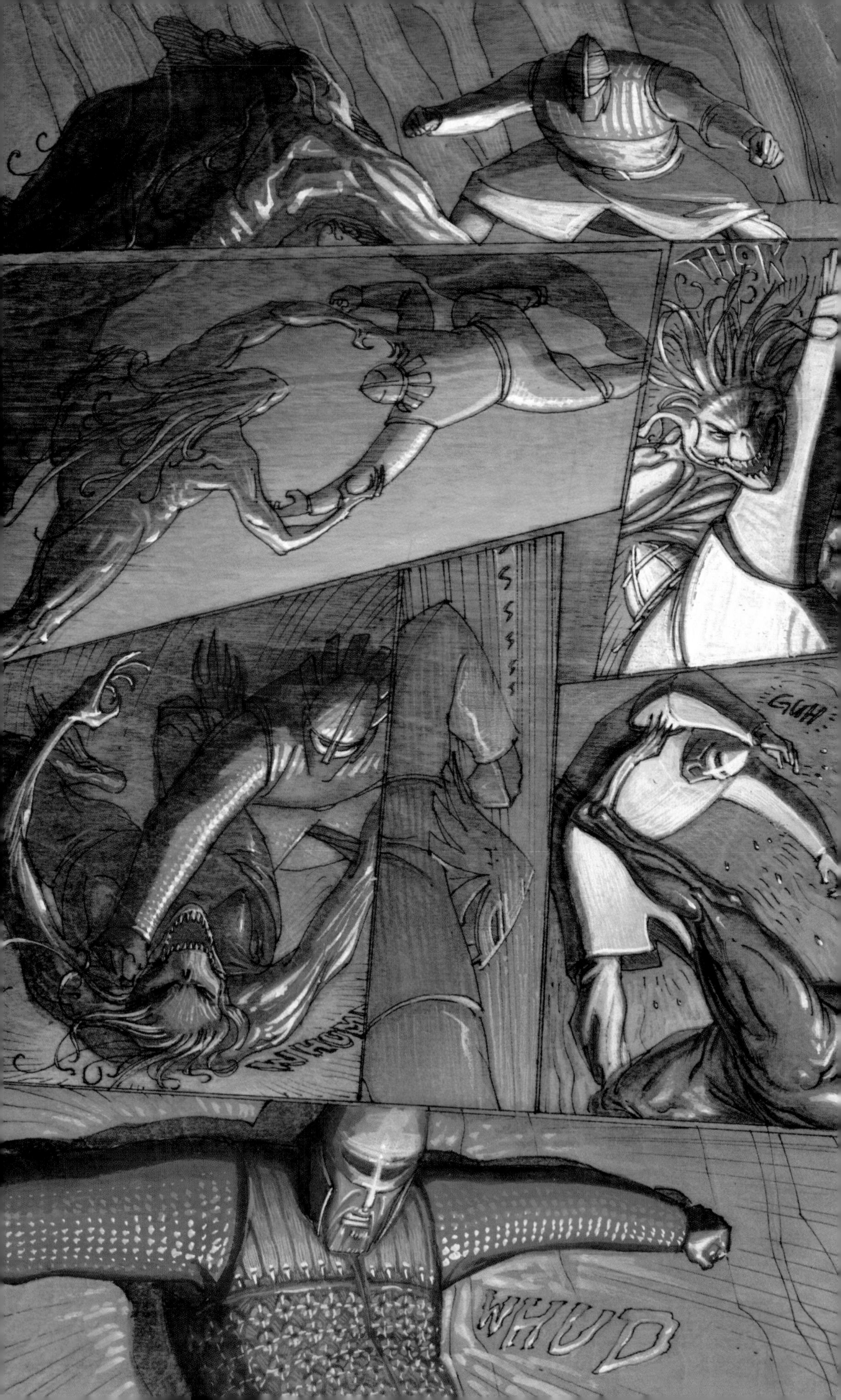
THOK
GUH
WHUD

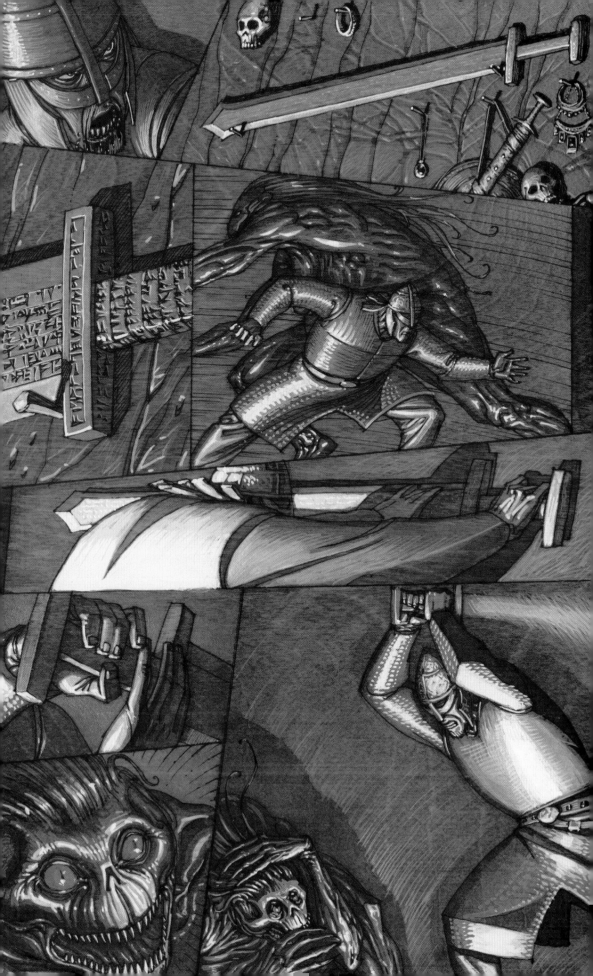

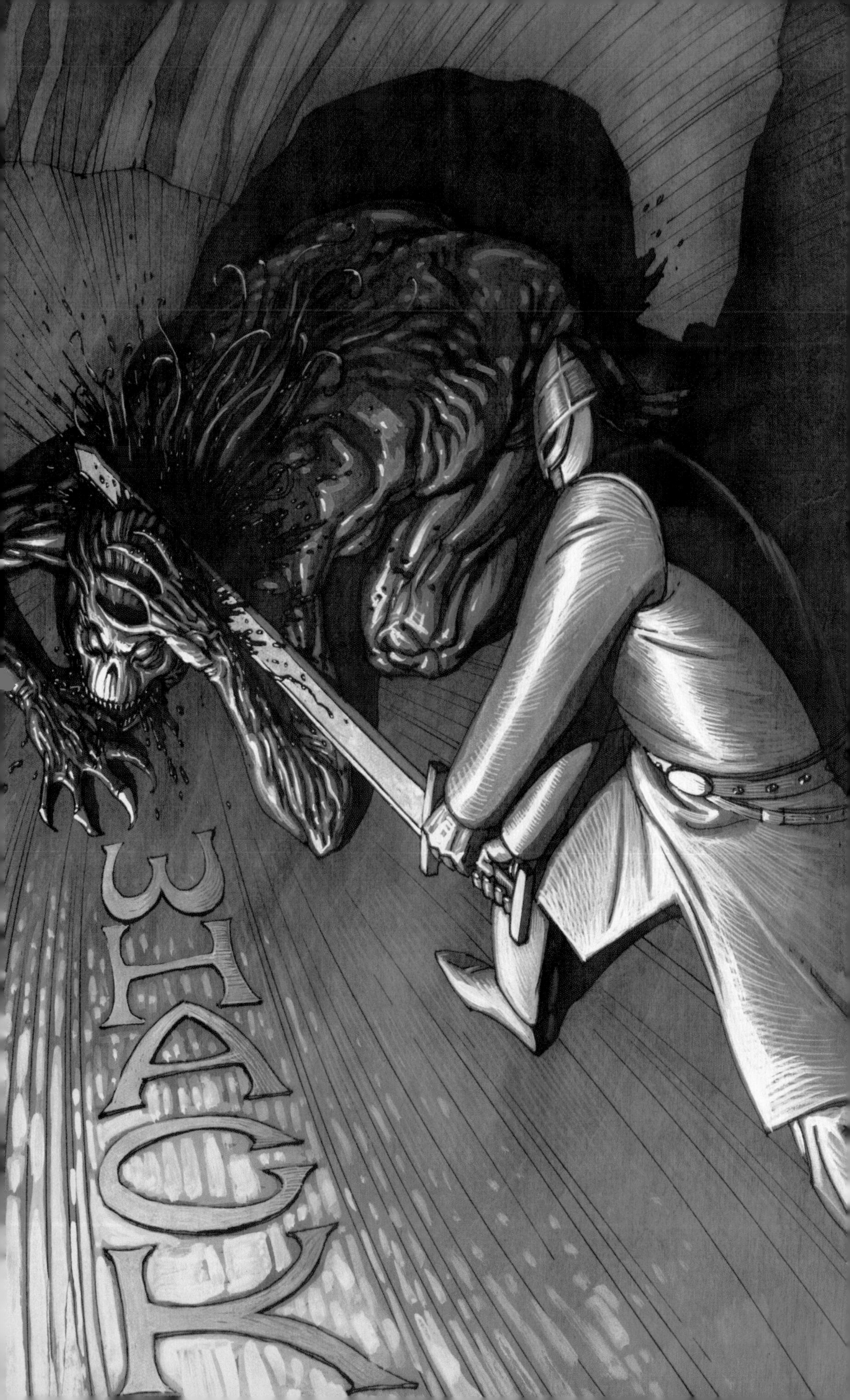
WHACK

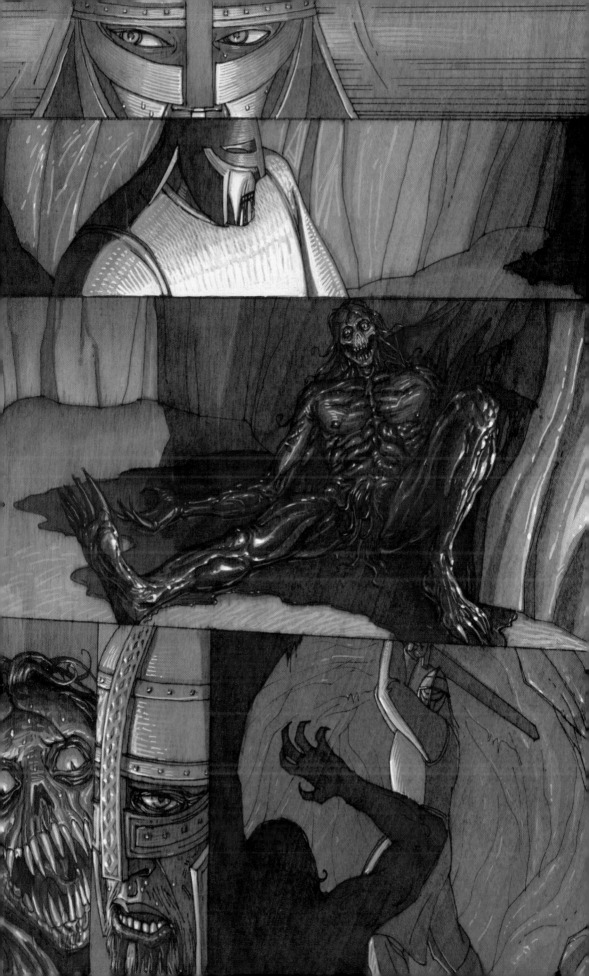

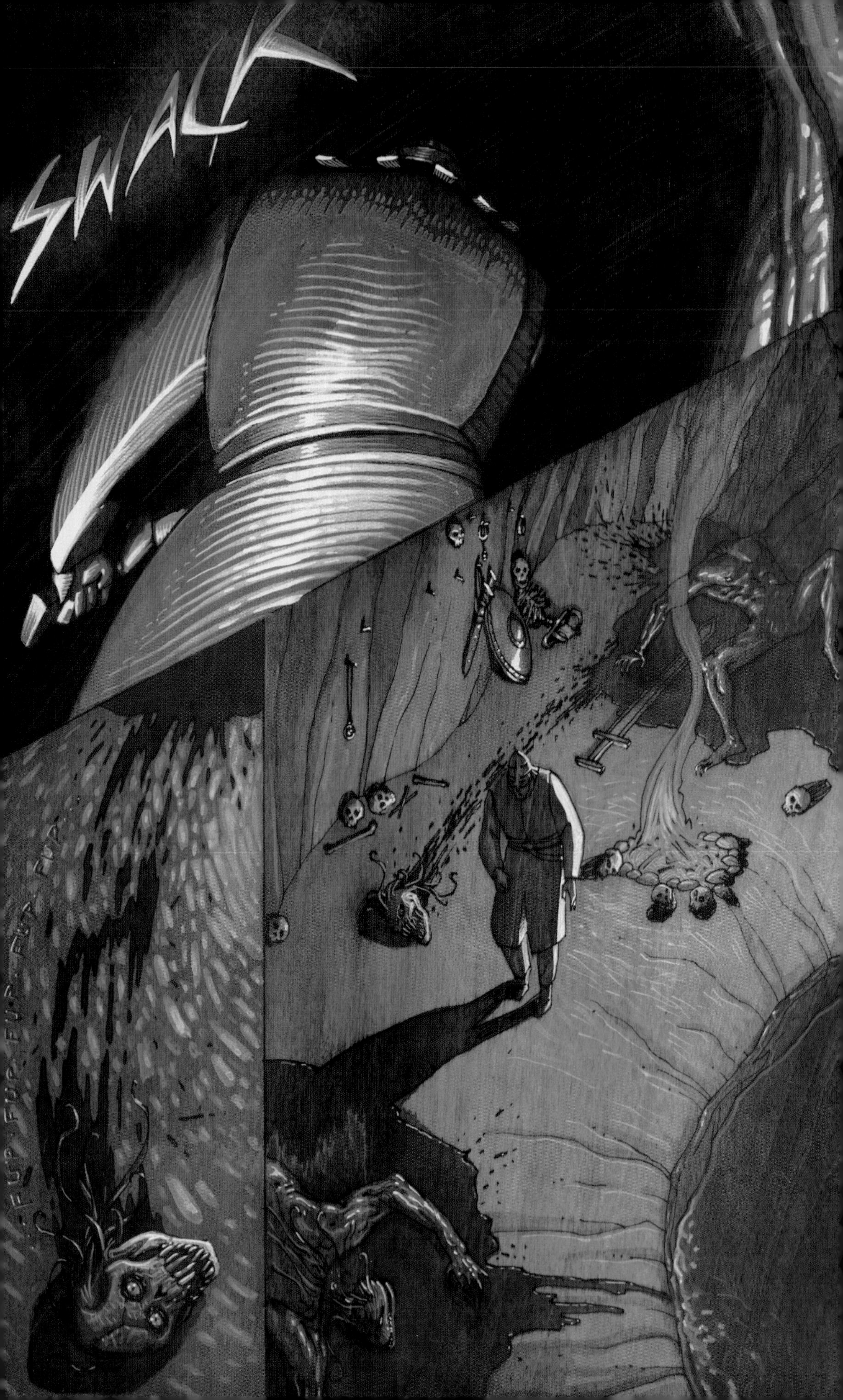
SWACK
FUP. FUP. FUP. FUP. FUP.

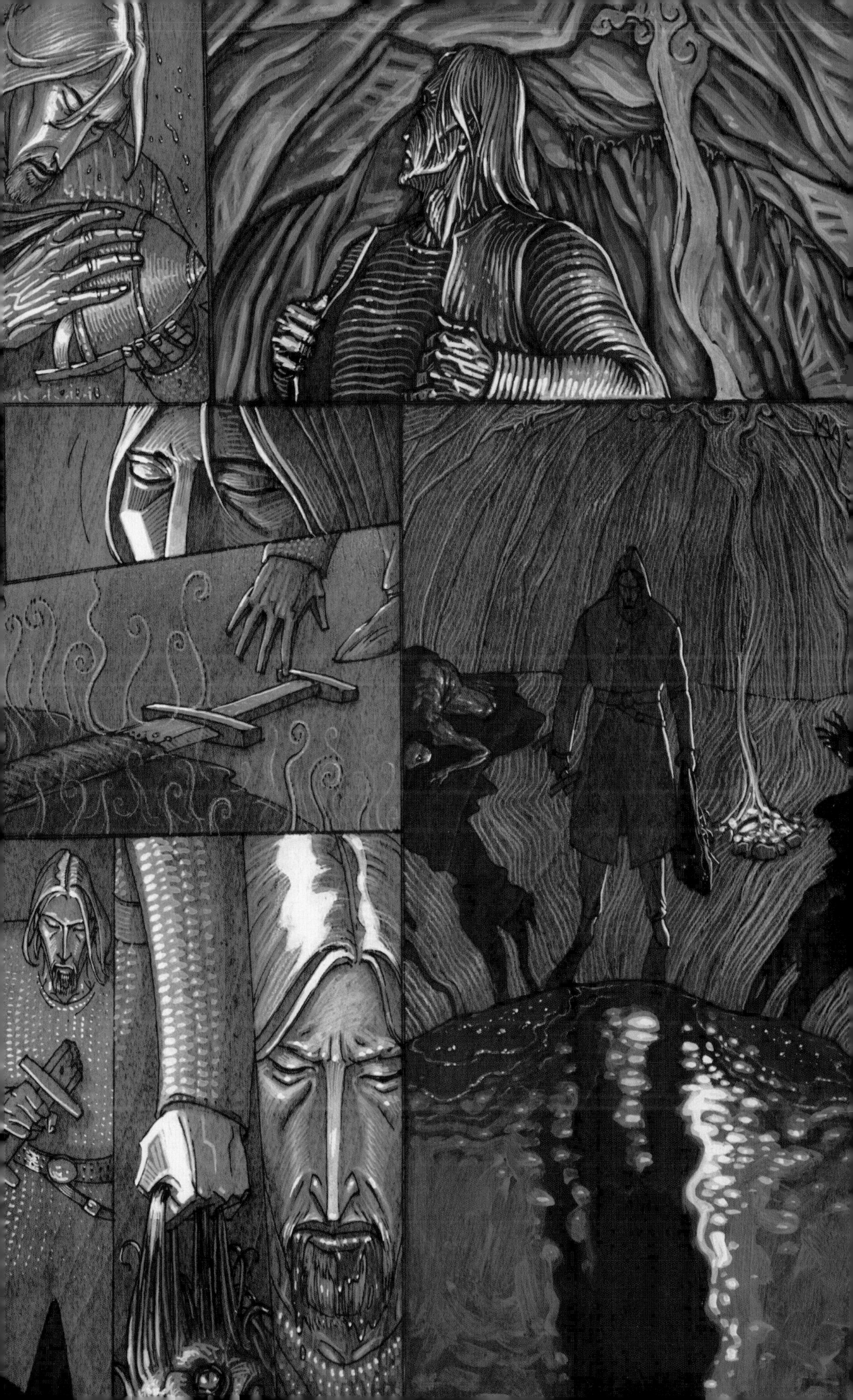

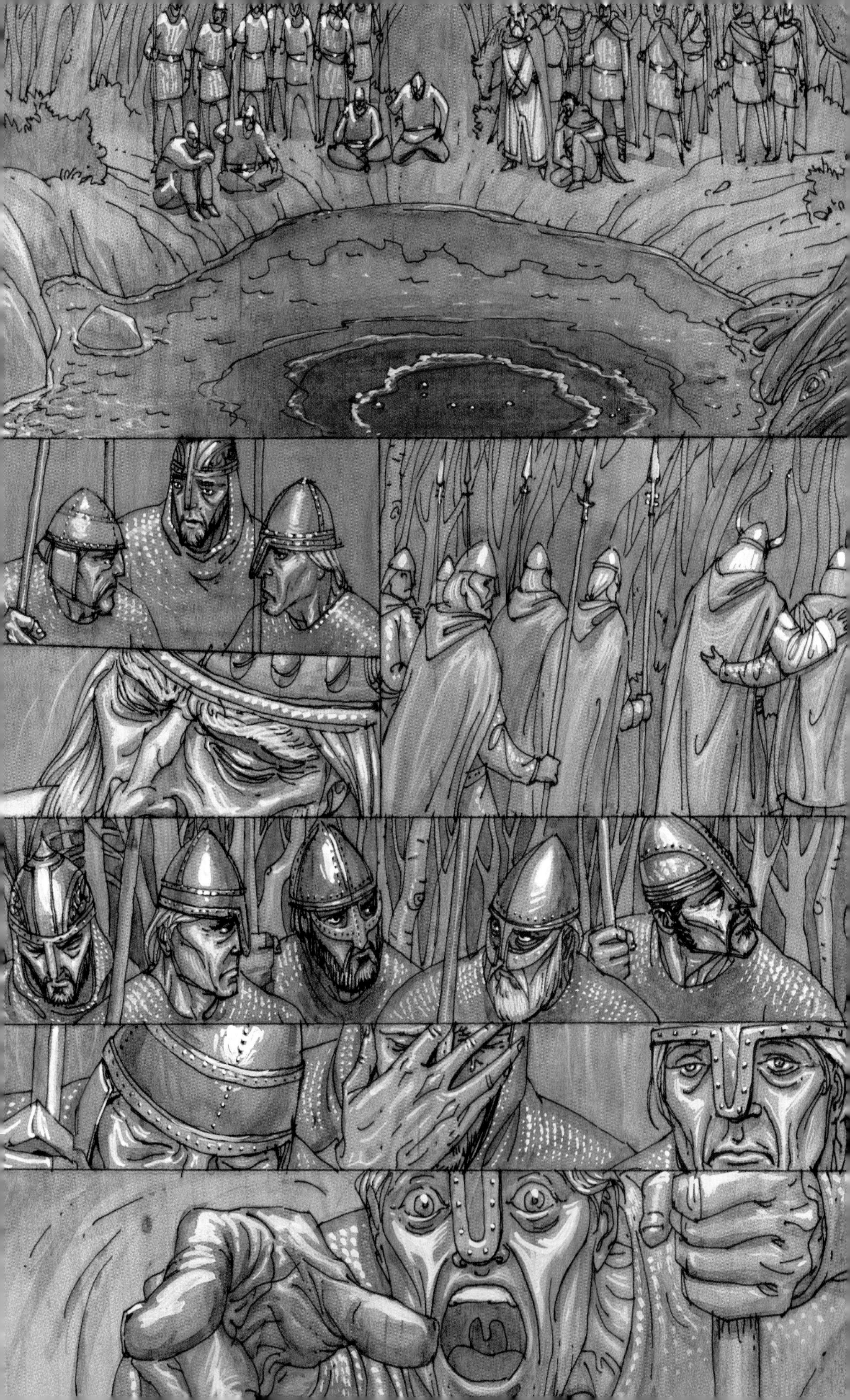

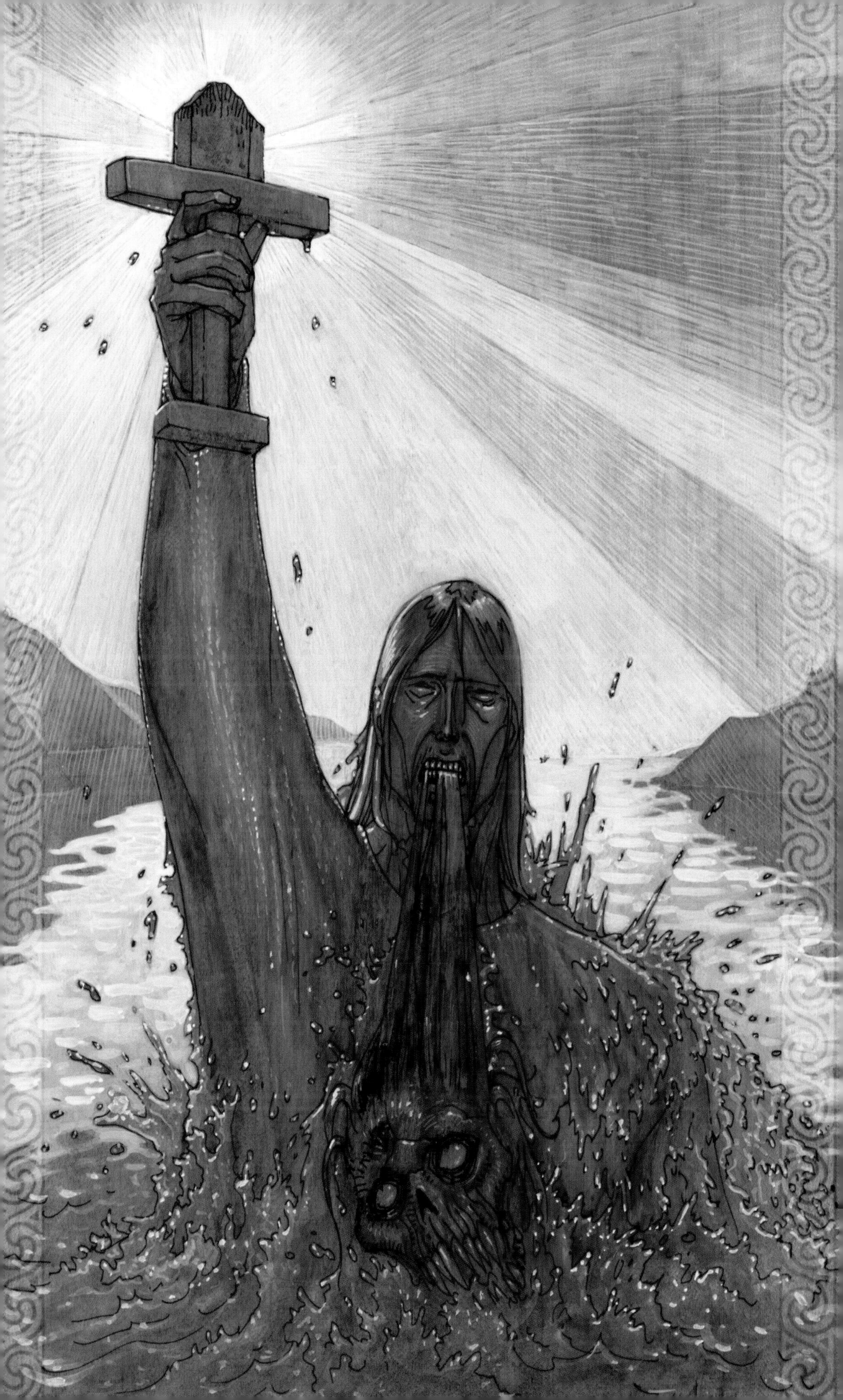

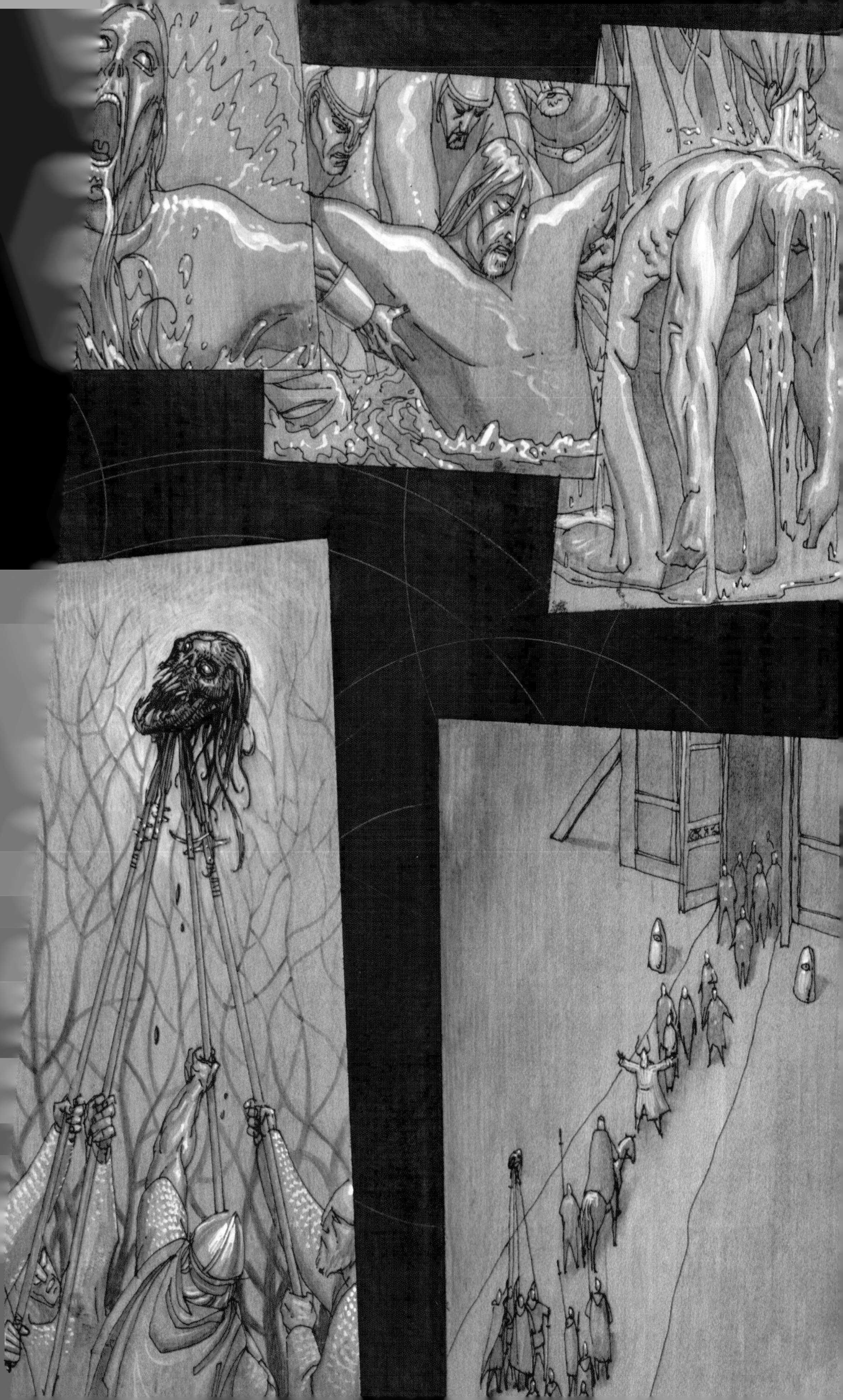

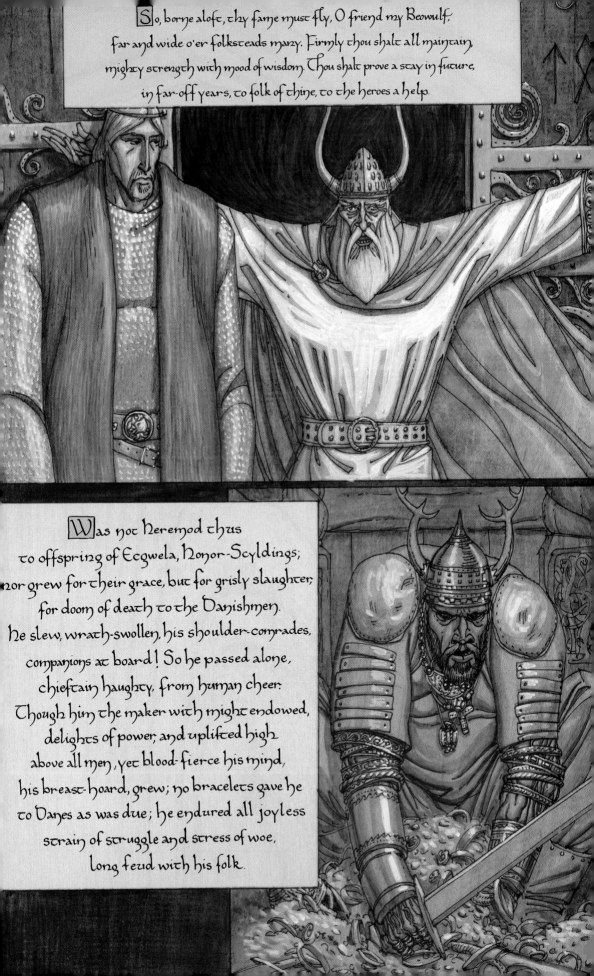

So, borne aloft, thy fame must fly, O friend my Beowulf,
far and wide o'er folksteads many. Firmly thou shalt all maintain,
mighty strength with mood of wisdom. Thou shalt prove a stay in future,
in far-off years, to folk of thine, to the heroes a help.

Was not Heremod thus
to offspring of Ecgwela, Honor-Scyldings;
nor grew for their grace, but for grisly slaughter,
for doom of death to the Danishmen.
He slew, wrath-swollen, his shoulder-comrades,
companions at board! So he passed alone,
chieftain haughty, from human cheer.
Though him the maker with might endowed,
delights of power, and uplifted high
above all men, yet blood-fierce his mind,
his breast-hoard, grew; no bracelets gave he
to Danes as was due; he endured all joyless
strain of struggle and stress of woe,
long feud with his folk.

Here find thy lesson! Wondrous seems
how to sons of men Almighty God
in the strength of his spirit sendeth wisdom,
estate, high station. He swayeth all things.
Whiles he letteth right lustily fare
the heart of the hero of high-born race, --
puts in his power great parts of the earth,
empire so ample, that end of it
this wanter-of-wisdom weeneth none.
Yet in the end it ever comes
that the frame of the body fragile yields,
fated falls; and there follows another
who joyously the jewels divides,
the royal riches, nor recks of his forebear.
Ban, then, such baleful thoughts, O Beowulf,
best of men, and the better part choose,
profit eternal; and temper thy pride,
Warrior famous! The flower of thy might
lasts now a while: but erelong it shall be
that sickness or sword thy strength shall minish,
or fang of fire, or flooding billow,
or bite of blade, or brandished spear,
or odious age; or the eyes' clear beam
wax dull and darken: Death even thee
shall o'erwhelm, thou hero of war!

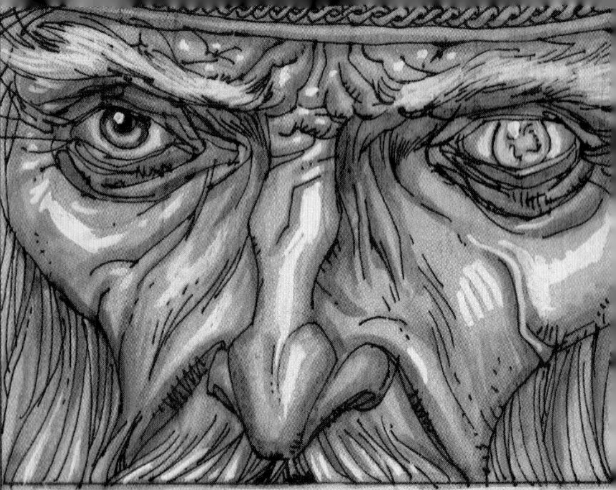

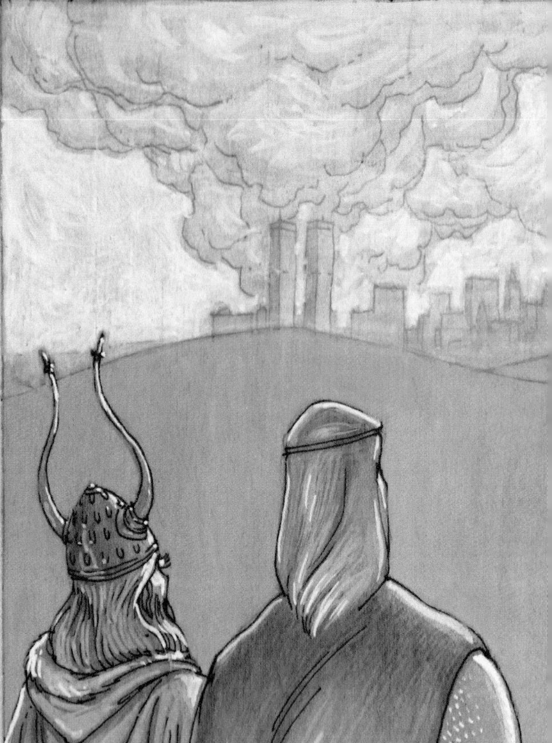

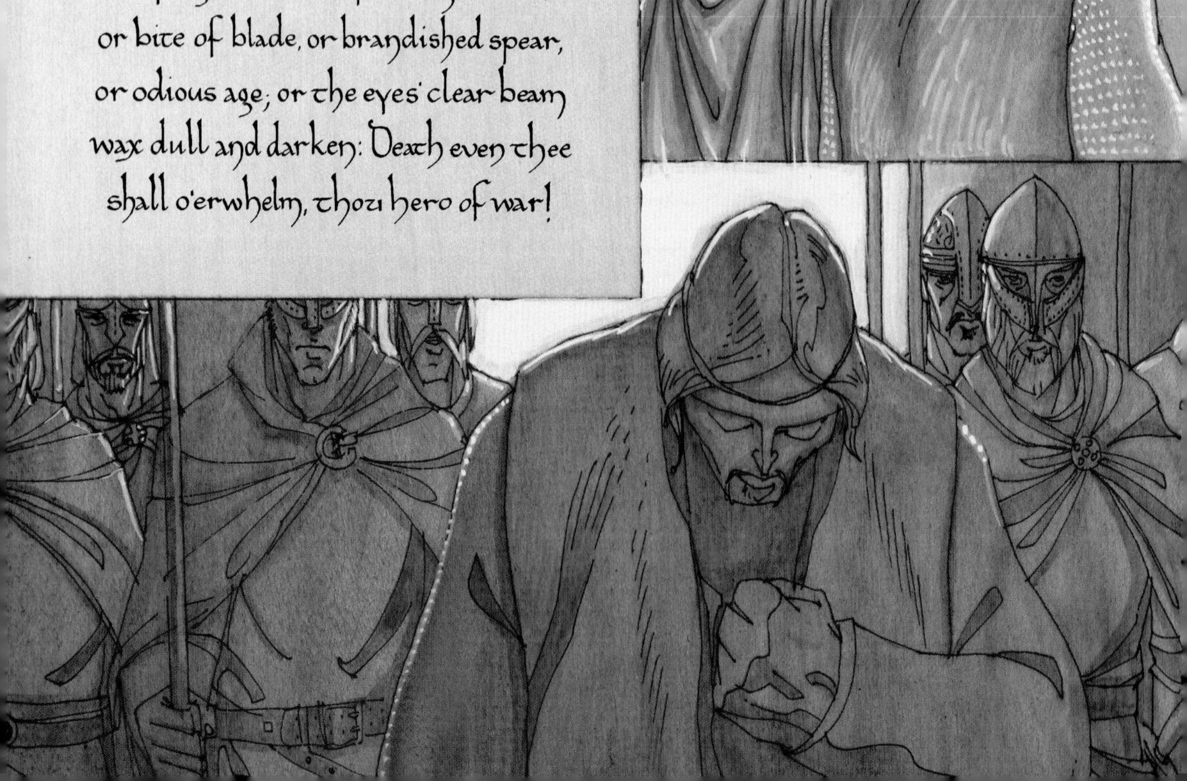

To him in the hall, then, Healfdeane's son
ave treasures twelve, and the trust-of-earls
ade him fare with the gifts to his folk beloved,
hale to his home, and in haste return.
hen on the strand, with steeds and treasure
nd armor their roomy and ring-dight ship
was heavily laden: high its mast
rose over Hrothgar's hoarded gems.
A sword to the boat-guard Beowulf gave,
ounted with gold. Their ocean-keel boarding,
ey drove through the deep, and Daneland left.

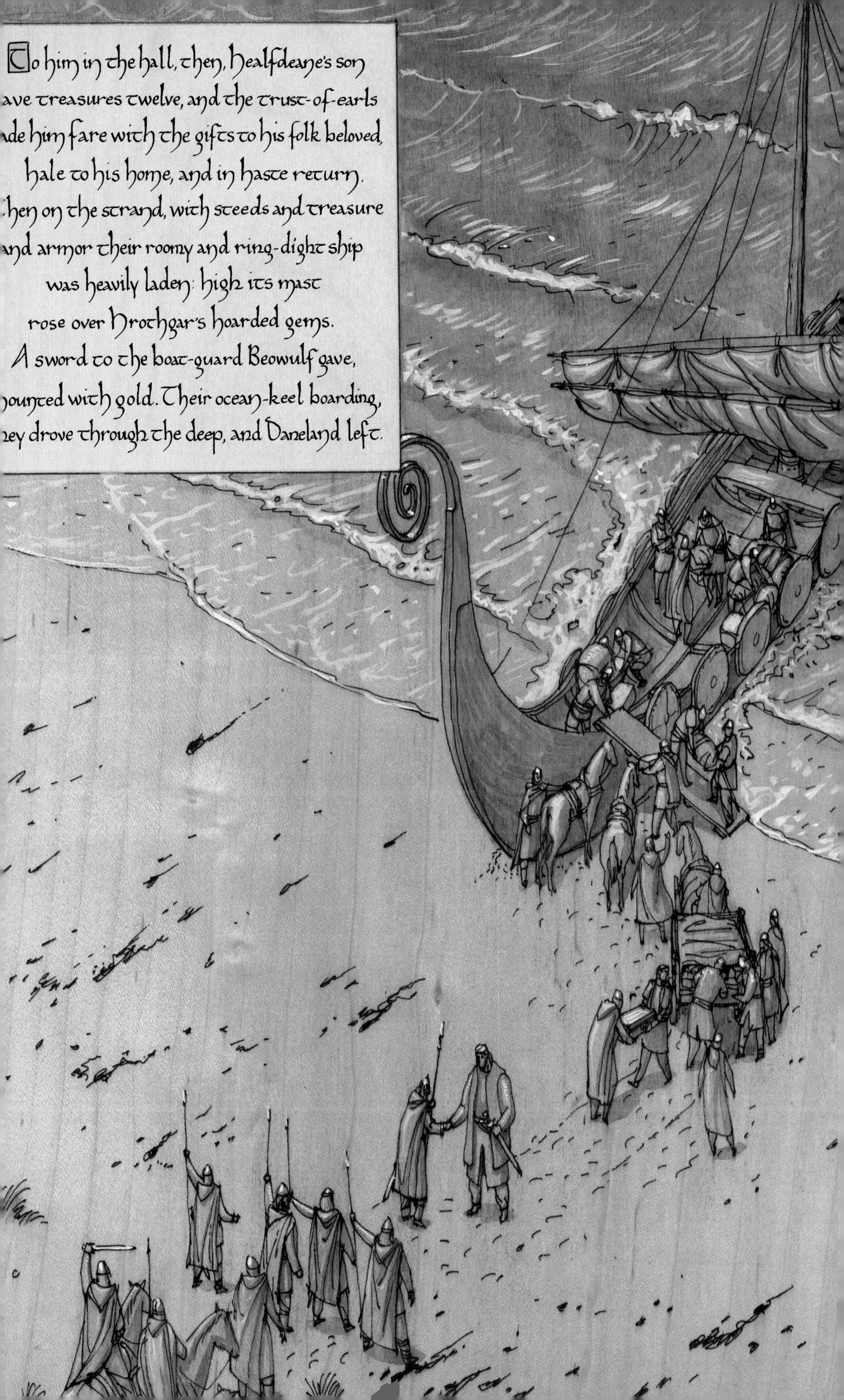

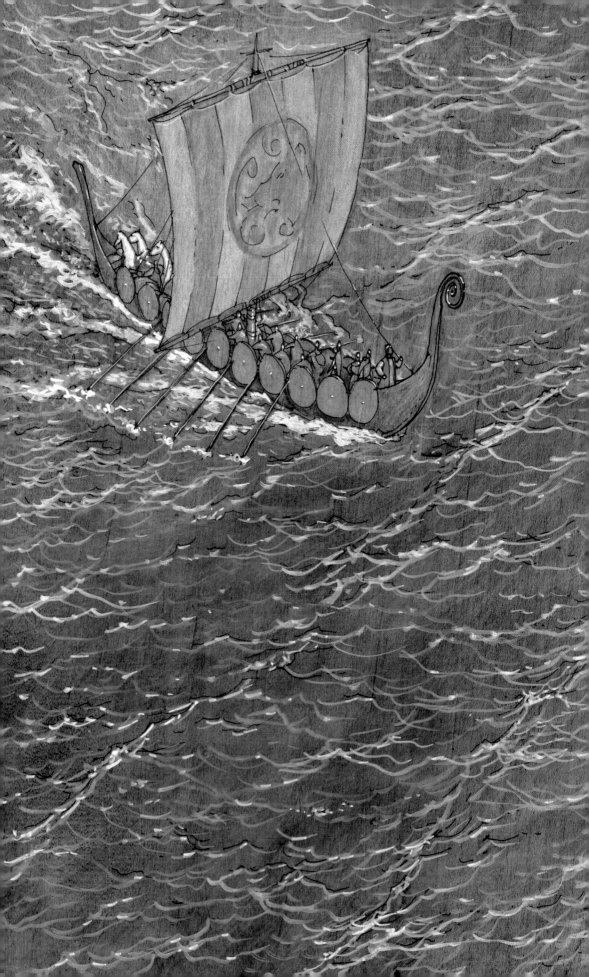

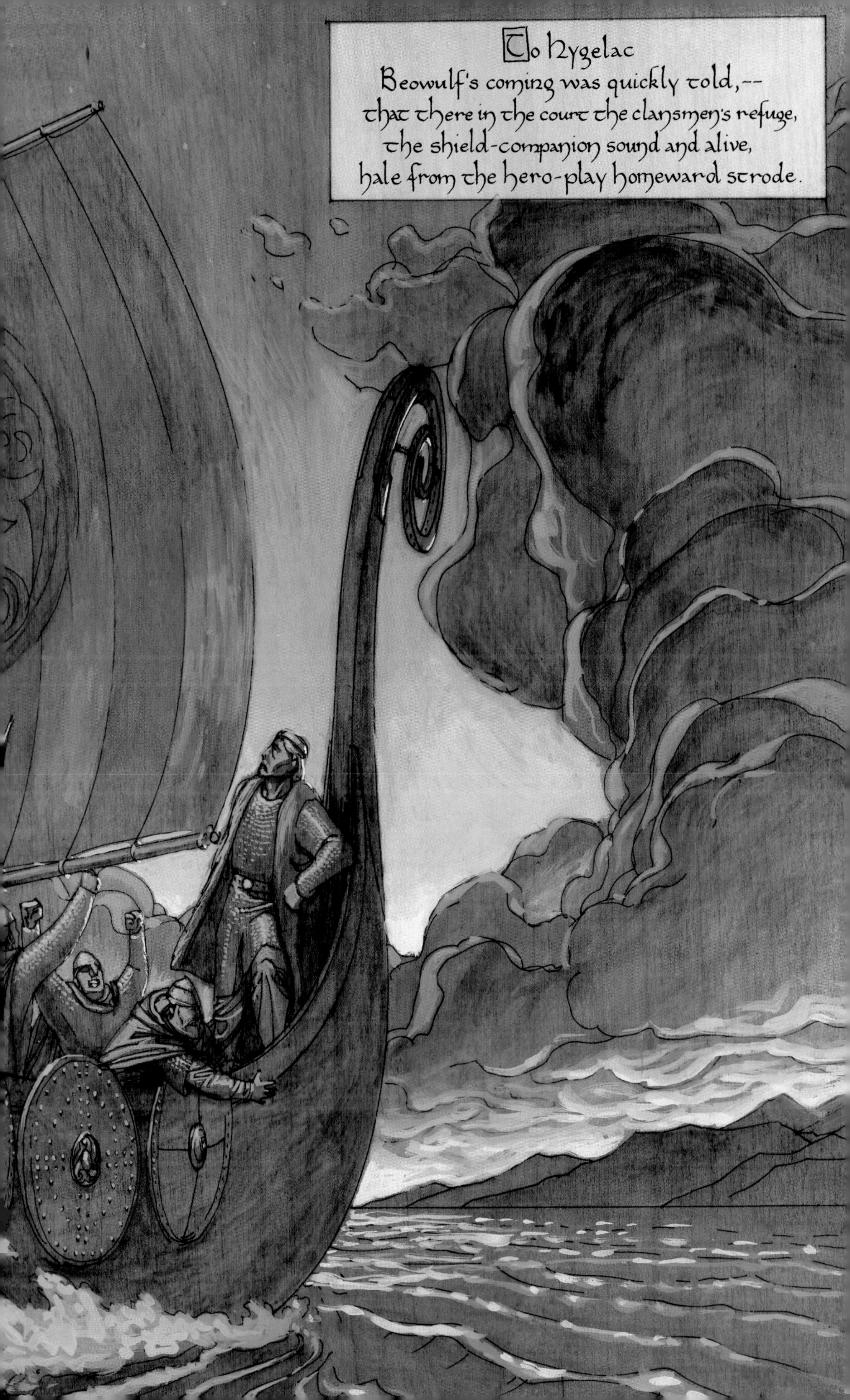
To Hygelac
Beowulf's coming was quickly told,--
that there in the court the clansmen's refuge,
the shield-companion sound and alive,
hale from the hero-play homeward strode.

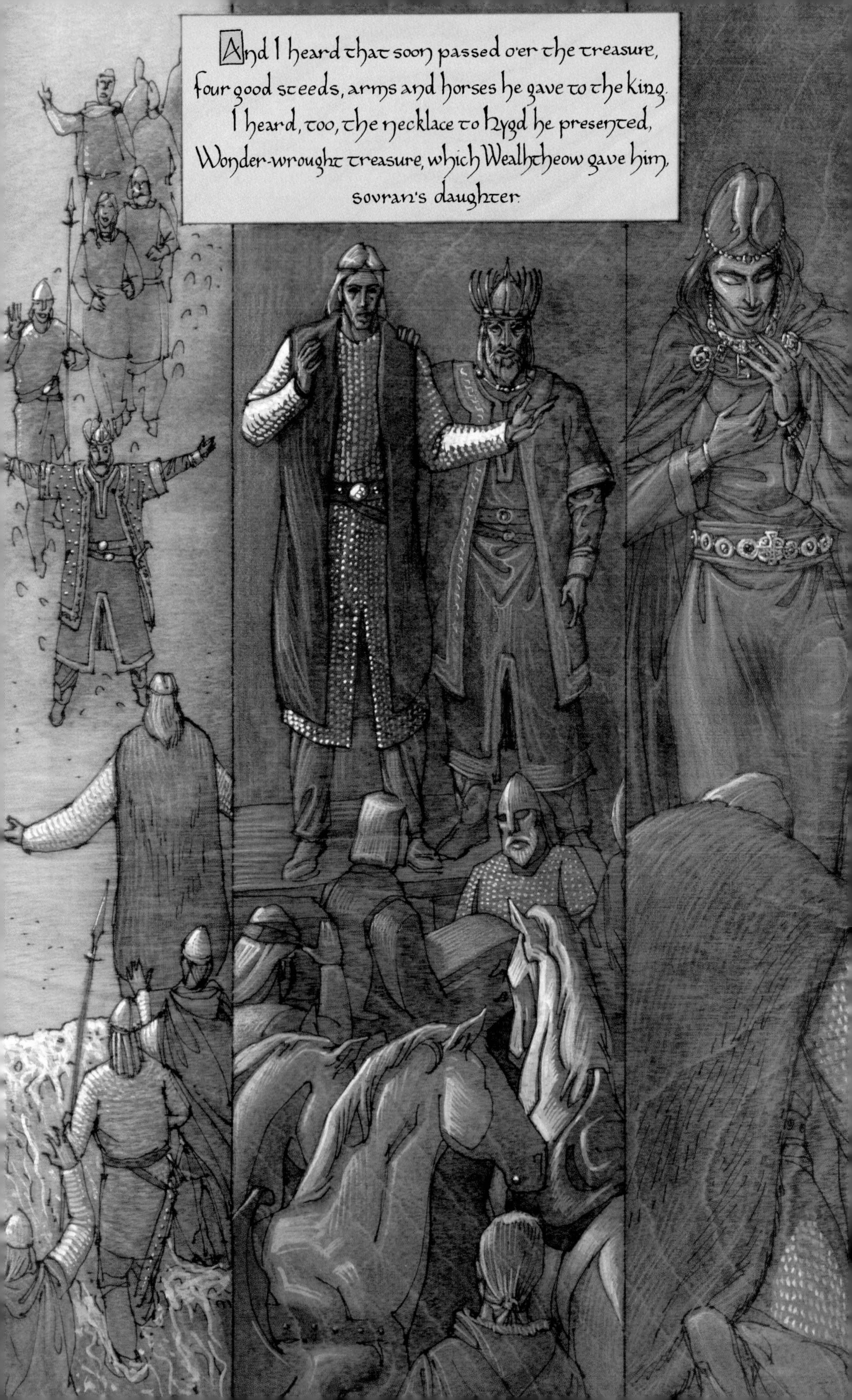
And I heard that soon passed o'er the treasure,
four good steeds, arms and horses he gave to the king.
I heard, too, the necklace to Hygd he presented,
Wonder-wrought treasure, which Wealhtheow gave him,
sovran's daughter.

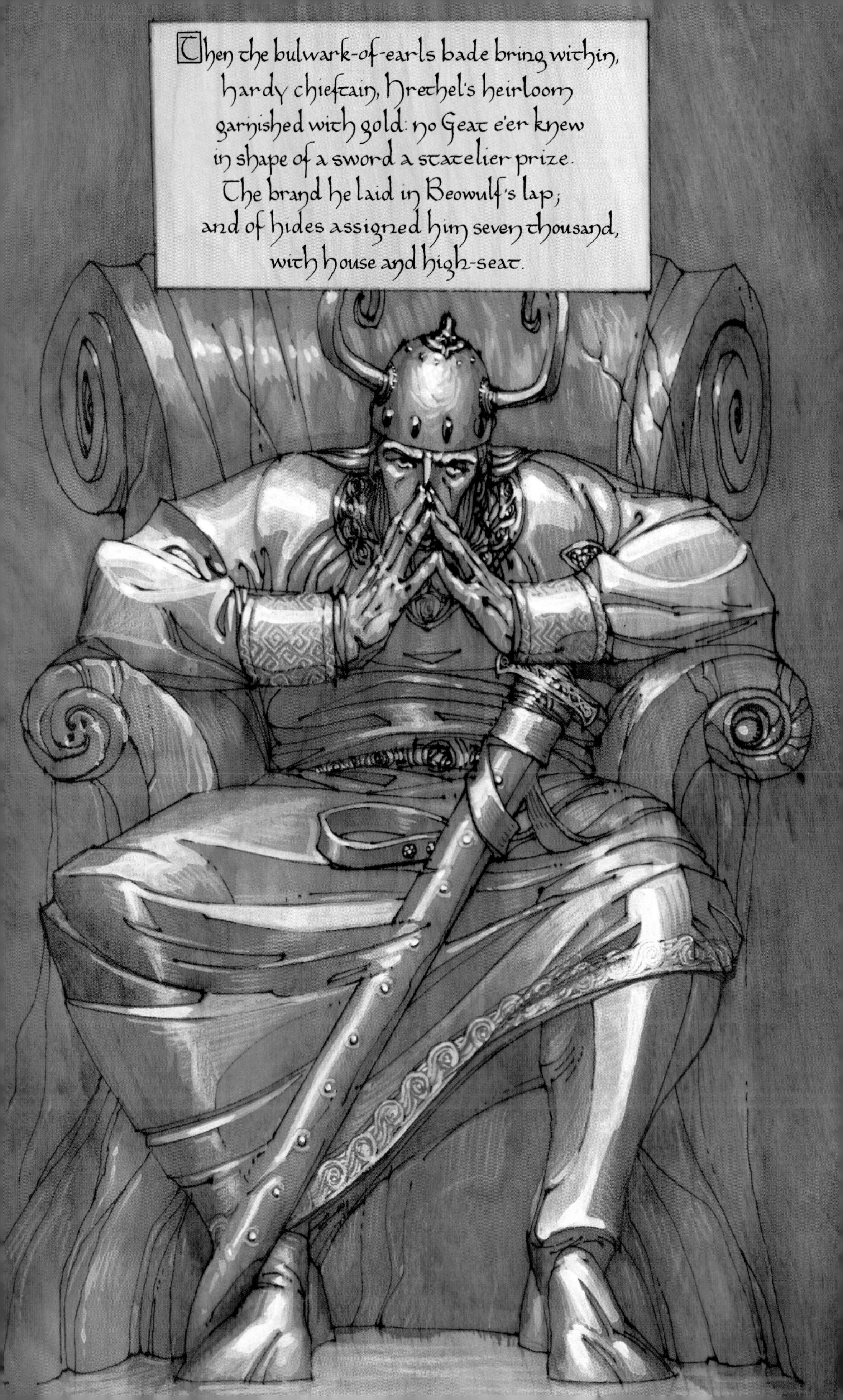
Then the bulwark-of-earls bade bring within,
hardy chieftain, Hrethel's heirloom
garnished with gold: no Geat e'er knew
in shape of a sword a statelier prize.
The brand he laid in Beowulf's lap;
and of hides assigned him seven thousand,
with house and high-seat.

Now further it fell with the flight of years,
with harryings horrid, that Hygelac perished,
and Heardred, too, by hewing of swords
under the shield-wall slaughtered lay.

Then Beowulf came as King this broad
realm to wield; and he ruled it well
fifty winters, a wise old prince,
warding his land, until One began
in the dark of night, a Dragon, to rage.

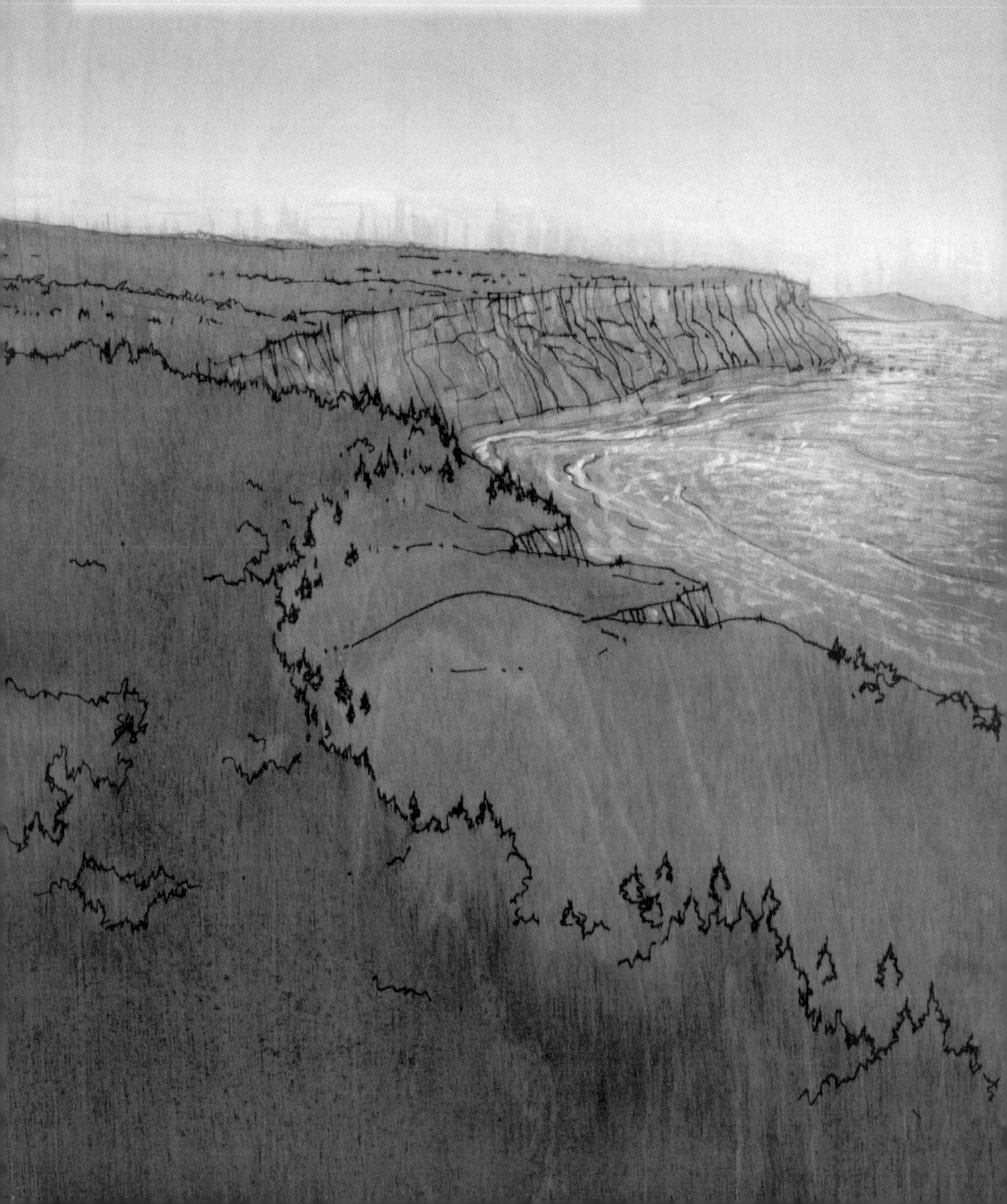

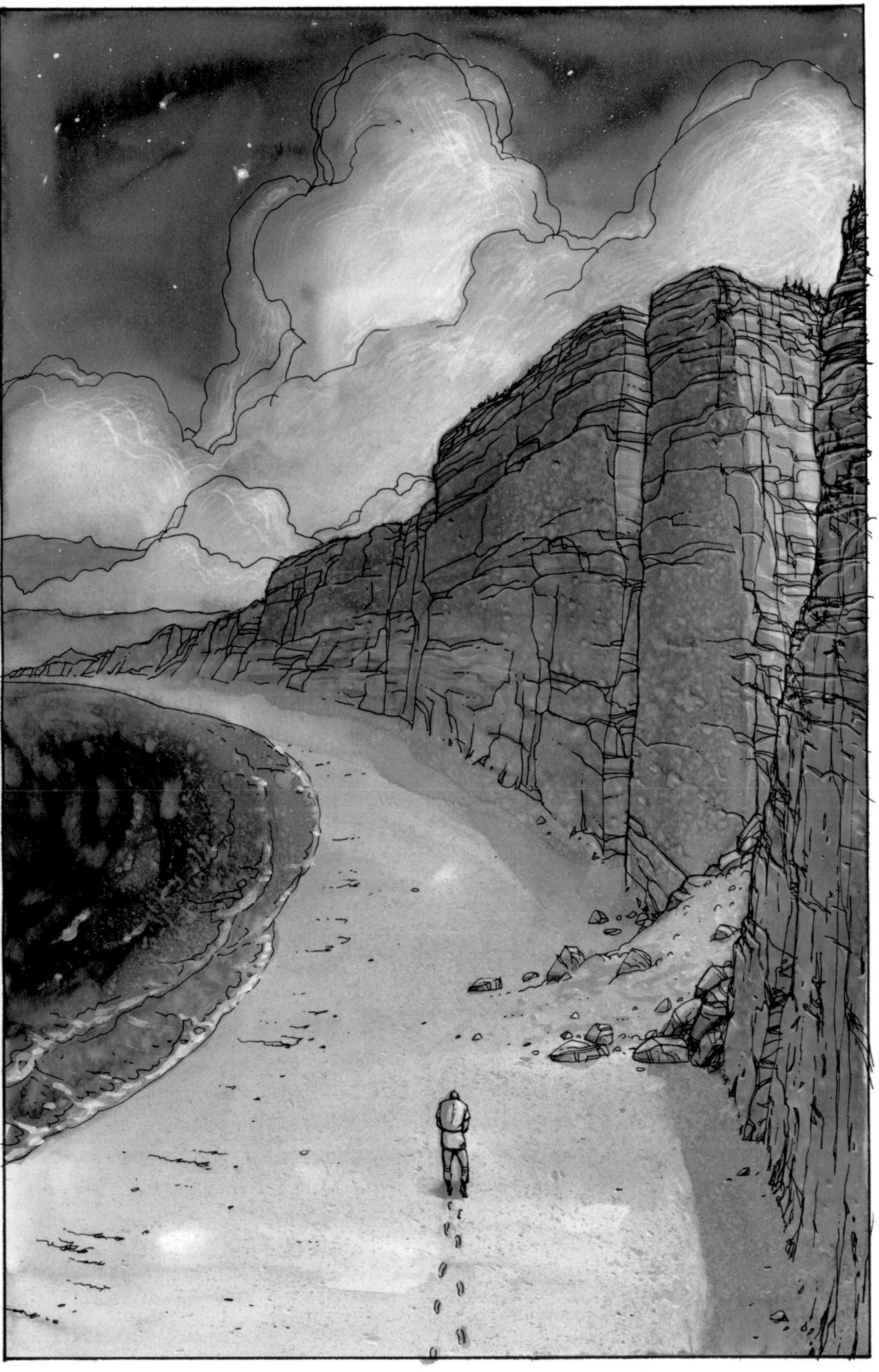

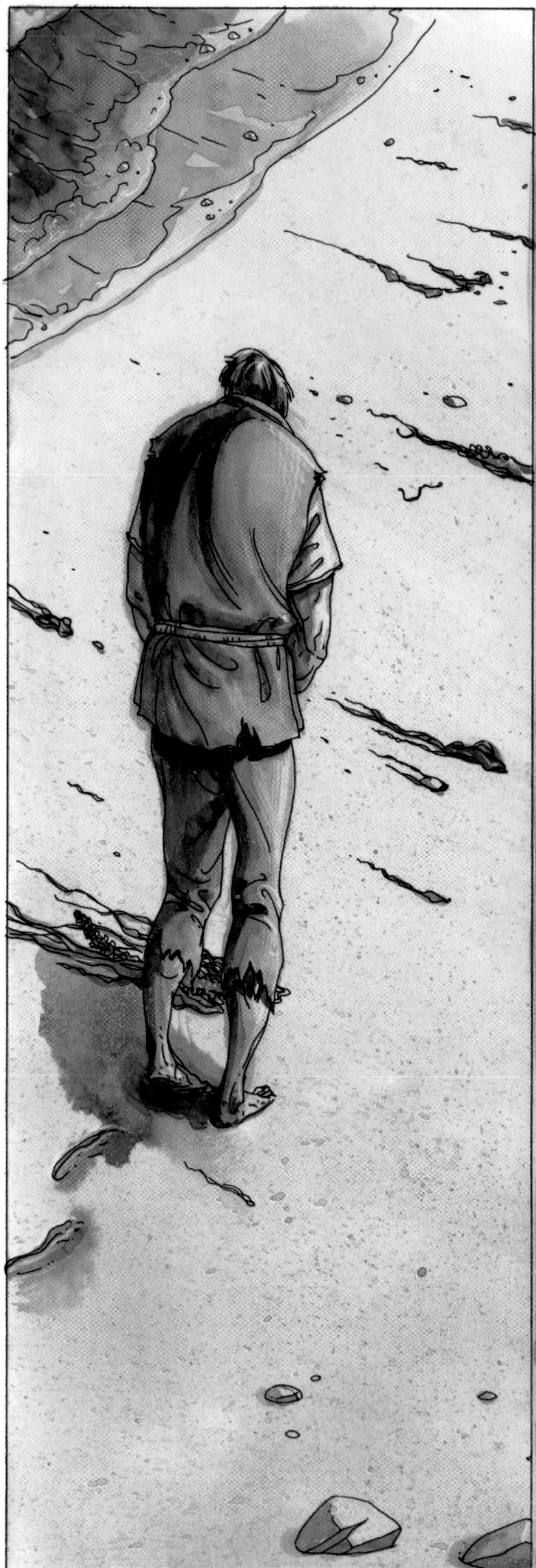
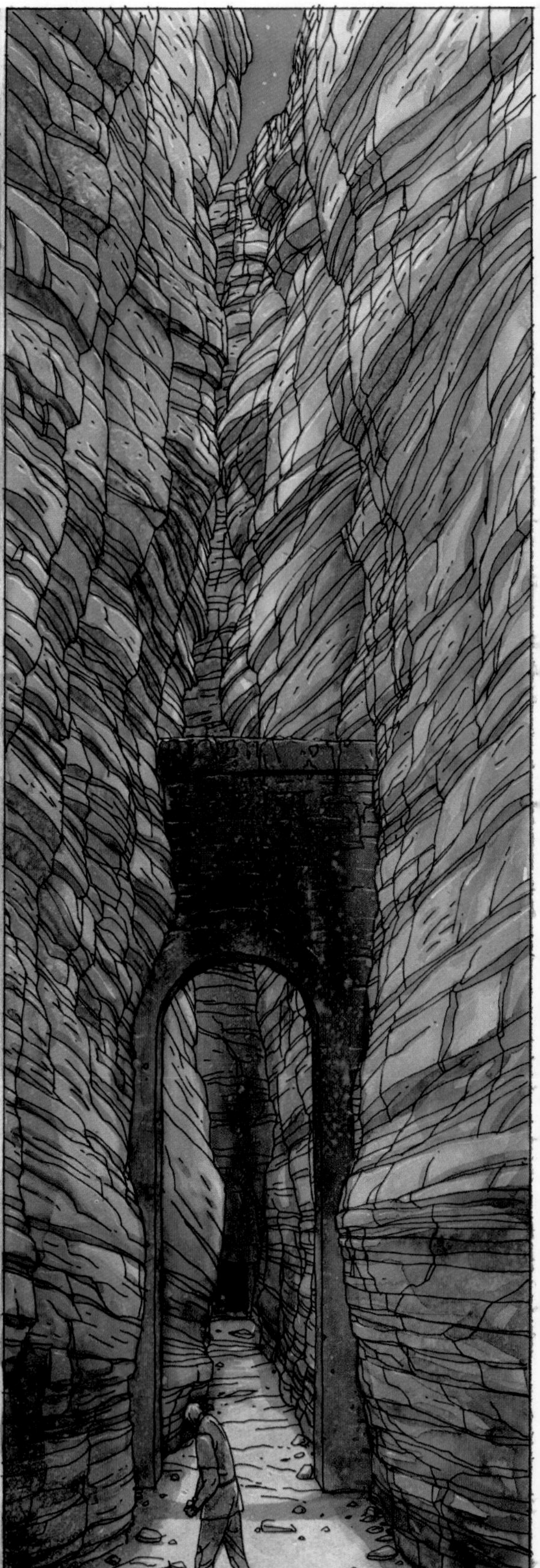

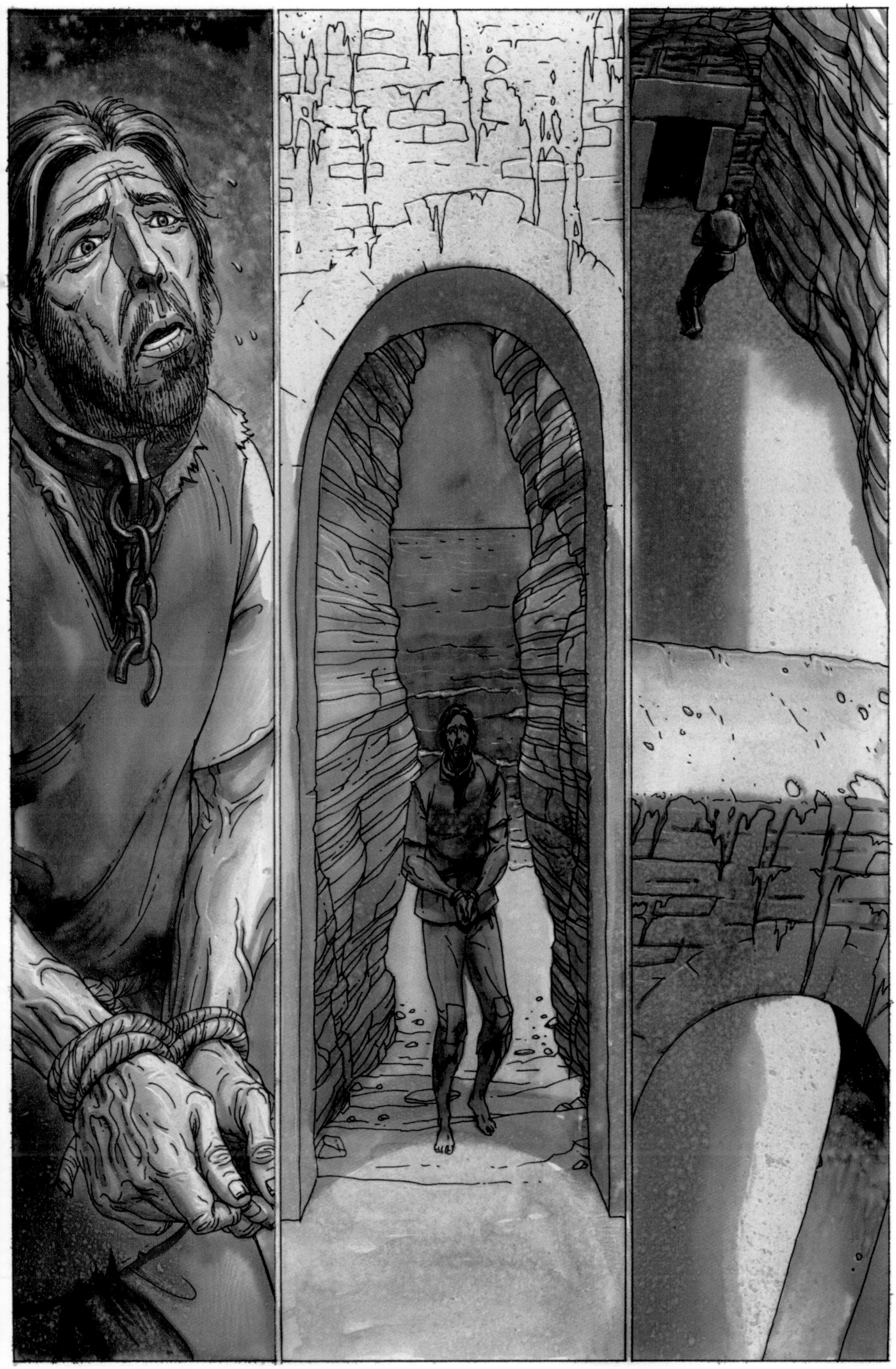

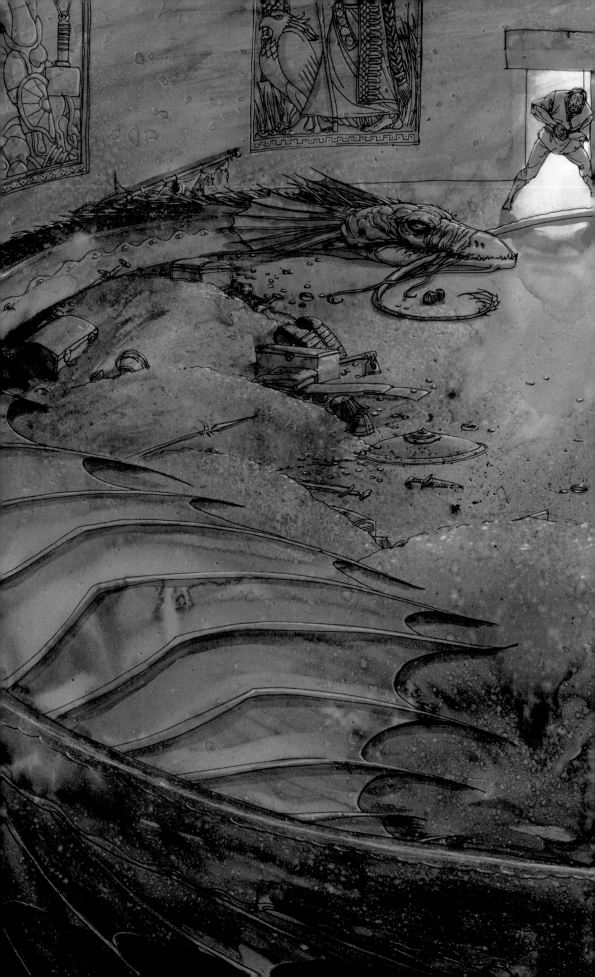

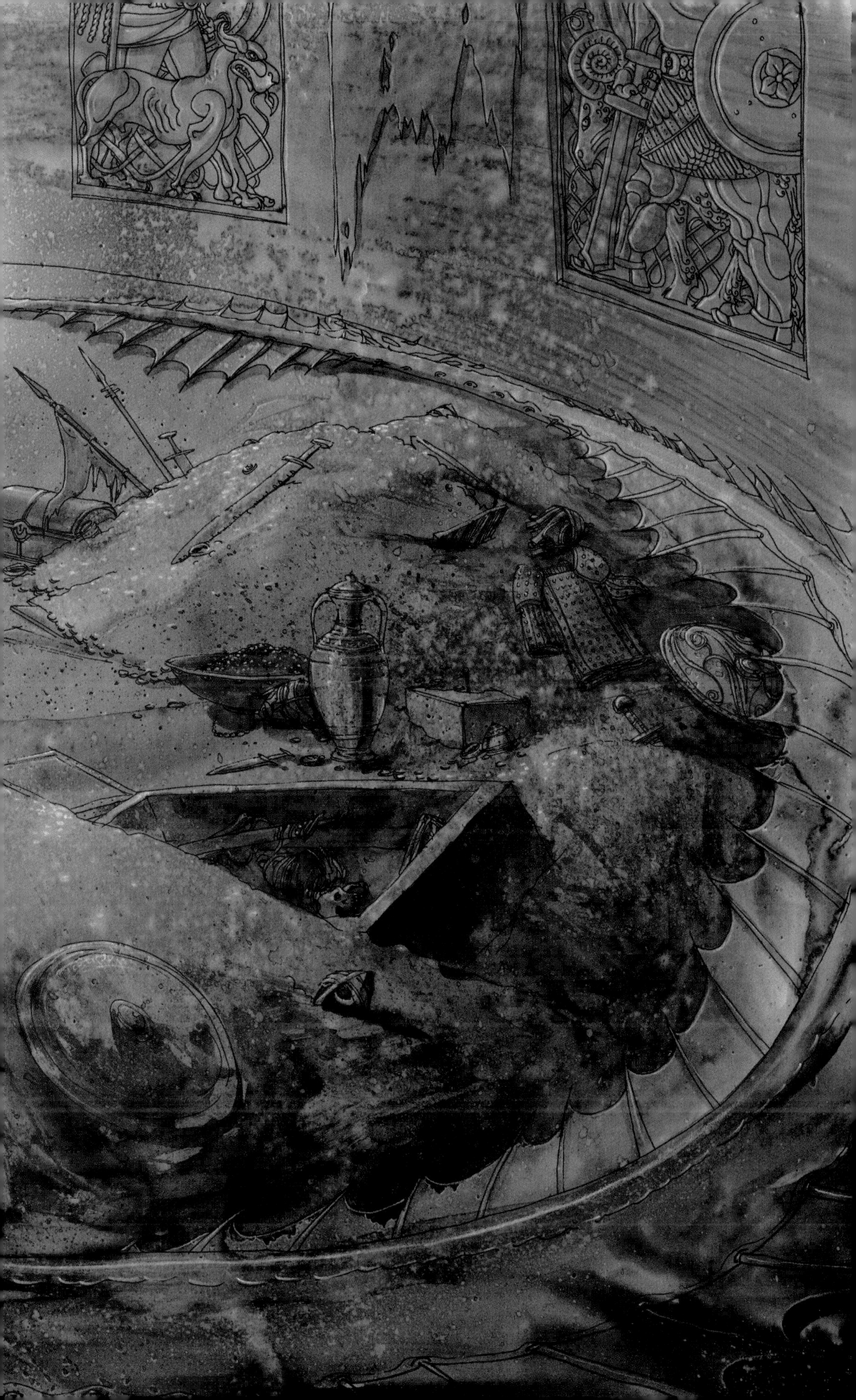

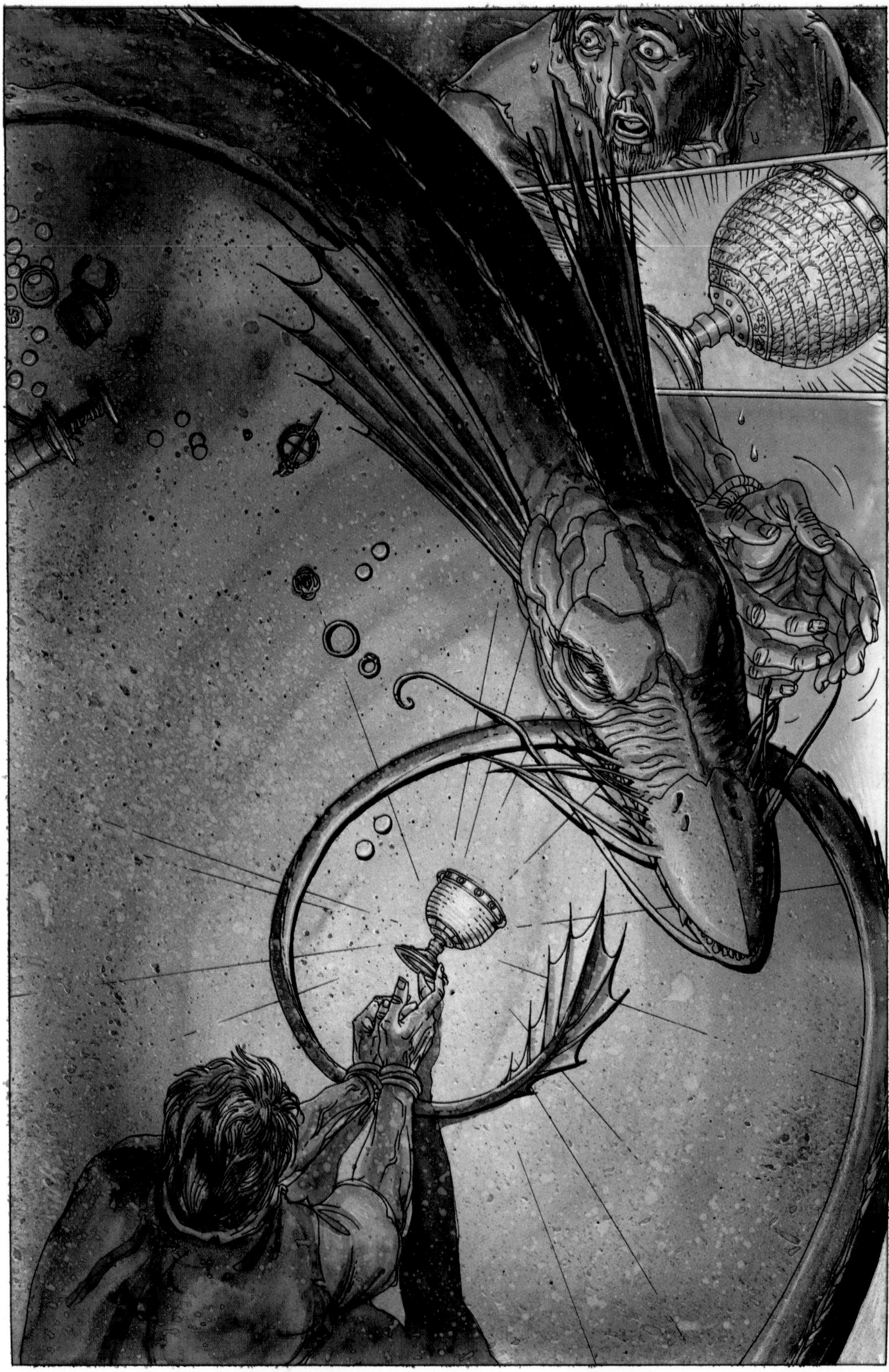

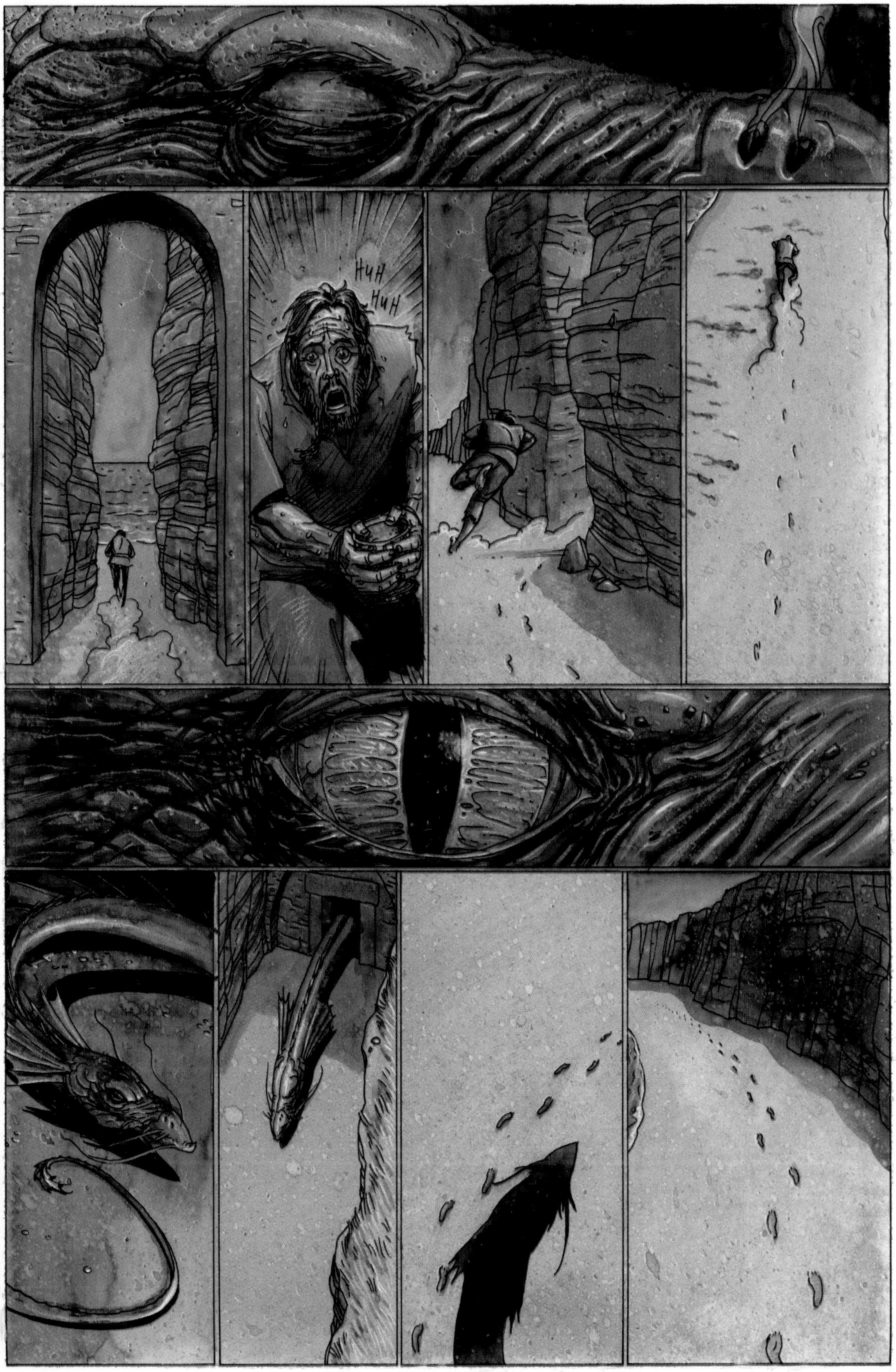
HUH
HUH

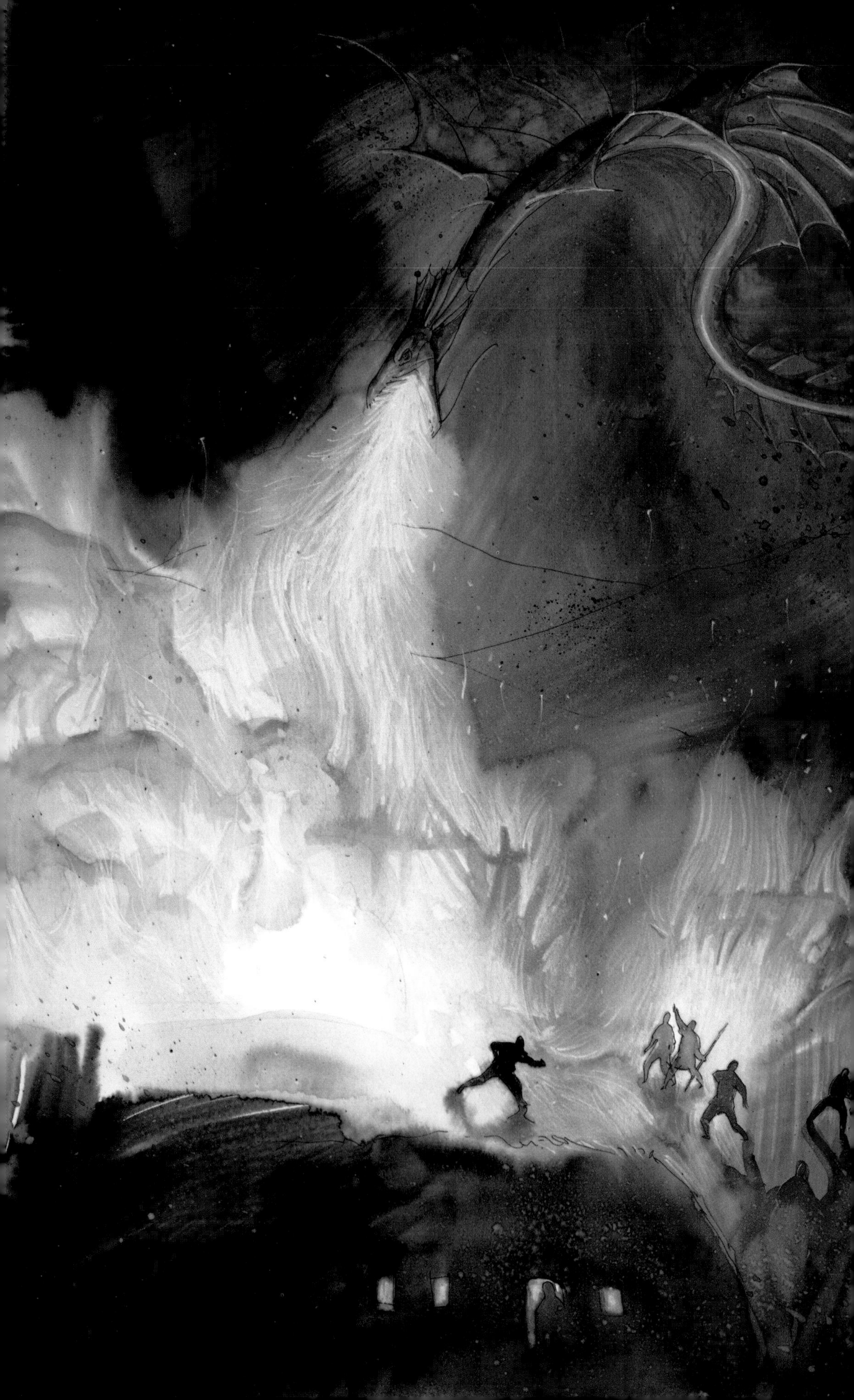

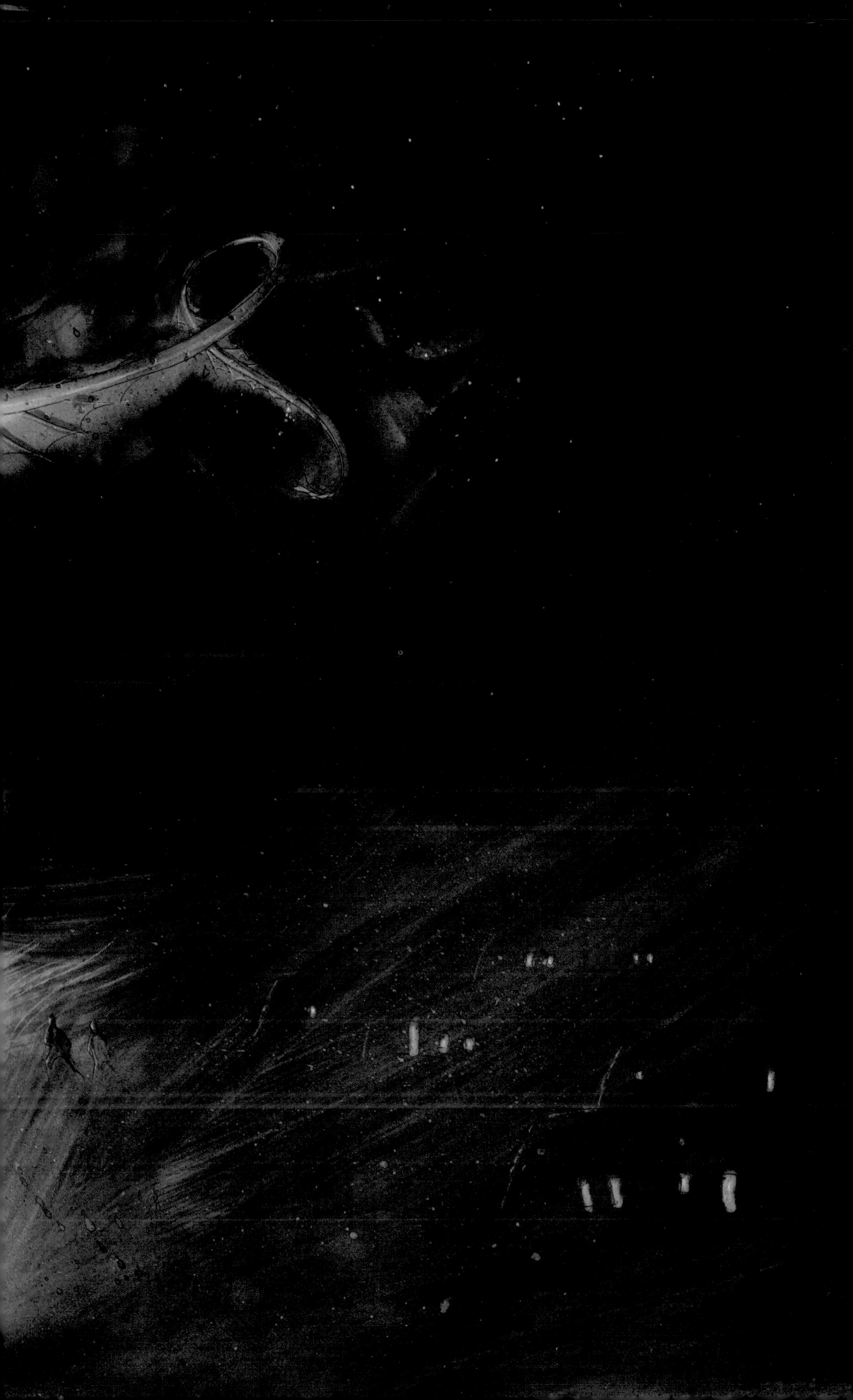

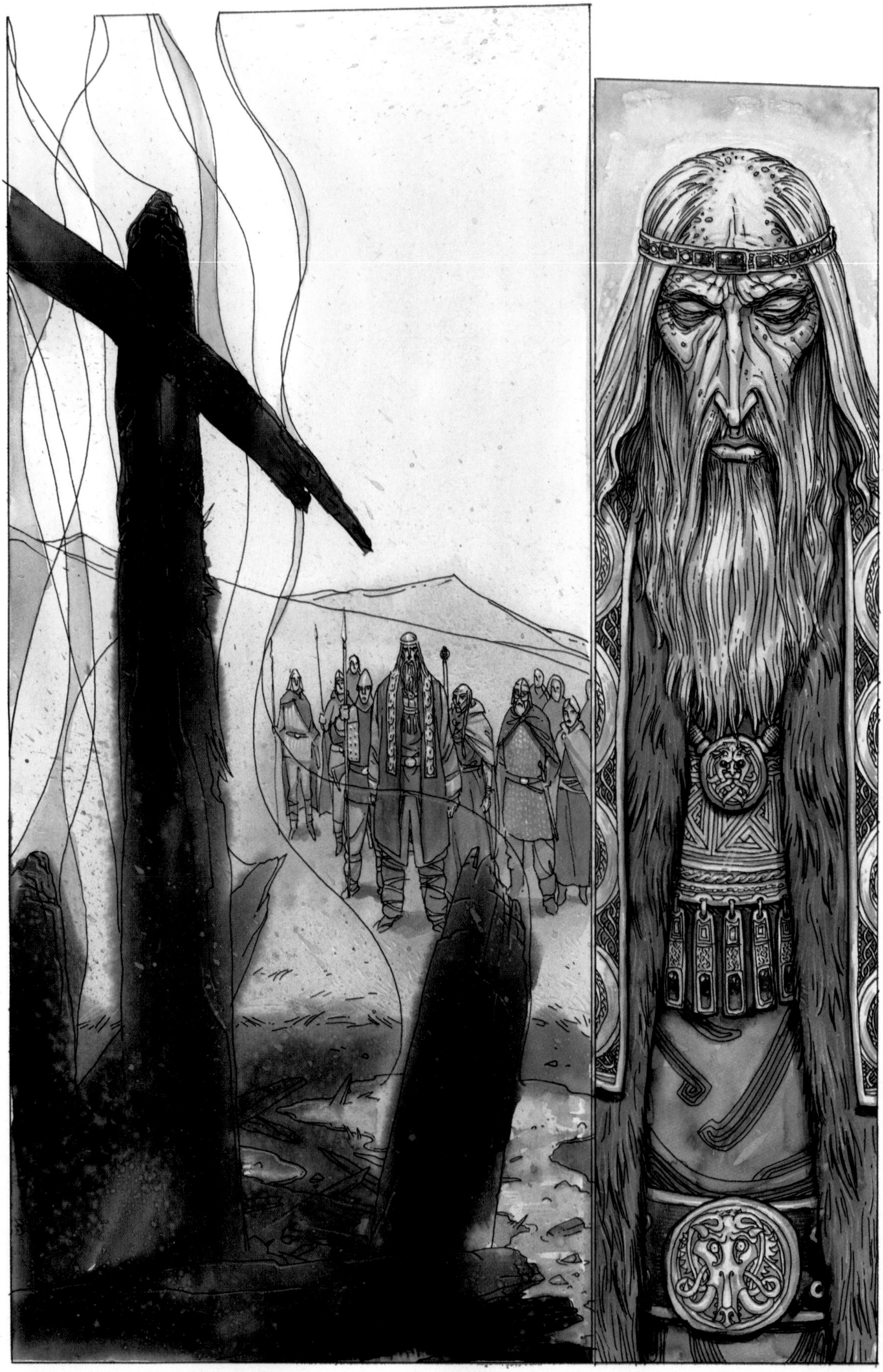

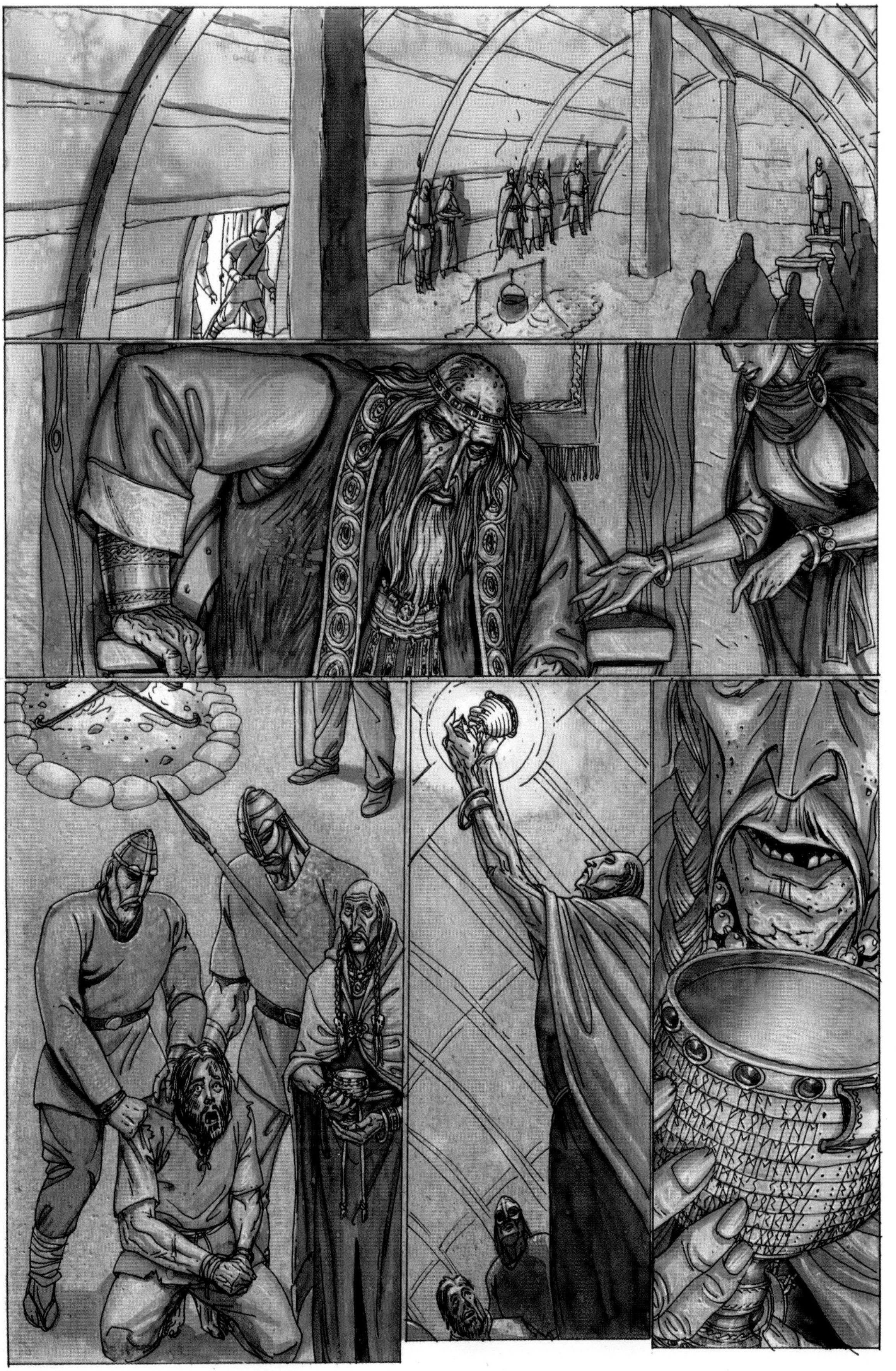

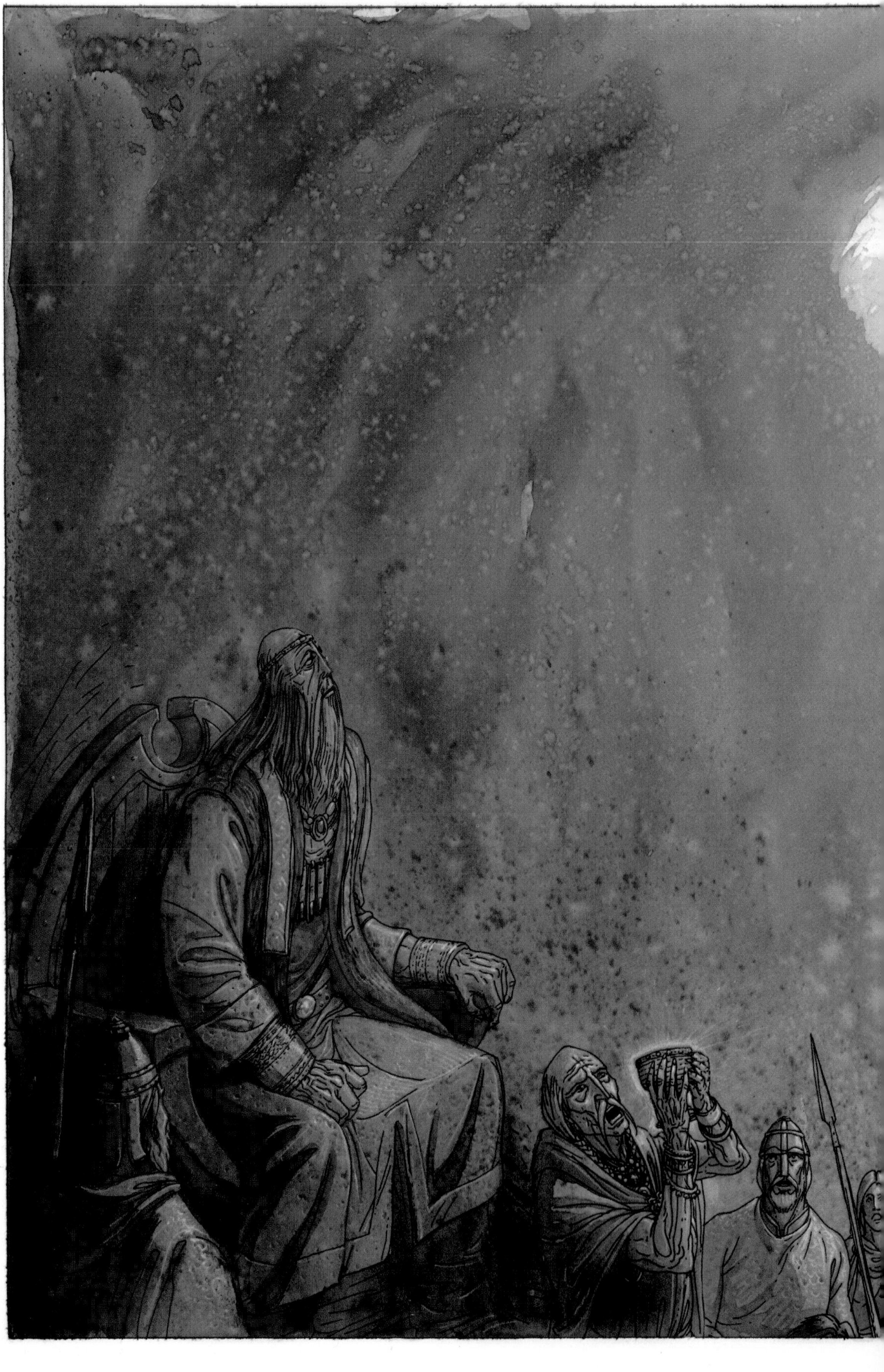

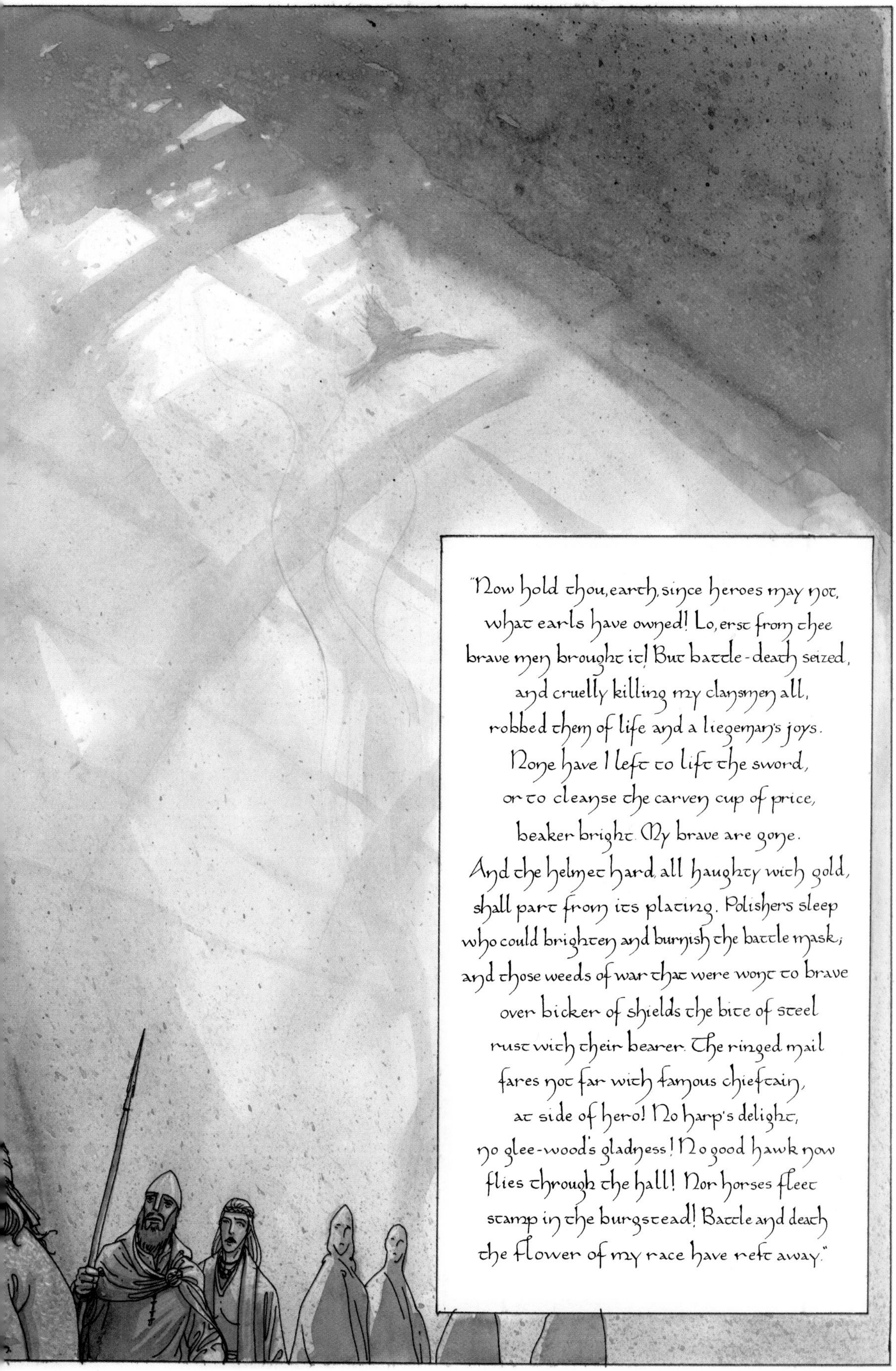
"Now hold thou, earth, since heroes may not,
what earls have owned! Lo, erst from thee
brave men brought it! But battle-death seized,
and cruelly killing my clansmen all,
robbed them of life and a liegeman's joys.
None have I left to lift the sword,
or to cleanse the carven cup of price,
beaker bright. My brave are gone.
And the helmet hard, all haughty with gold,
shall part from its plating. Polishers sleep
who could brighten and burnish the battle mask;
and those weeds of war that were wont to brave
over bicker of shields the bite of steel
rust with their bearer. The ringed mail
fares not far with famous chieftain,
at side of hero! No harp's delight,
no glee-wood's gladness! No good hawk now
flies through the hall! Nor horses fleet
stamp in the burgstead! Battle and death
the flower of my race have reft away."

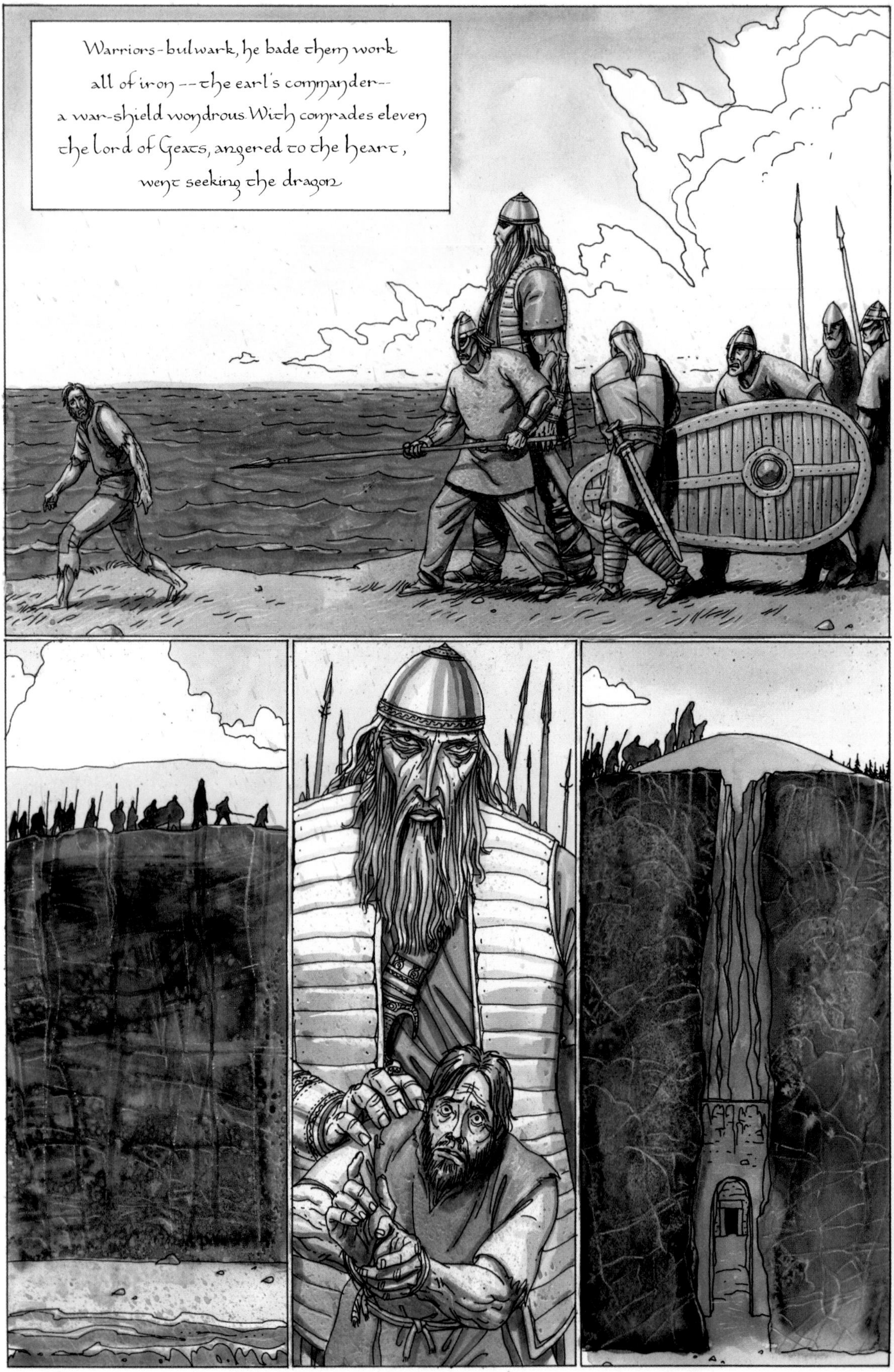
Warriors-bulwark, he bade them work
all of iron --the earl's commander--
a war-shield wondrous. With comrades eleven
the lord of Geats, angered to the heart,
went seeking the dragon

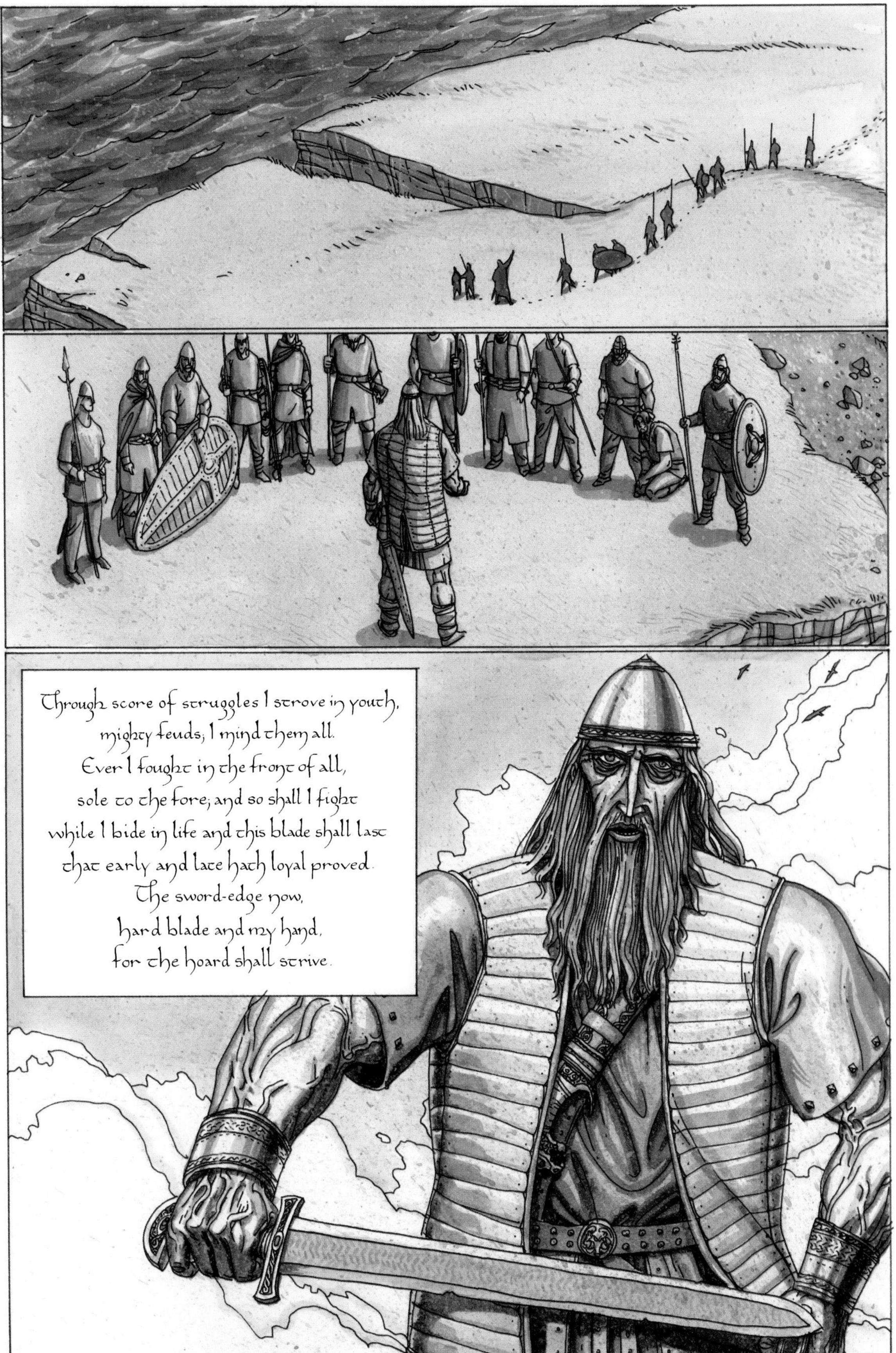
Through score of struggles I strove in youth,
mighty feuds; I mind them all.
Ever I fought in the front of all,
sole to the fore; and so shall I fight
while I bide in life and this blade shall last
that early and late hath loyal proved.
The sword-edge now,
hard blade and my hand,
for the hoard shall strive.

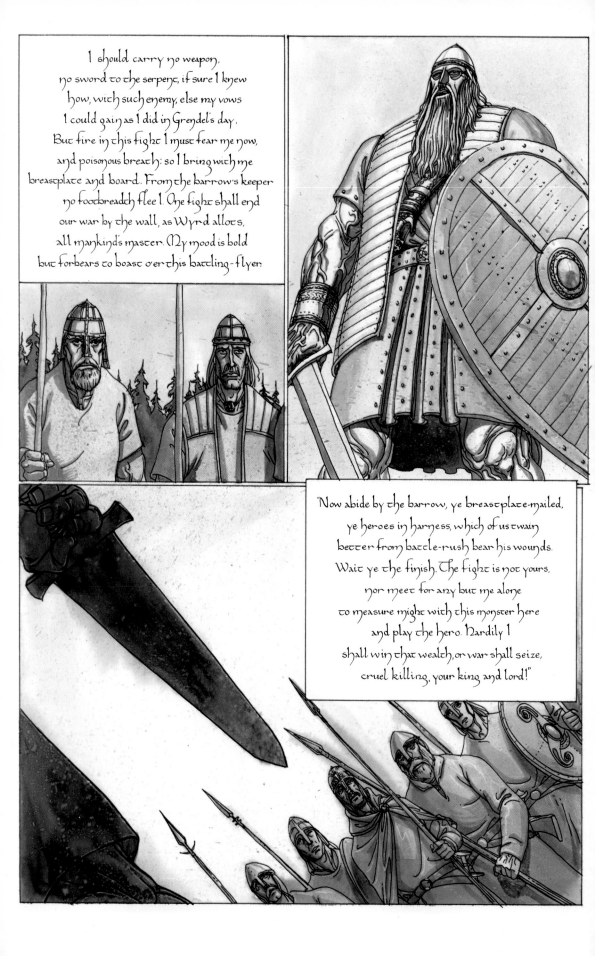

I should carry no weapon,
no sword to the serpent, if sure I knew
how, with such enemy, else my vows
I could gain as I did in Grendel's day.
But fire in this fight I must fear me now,
and poisonous breath: so I bring with me
breastplate and board. From the barrow's keeper
no footbreadth flee I. One fight shall end
our war by the wall, as Wyrd allots,
all mankind's master. My mood is bold
but forbears to boast o'er this battling-flyer.

"Now abide by the barrow, ye breastplate-mailed,
ye heroes in harness, which of us twain
better from battle-rush bear his wounds.
Wait ye the finish. The fight is not yours,
nor meet for any but me alone
to measure might with this monster here
and play the hero. Hardily I
shall win that wealth, or war shall seize,
cruel killing, your king and lord!"

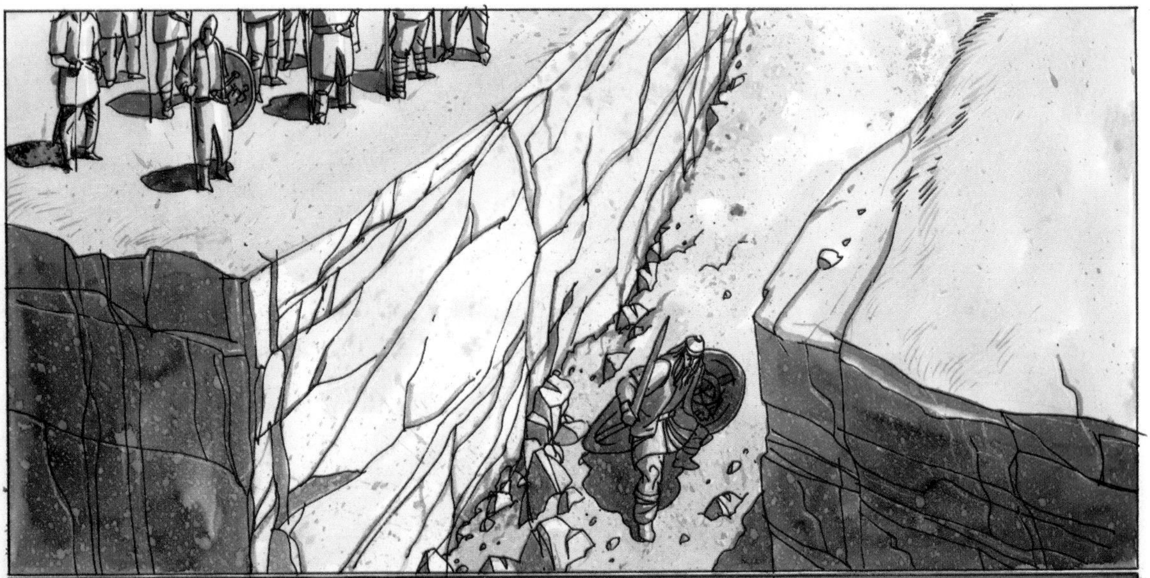

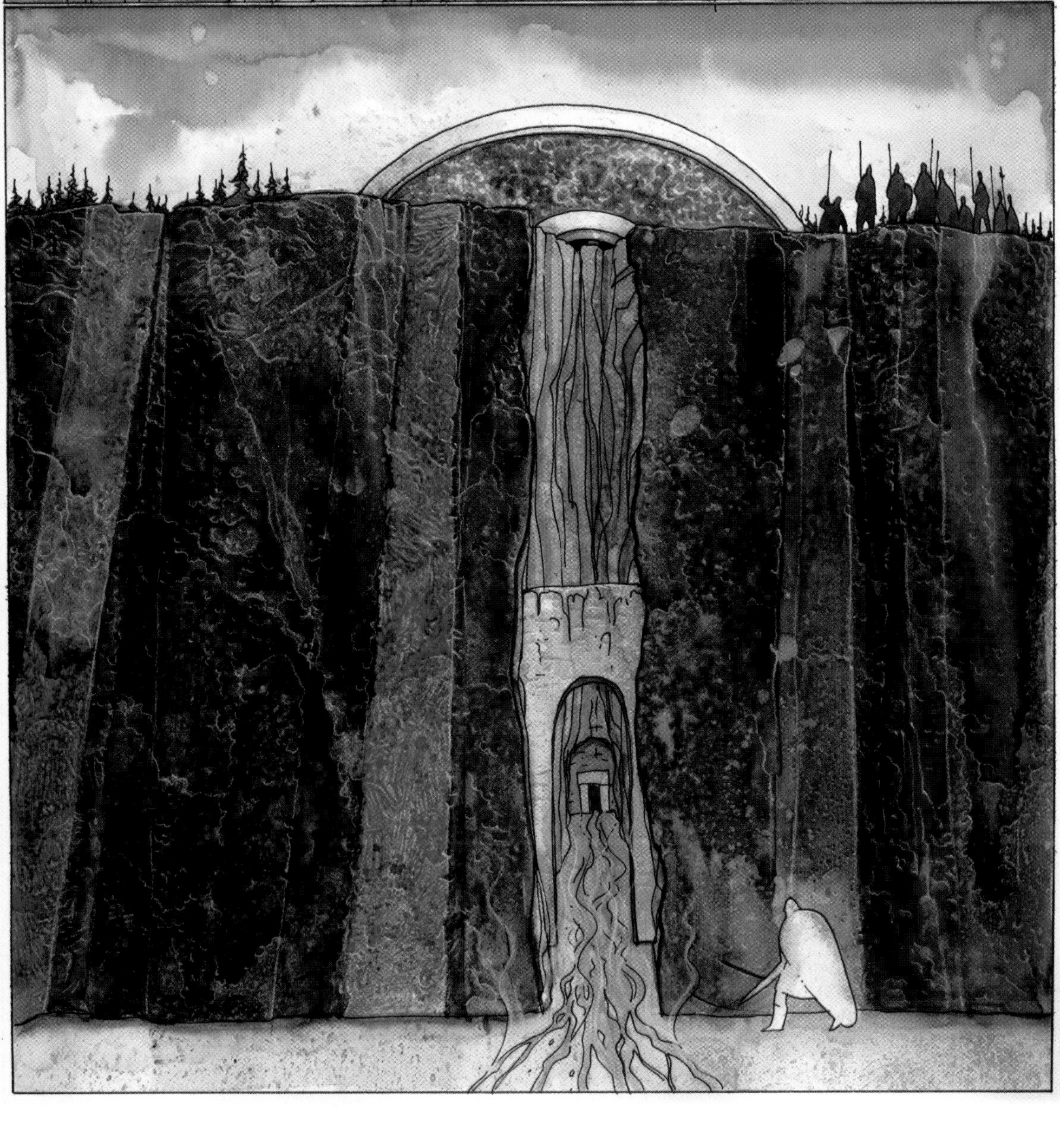

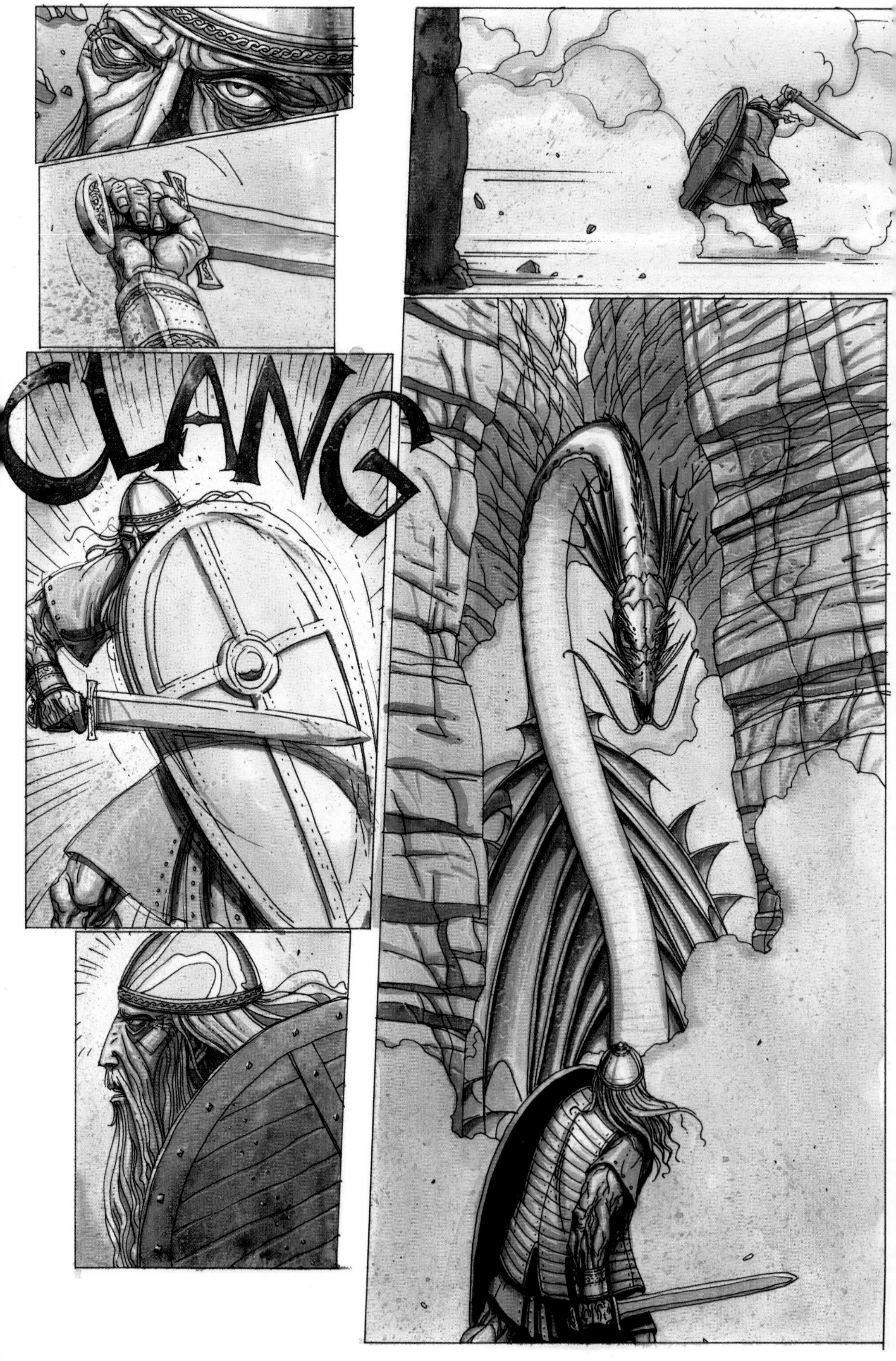
CLANG

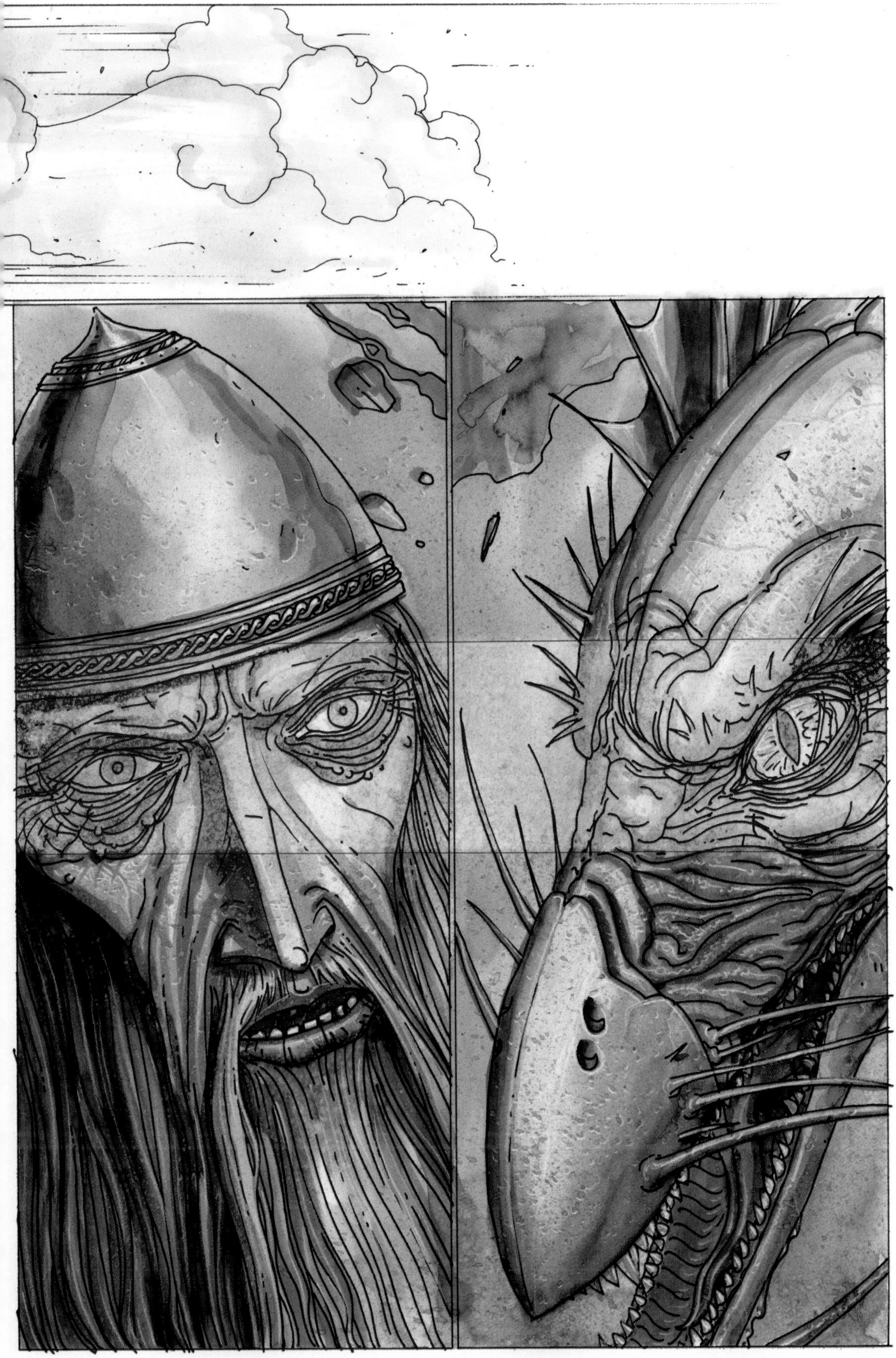

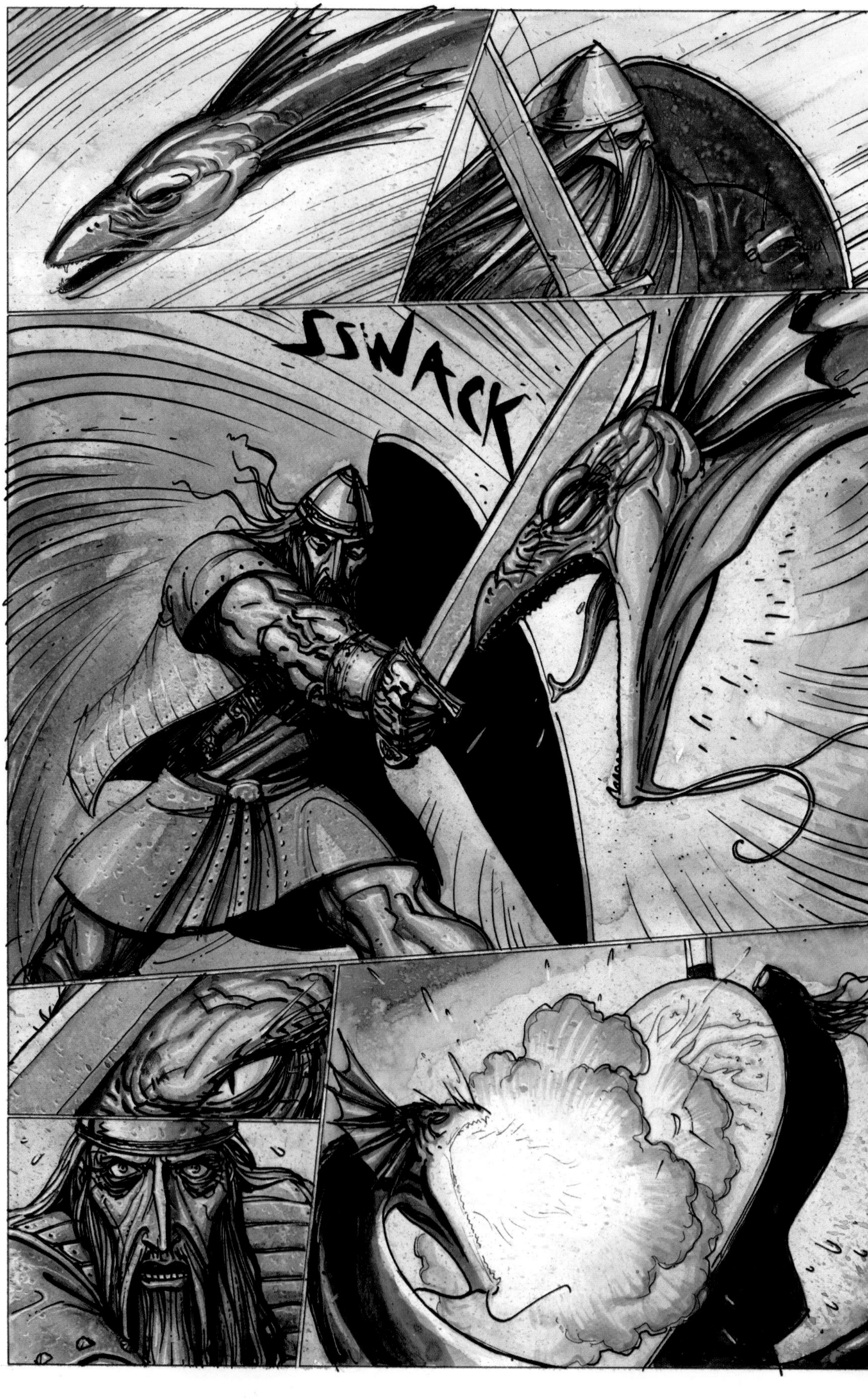
SSWACK

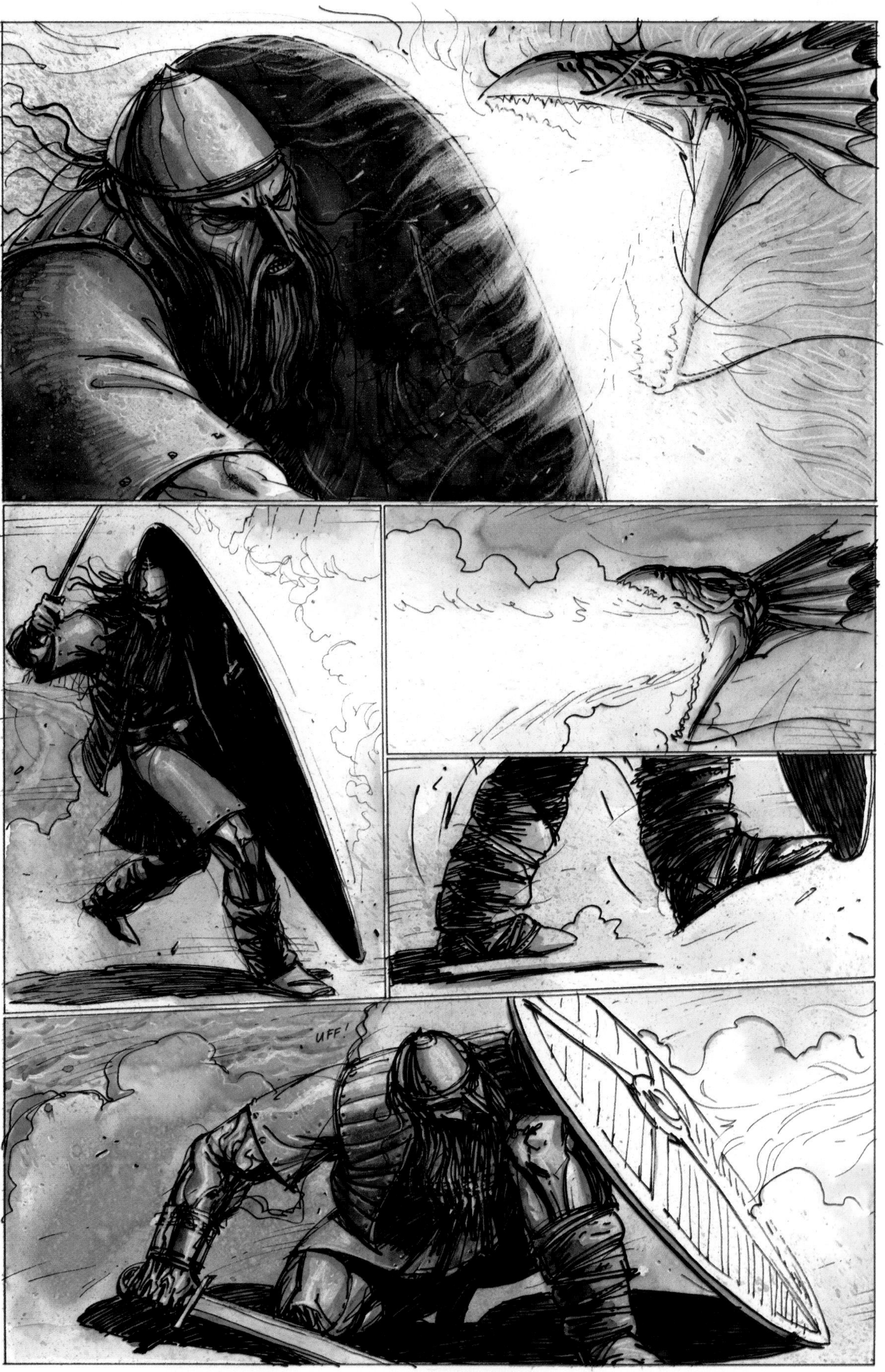
UFF!

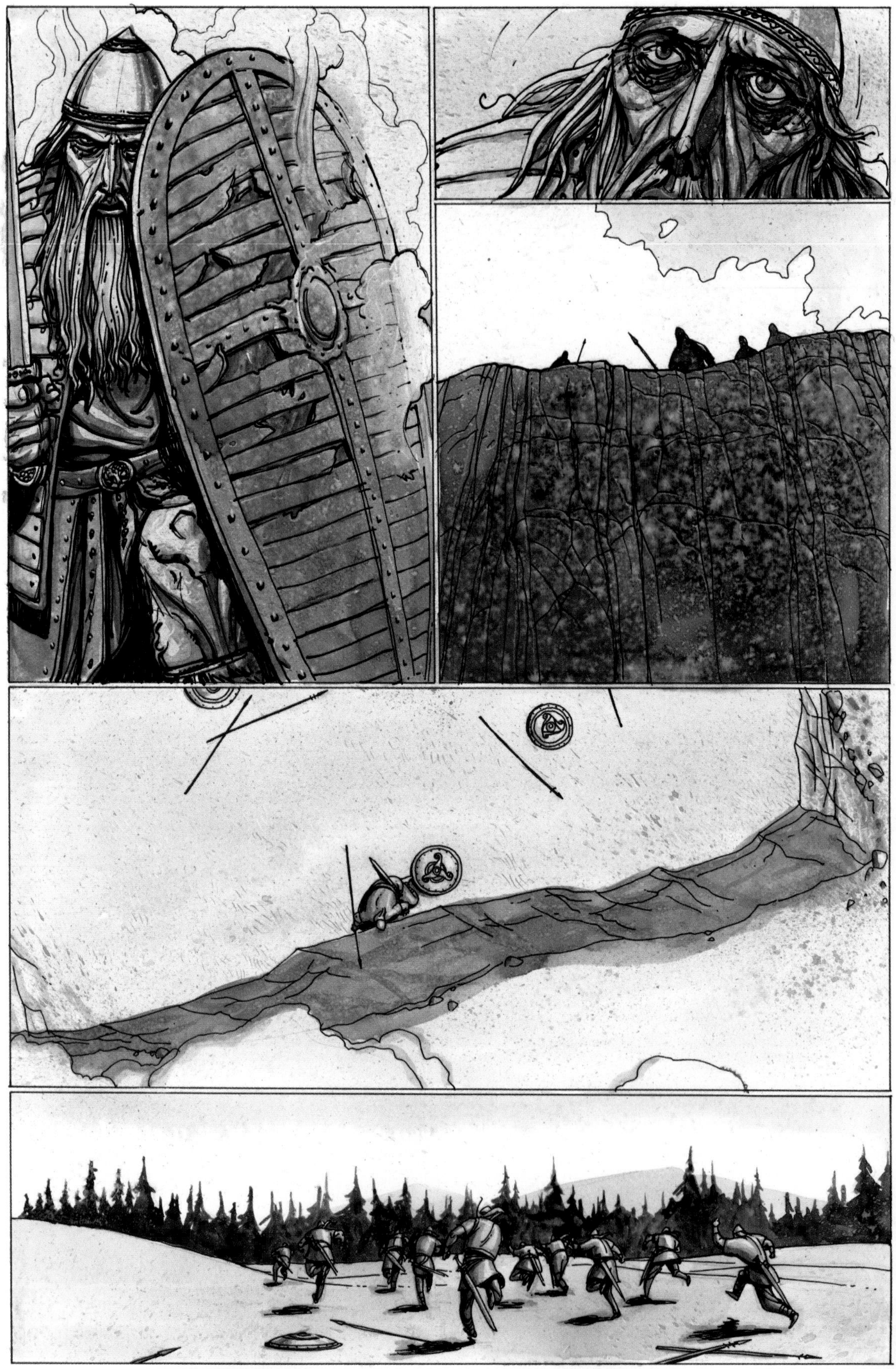

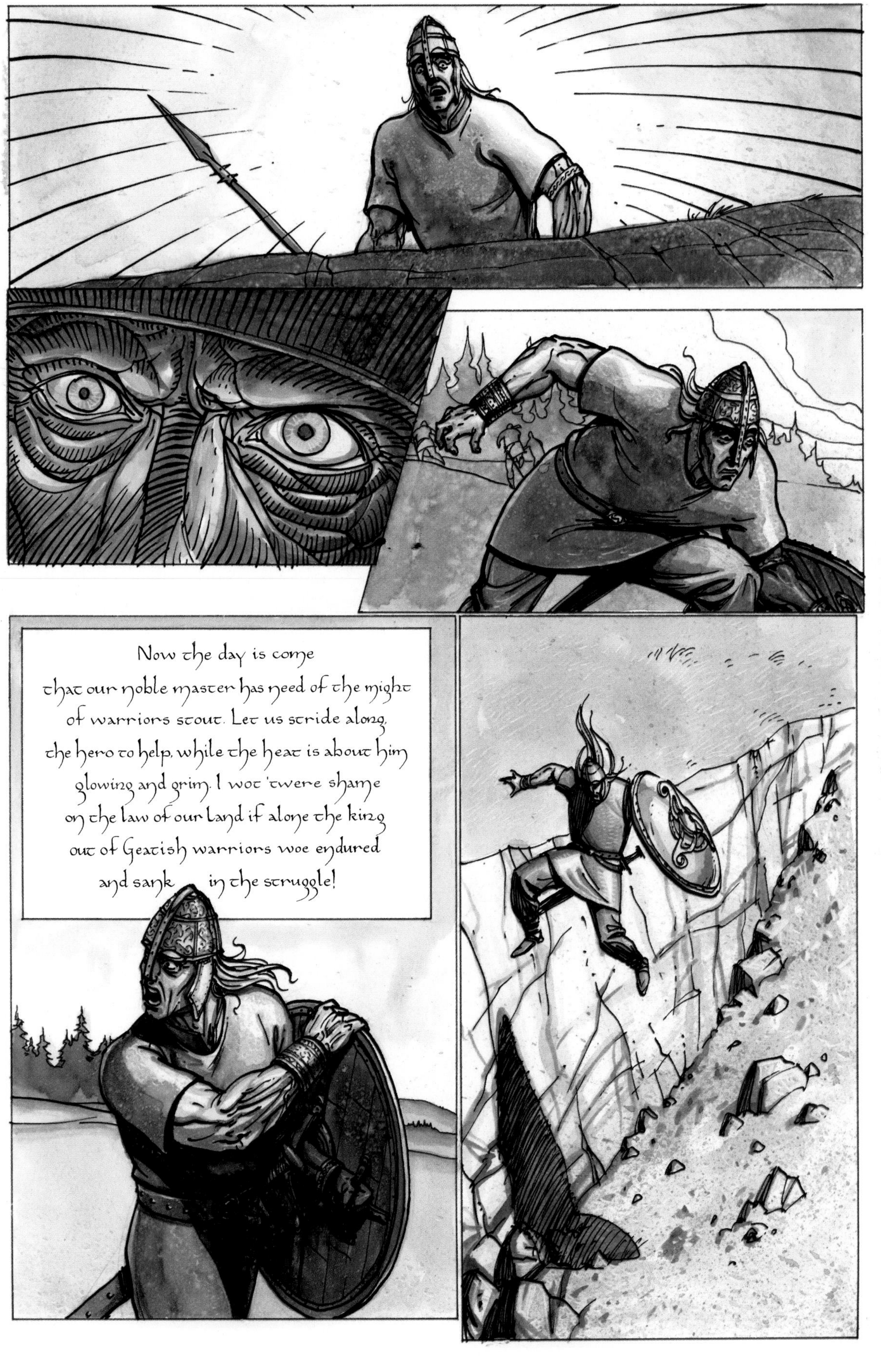
Now the day is come
that our noble master has need of the might
of warriors stout. Let us stride along,
the hero to help, while the heat is about him
glowing and grim. I wot 'twere shame
on the law of our land if alone the king
out of Geatish warriors woe endured
and sank in the struggle!

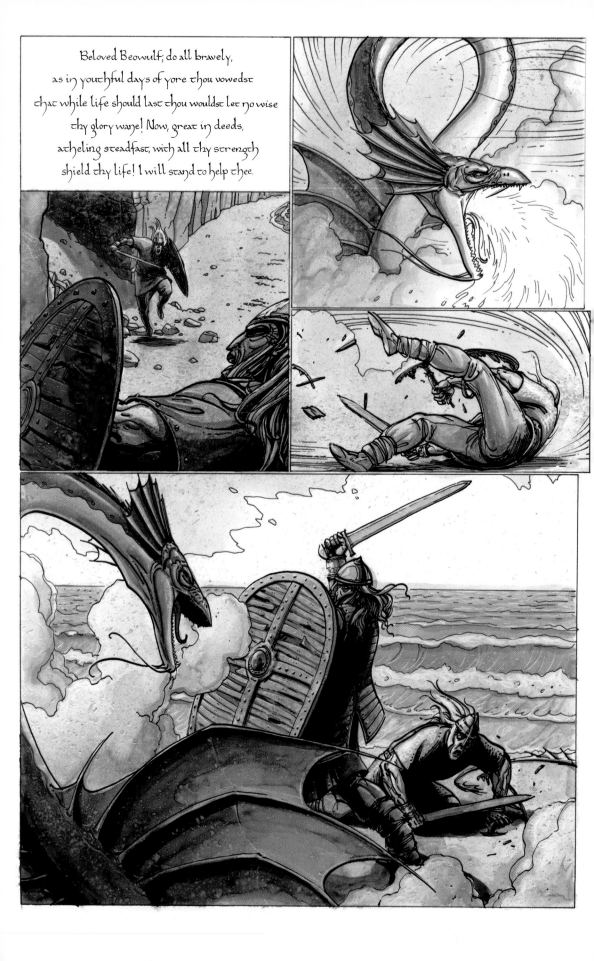

Beloved Beowulf, do all bravely,
as in youthful days of yore thou vowedst
that while life should last thou wouldst let no wise
thy glory wane! Now, great in deeds,
atheling steadfast, with all thy strength
shield thy life! I will stand to help thee.

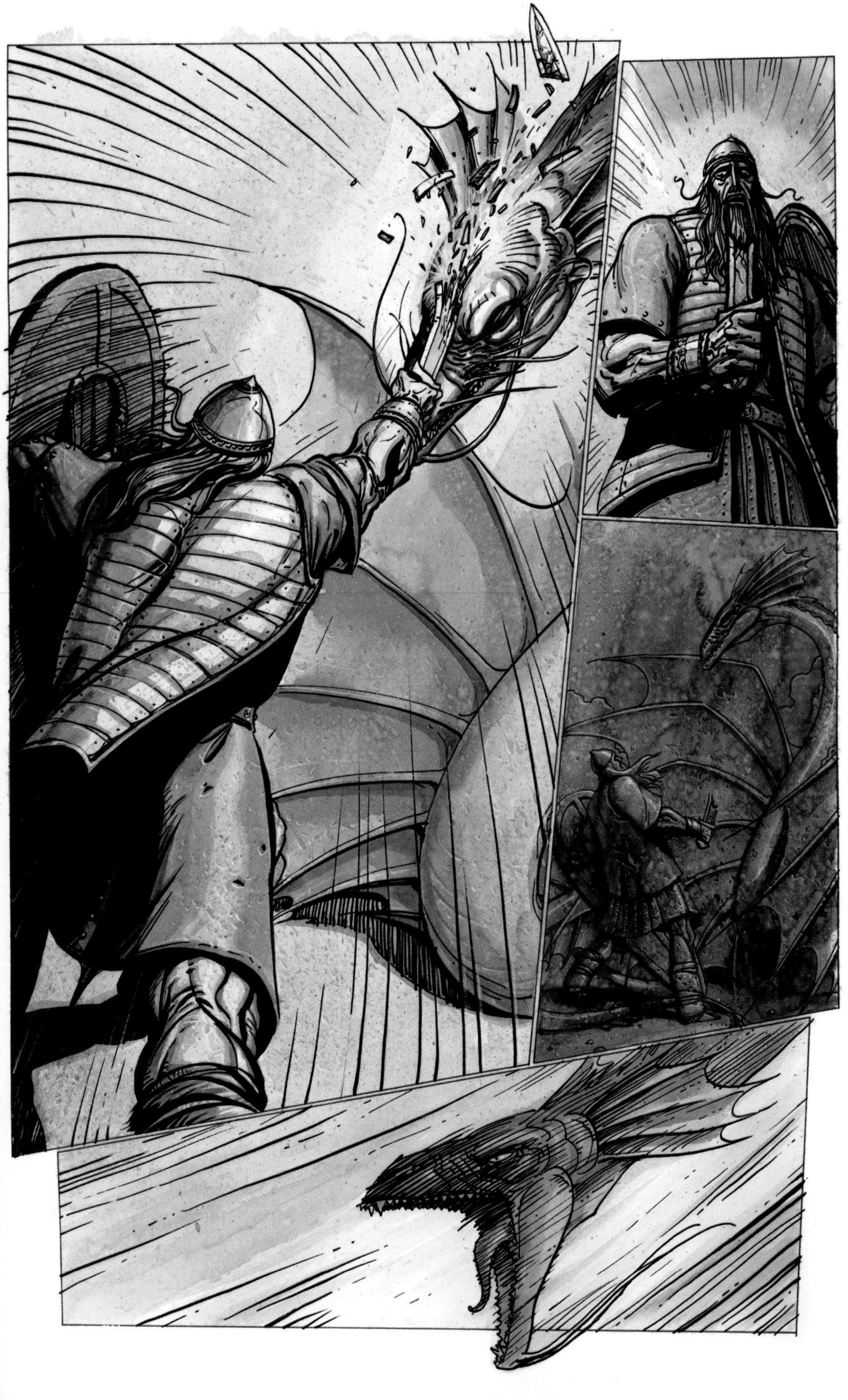

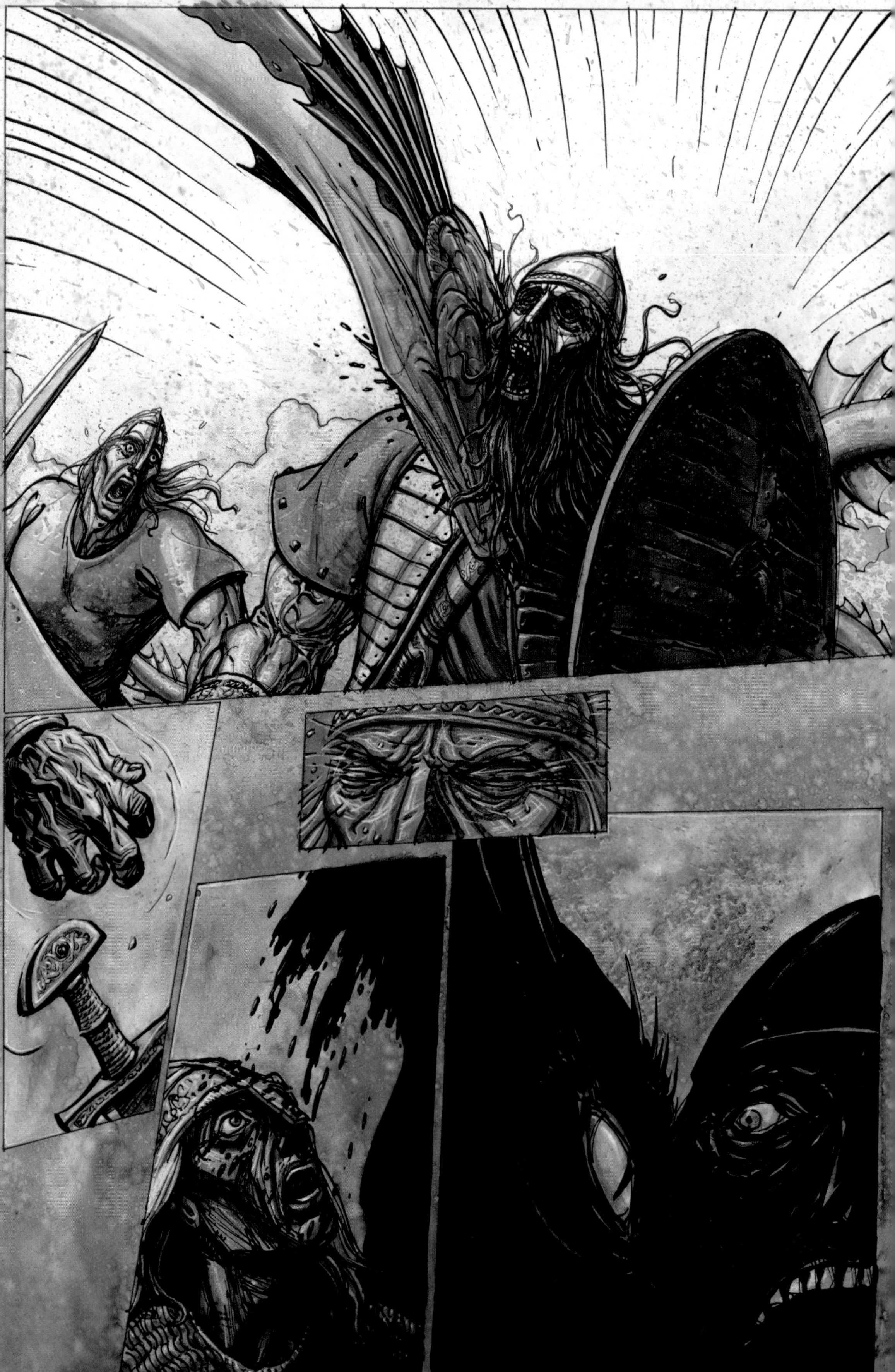

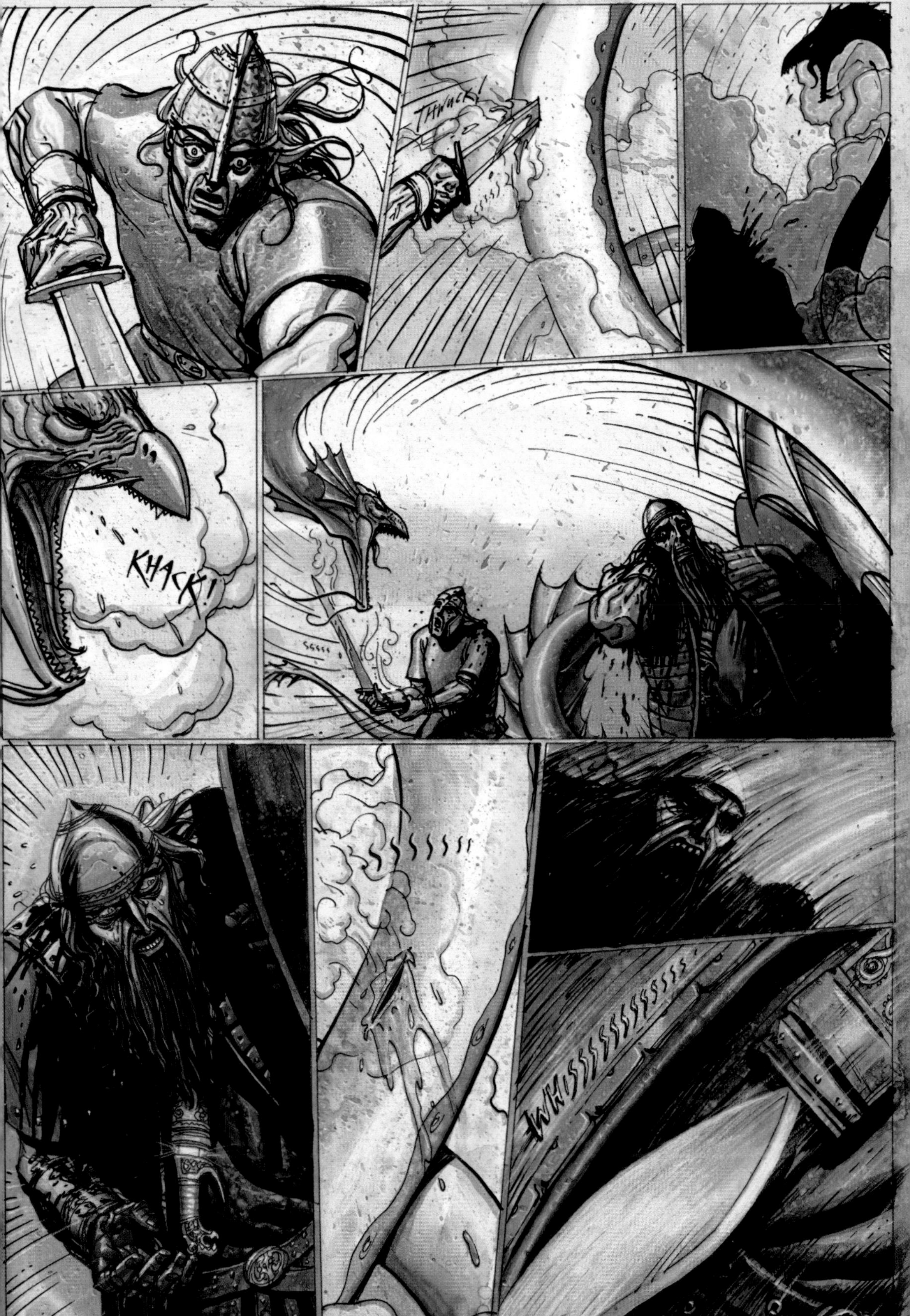

THWACK!
KHACK!
WHISSSSSSSSSSSS

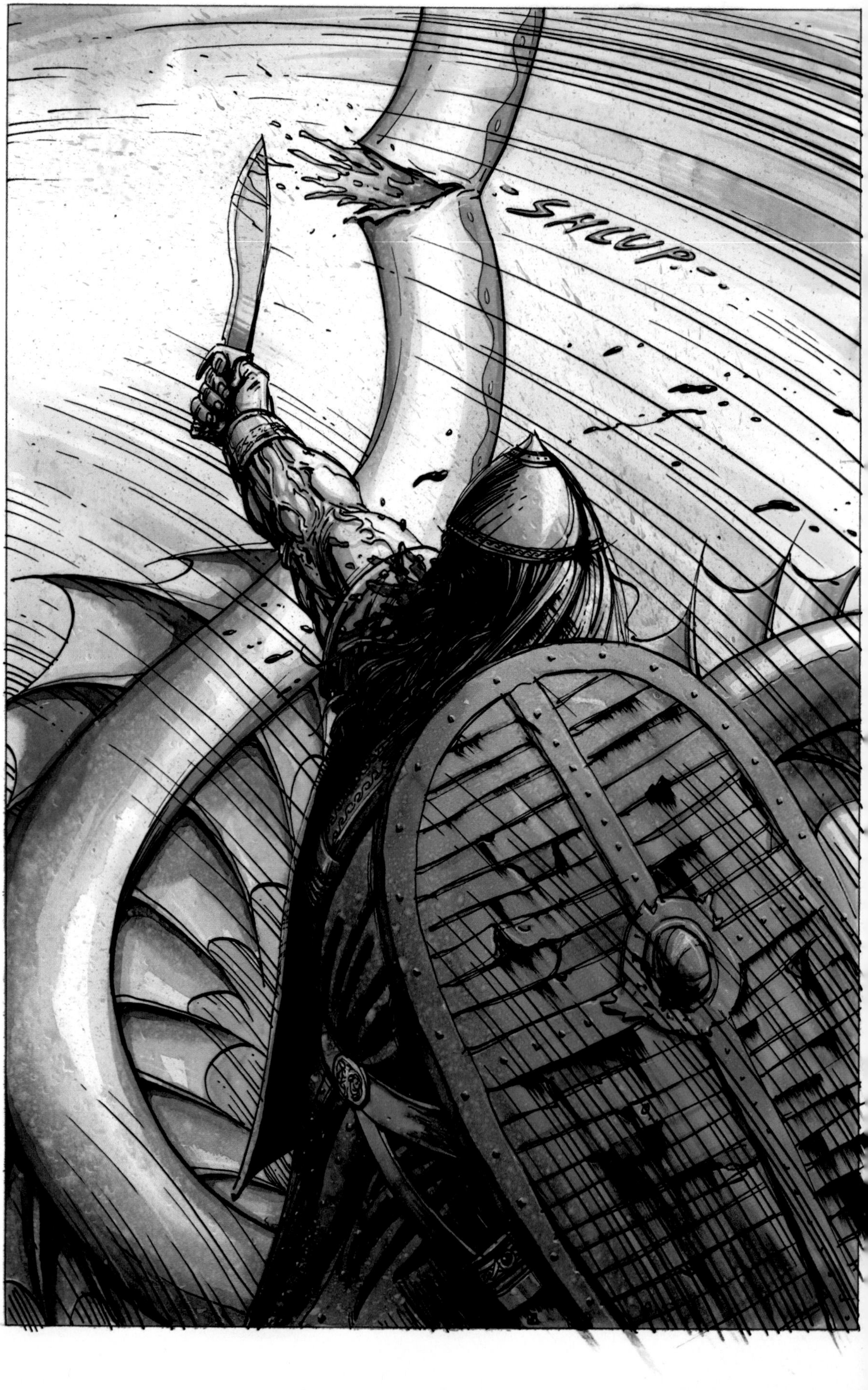
SHLUP...

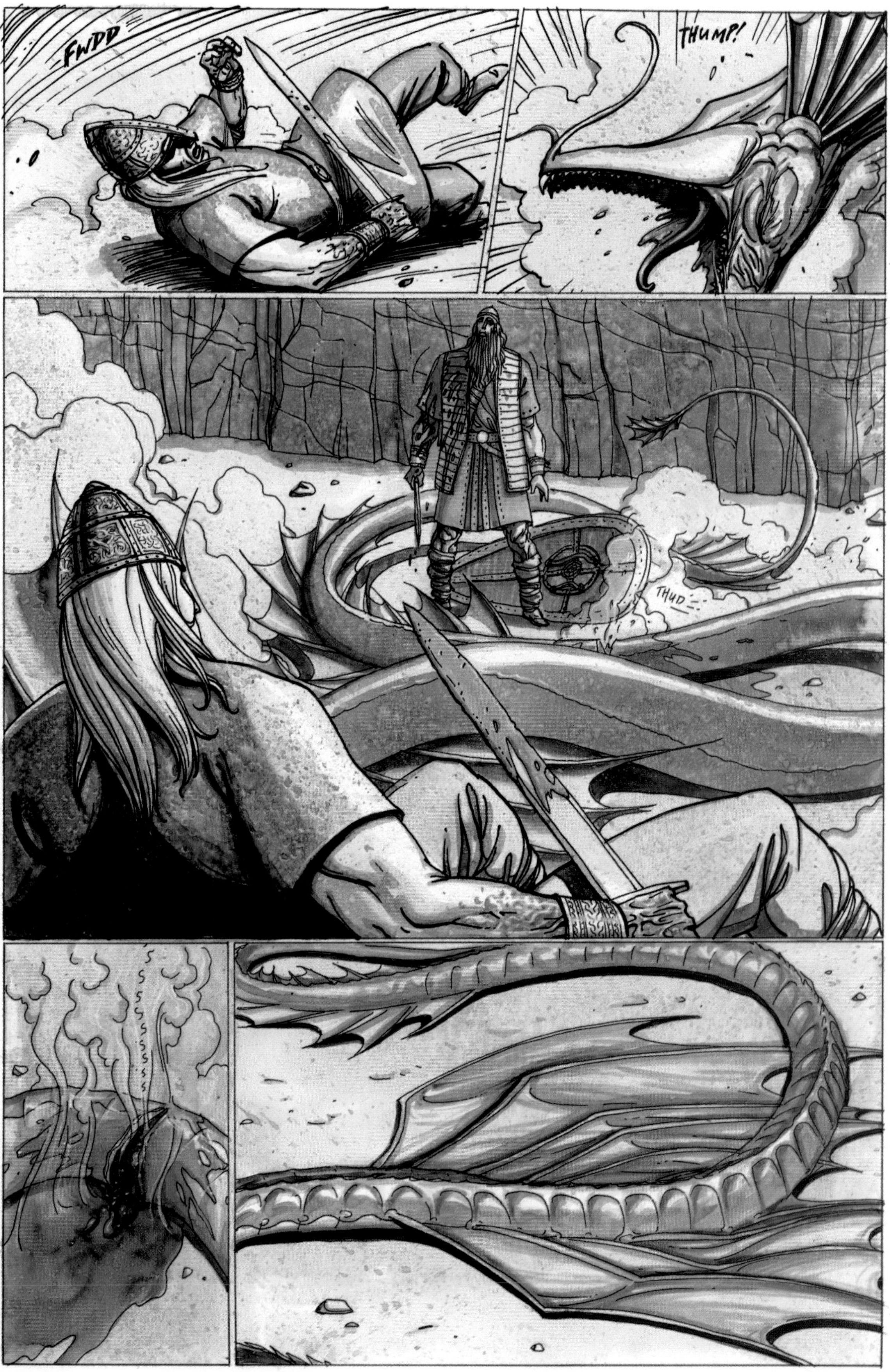
FWDD
THUMP!
THUD
SSSSSSSSSS

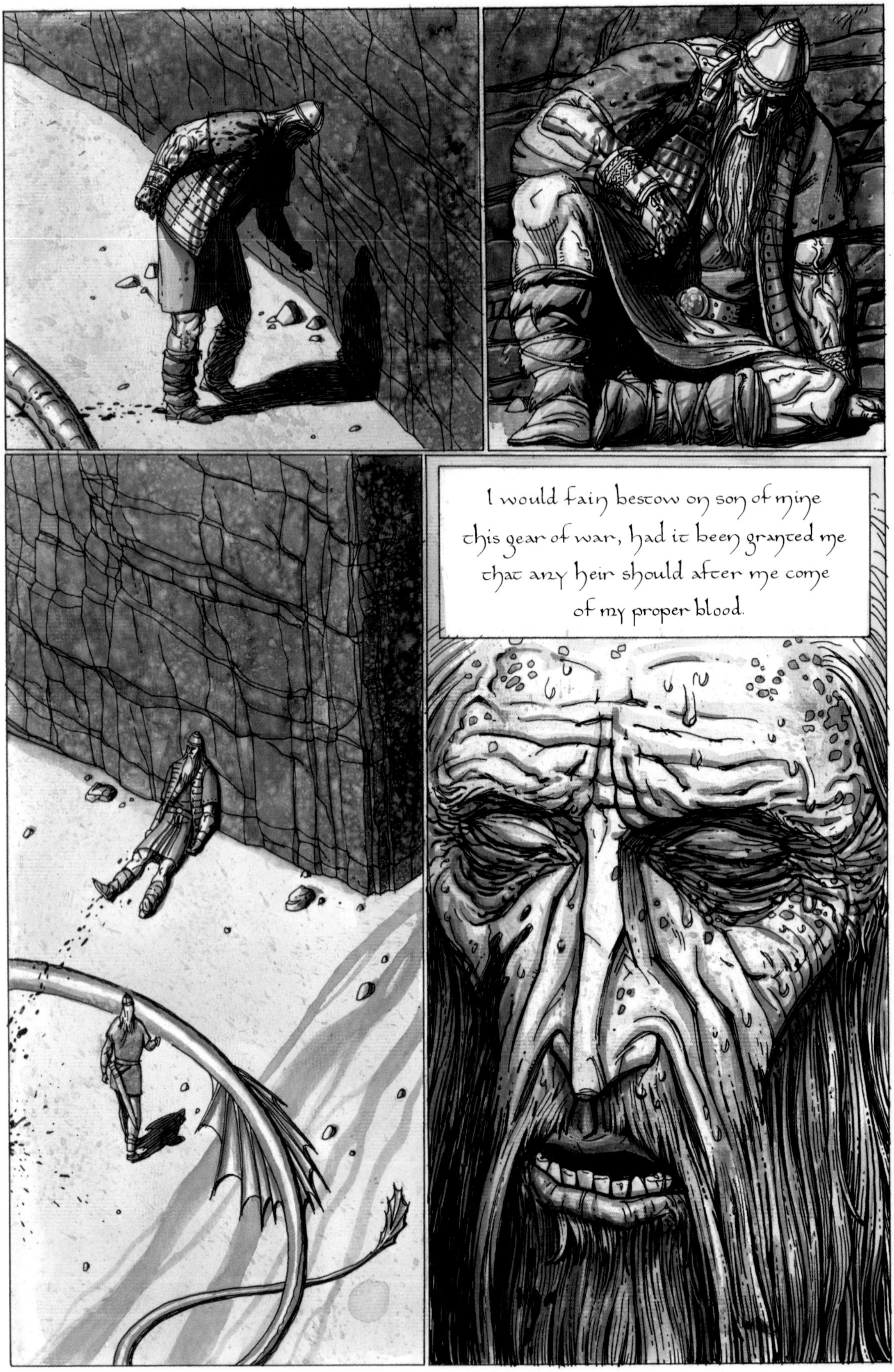
I would fain bestow on son of mine
this gear of war, had it been granted me
that any heir should after me come
of my proper blood.

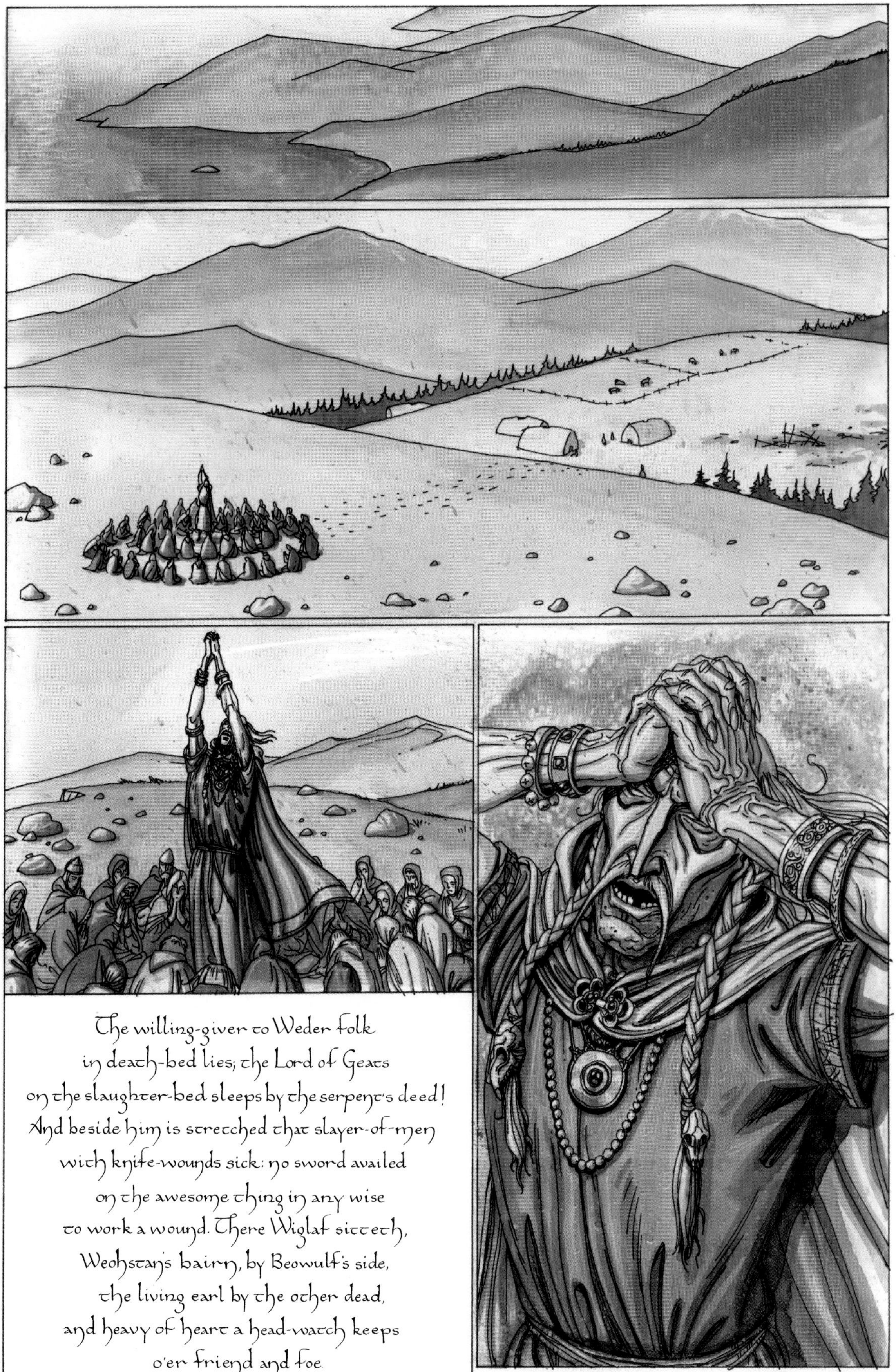
The willing-giver to Weder folk
in death-bed lies; the Lord of Geats
on the slaughter-bed sleeps by the serpent's deed!
And beside him is stretched that slayer-of-men
with knife-wounds sick: no sword availed
on the awesome thing in any wise
to work a wound. There Wiglaf sitteth,
Weohstan's bairn, by Beowulf's side,
the living earl by the other dead,
and heavy of heart a head-watch keeps
o'er friend and foe.

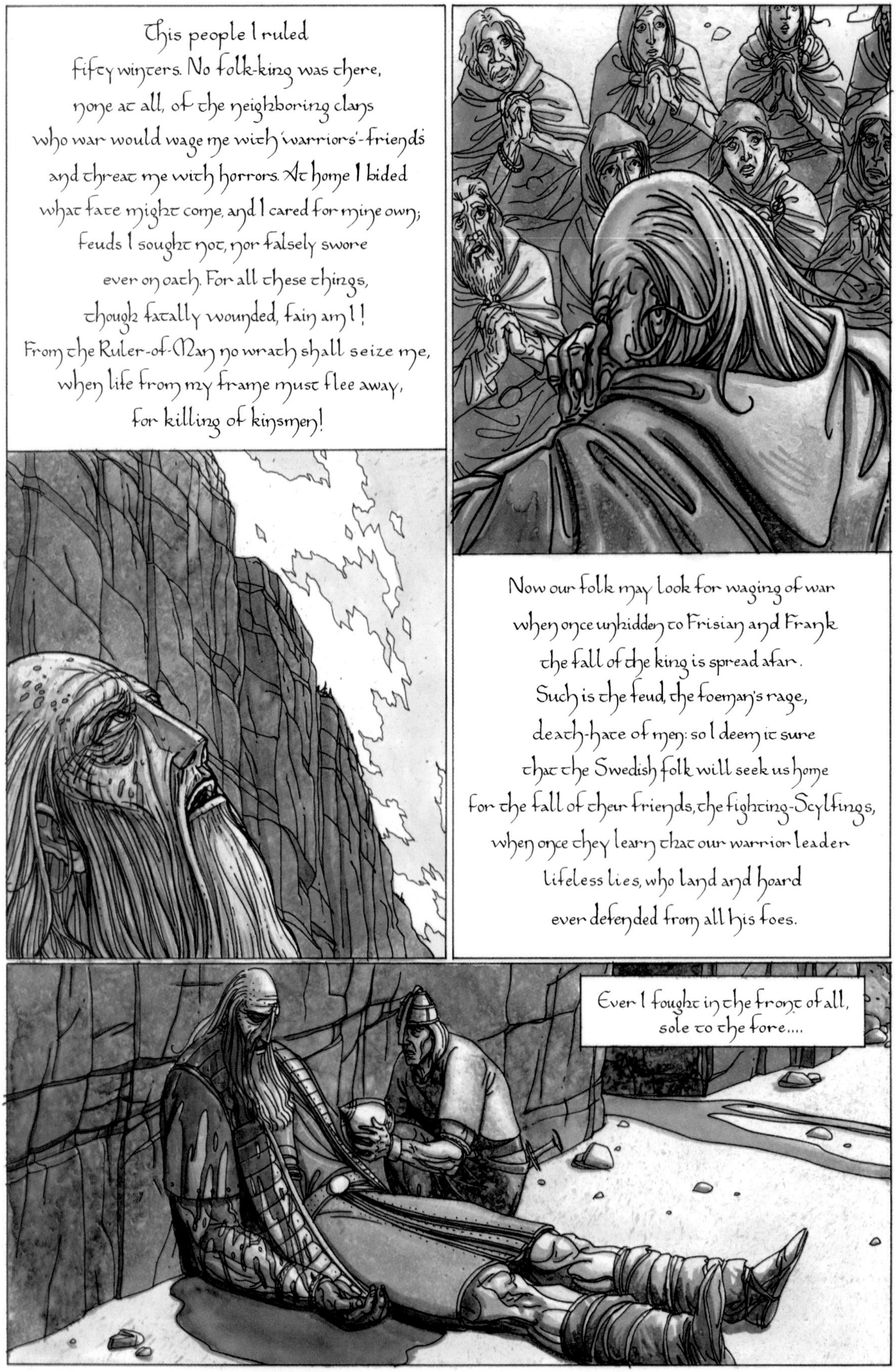
This people I ruled
fifty winters. No folk-king was there,
none at all, of the neighboring clans
who war would wage me with 'warriors'-friends'
and threat me with horrors. At home I bided
what fate might come, and I cared for mine own;
feuds I sought not, nor falsely swore
ever on oath. For all these things,
though fatally wounded, fain am I!
From the Ruler-of-Man no wrath shall seize me,
when life from my frame must flee away,
for killing of kinsmen!
Now our folk may look for waging of war
when once unhidden to Frisian and Frank
the fall of the king is spread afar.
Such is the feud, the foeman's rage,
death-hate of men: so I deem it sure
that the Swedish folk will seek us home
for the fall of their friends, the fighting-Scylfings,
when once they learn that our warrior leader
lifeless lies, who land and hoard
ever defended from all his foes.
Ever I fought in the front of all,
sole to the fore....

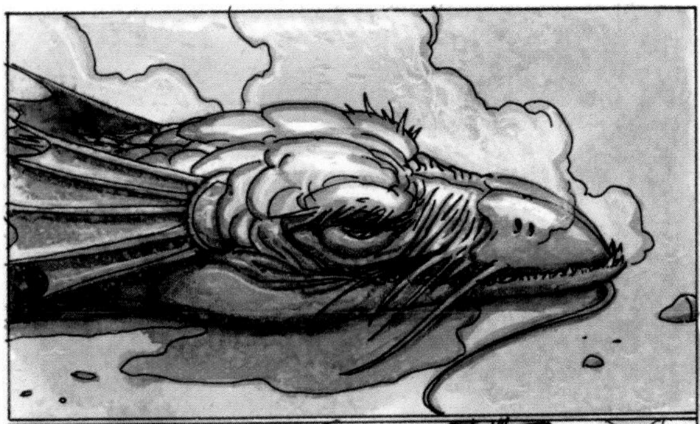

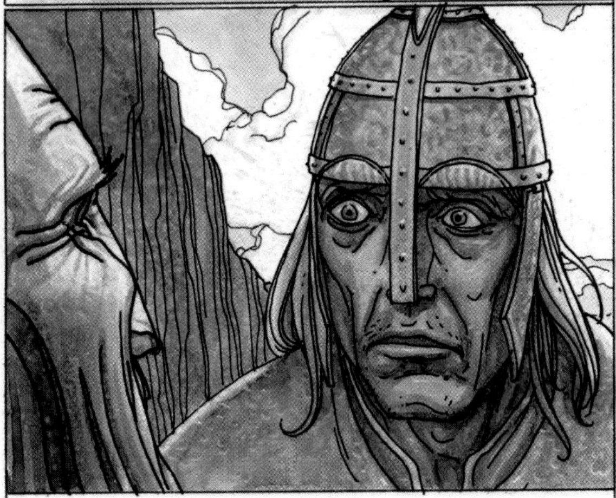

Oh, quickly go
and gaze on that hoard 'neath the hoary rock
Wiglaf loved, now the worm lies low,
sleeps, heart-sore, of his spoil bereaved.
And fare in haste. I would fain behold
the gorgeous heirlooms, golden store,
have joy in the jewels and gems; lay down
softlier, for sight of this splendid hoard,
my life and the lordship I long have held.

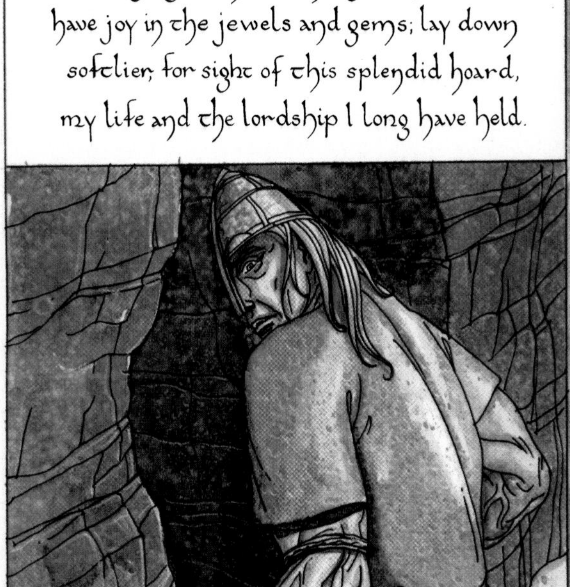

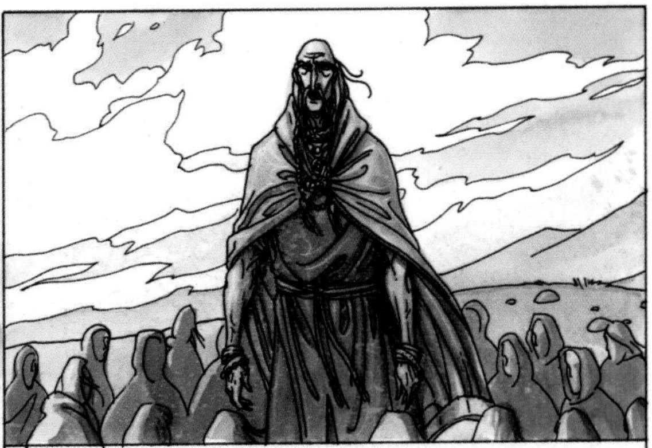

Now haste is best,
that we go to gaze on our Geatish lord,
and bear the bountiful breaker-of-rings
to the funeral pyre. No fragments merely
shall burn with the warrior. Wealth of jewels,
gold untold and gained in terror,
fire shall eat it. No earl must carry
memorial jewel. No maiden fair
shall wreathe her neck with noble ring:
nay, sad in spirit and shorn of her gold,
oft shall she pass o'er paths of exile
now our Lord all laughter has laid aside,
all mirth and revel.

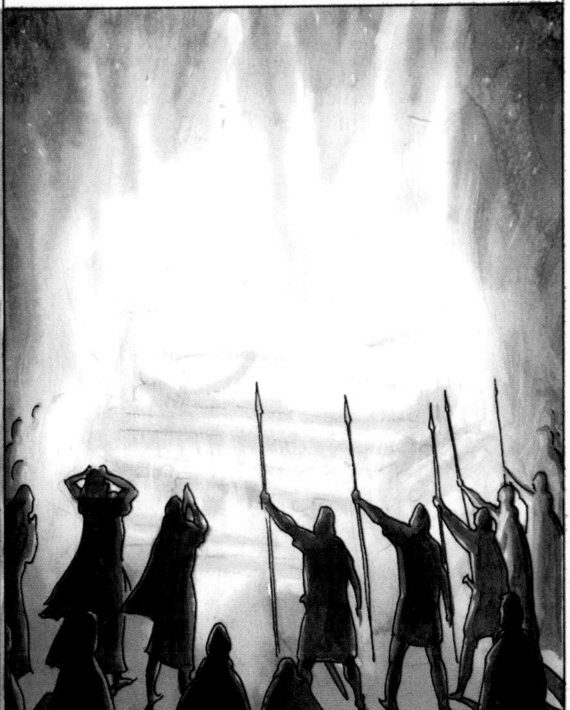

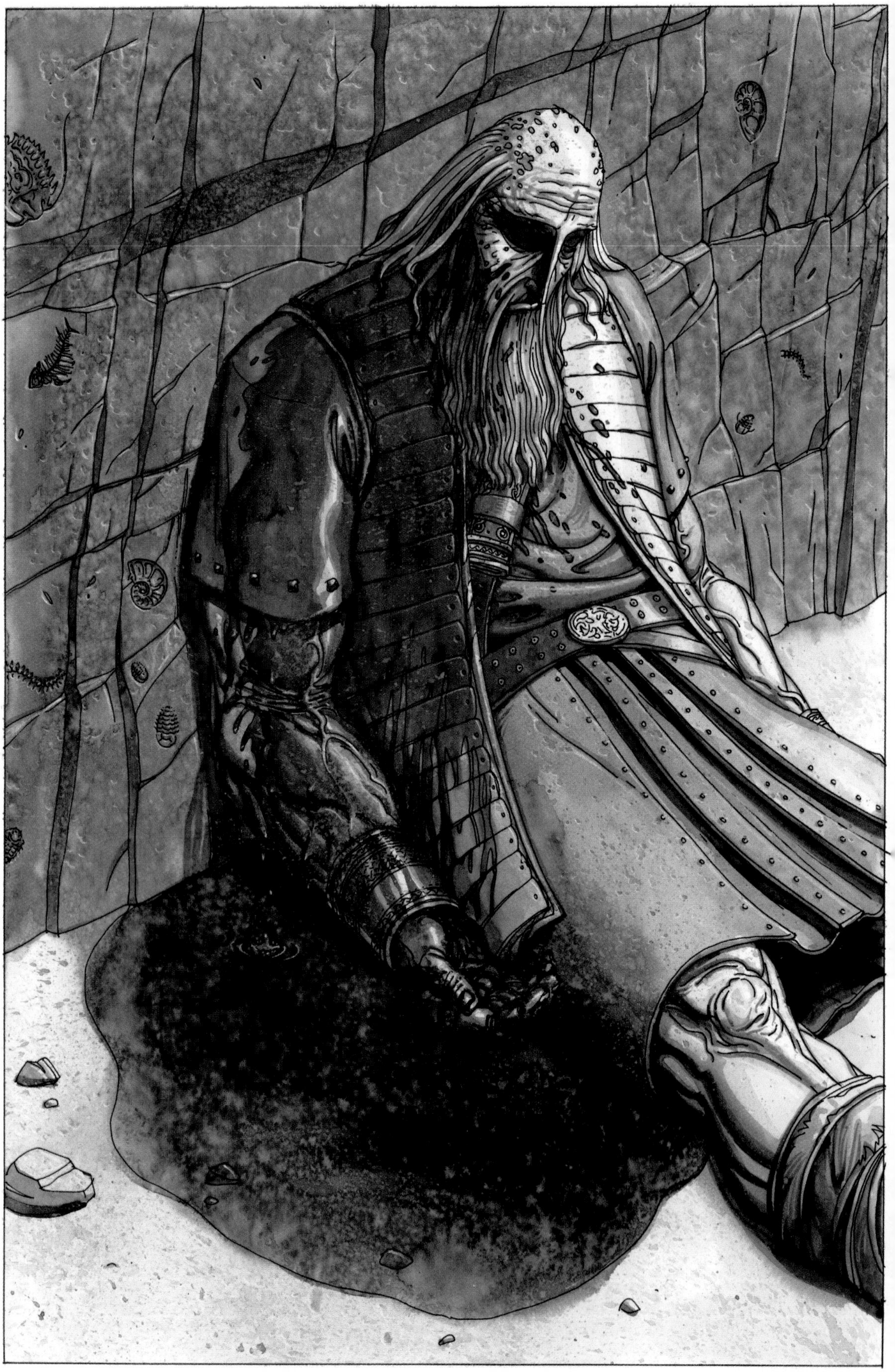

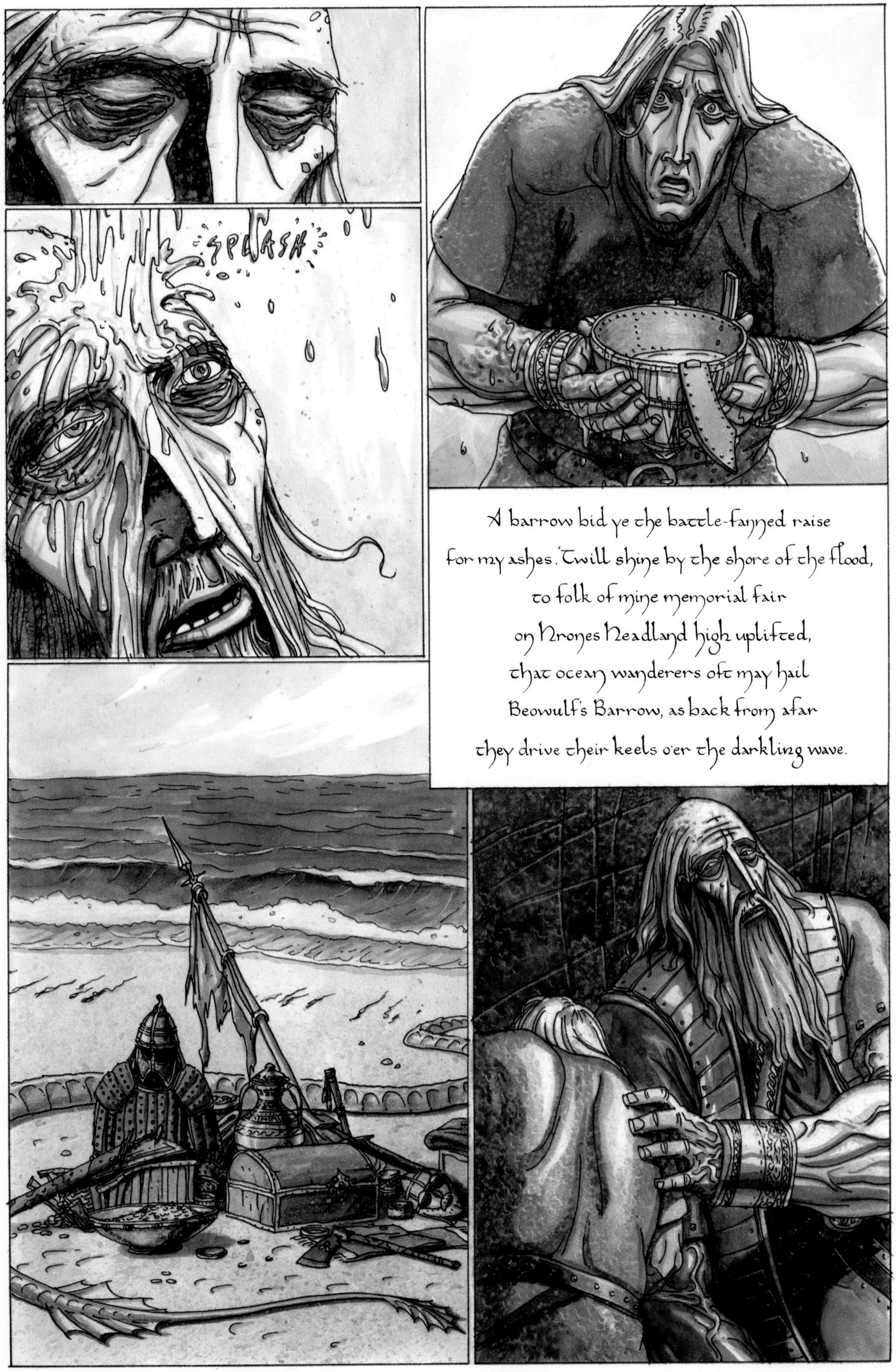
SPLASH
A barrow bid ye the battle-fanned raise
for my ashes. 'Twill shine by the shore of the flood,
to folk of mine memorial fair
on Hrones Headland high uplifted,
that ocean wanderers oft may hail
Beowulf's Barrow, as back from afar
they drive their keels o'er the darkling wave.

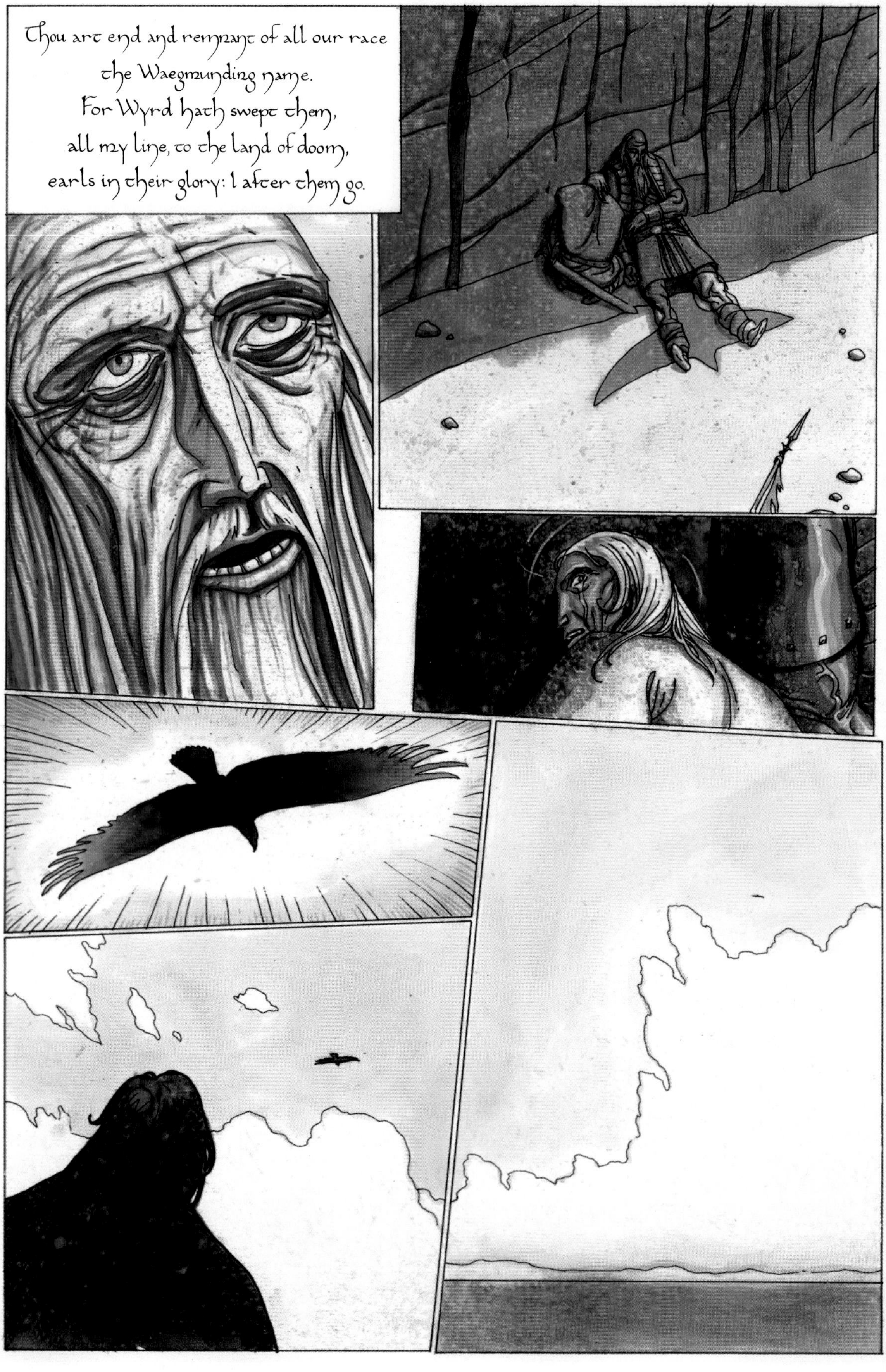
Thou art end and remnant of all our race
the Waegmunding name.
For Wyrd hath swept them,
all my line, to the land of doom,
earls in their glory: I after them go.

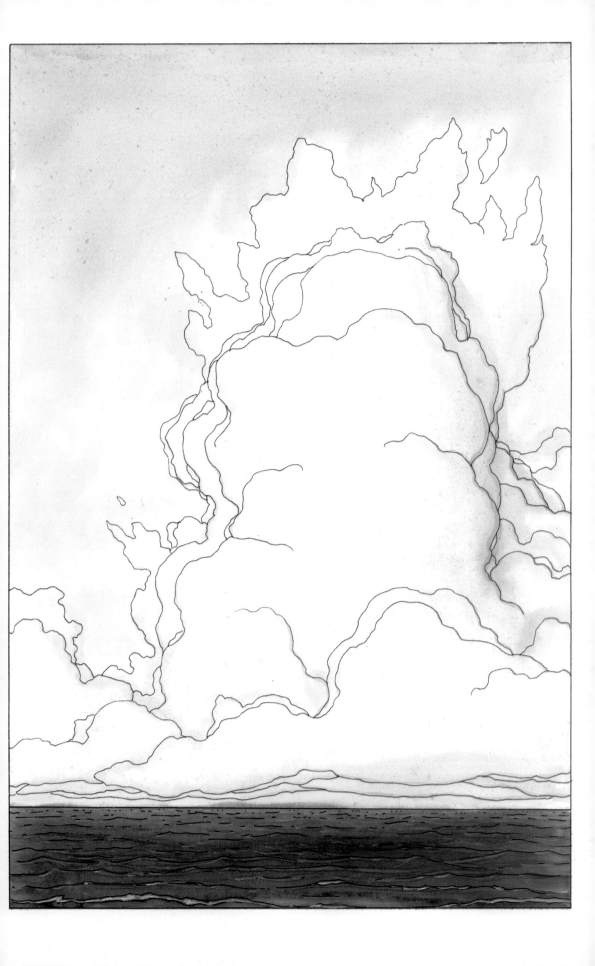

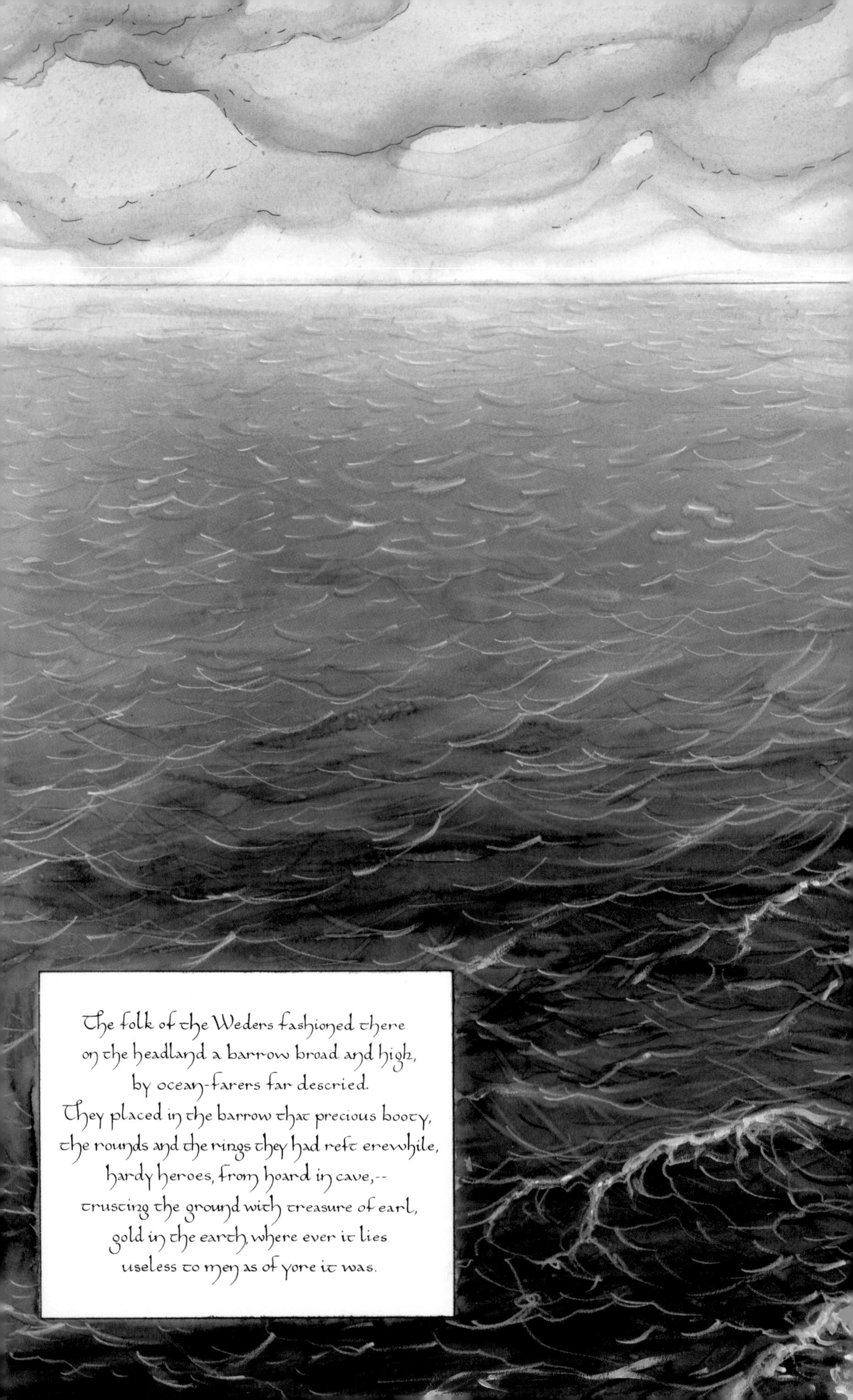

The folk of the Weders fashioned there
on the headland a barrow broad and high,
by ocean-farers far descried.
They placed in the barrow that precious booty,
the rounds and the rings they had reft erewhile,
hardy heroes, from hoard in cave,--
trusting the ground with treasure of earl,
gold in the earth, where ever it lies
useless to men as of yore it was.

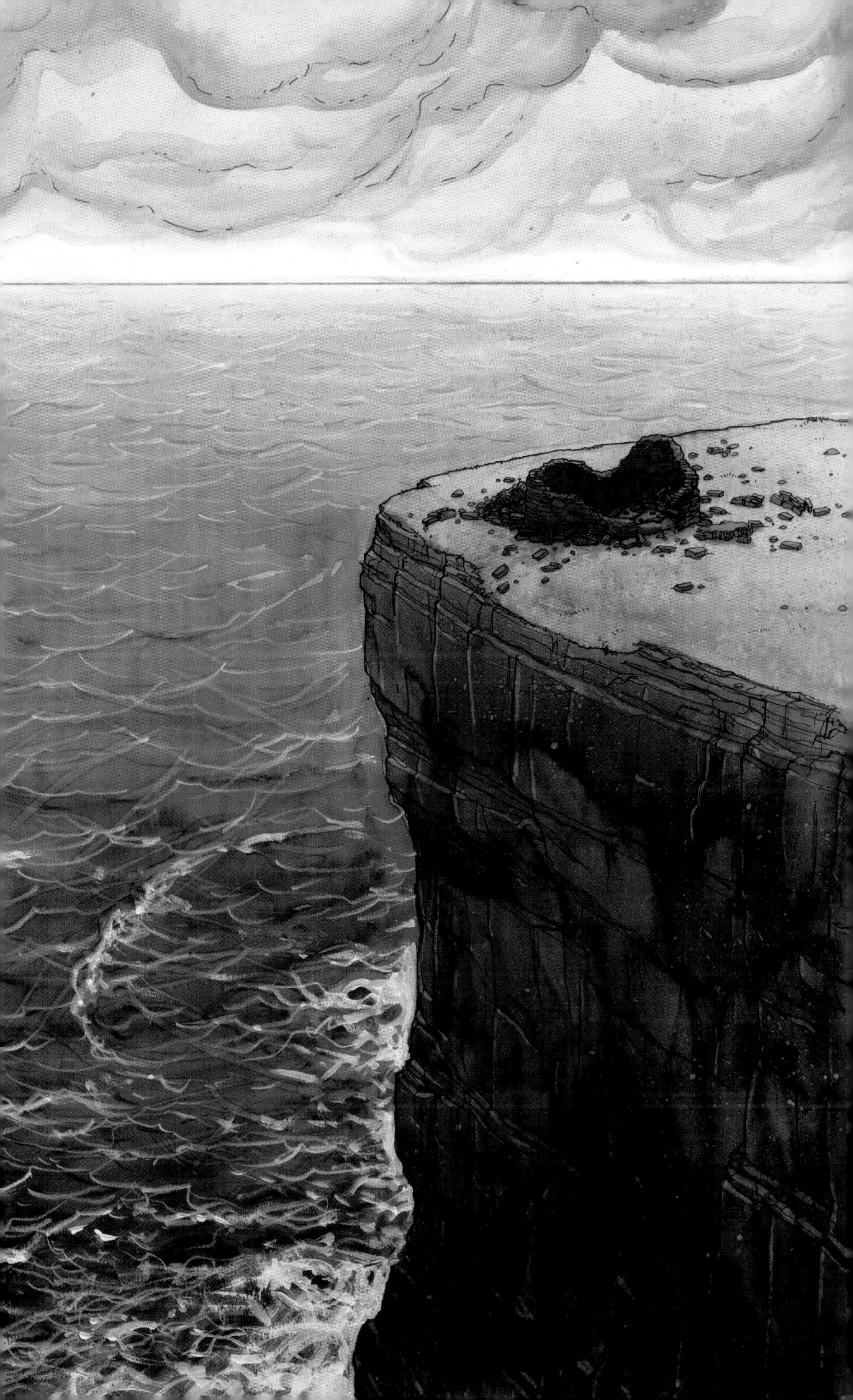

The End

Afterword

"Now our folk may look for waging of war
when once unhidden to Frisian and Frank
the fall of the king is spread afar.
Such is the feud, the foeman's rage,
death-hate of men: so I deem it sure
that the Swedish folk will seek us home
for the fall of their friends, the fighting-Scylfings,
when once they learn that our warrior leader
lifeless lies, who land and hoard
ever defended from all his foes."

This passage is a foretelling of the fate of the Geats. There was an old feud between the Geats and the Swedes. Since the Geats occupied what is now the southern part of Sweden, it is fairly clear what happened. No further reference to them is found in history or legend after the burial of Beowulf. Some scholars believe the Wuffing dynasty in Denmark was founded by exiled Geats, but nothing is known for sure.

A note on the adaptation: For books 1 and 2, the script was prepared exclusively by subtraction. That is, I only removed material from the Gummere translation, never rewrote or added material. For book 3, however, there were places where the particular shade of meaning suggested in the Gummere translation did not fit my purposes. In those cases, I consulted several other translations, including those of Howell Chickering, Burton Raffel, Michael Alexander, and Constance Hieatt, before swapping in a few words or phrases which I liked better.

I also took a few more liberties with the story in Book 3; principally by replacing the herald with the seer, so I could achieve a more dramatic narrative flow at the end of the book. The herald has always been a strange and interesting figure to me, and I hope that the loss of that archetype is made up for by the improved pacing.

The other change is that I have somewhat downplayed Wiglaf's heroism. This may be a sore point for some readers who feel that Wiglaf is the true hero of the epic, since he is brave enough to face the dragon without the benefit of Beowulf's size, strength, or iron shield. I wanted to drive home the point that Beowulf has protected his people too completely, leaving them helpless in his absence. Therefore I chose to portray Wiglaf's bravery (which is undeniable) as being dependent for support on Beowulf's strength.

The Collected Beowulf features a new three-page introduction. I had the idea to do this as I was working on Beowulf's death scene at the end of Book 3. I realized that, in the original, part of what lends weight to the scene is that it mirrors (or closes the circle with) the death-scene of the Danish chief Scyld described at the beginning of the poem. In my initial editing, I had removed that scene as unnecessary to the narrative. I hope that adding it back strengthens the overall structure, and that it does not look like an afterthought.

In any case, I hope you have enjoyed the product of my labors. Until the next project, so long.

- GH

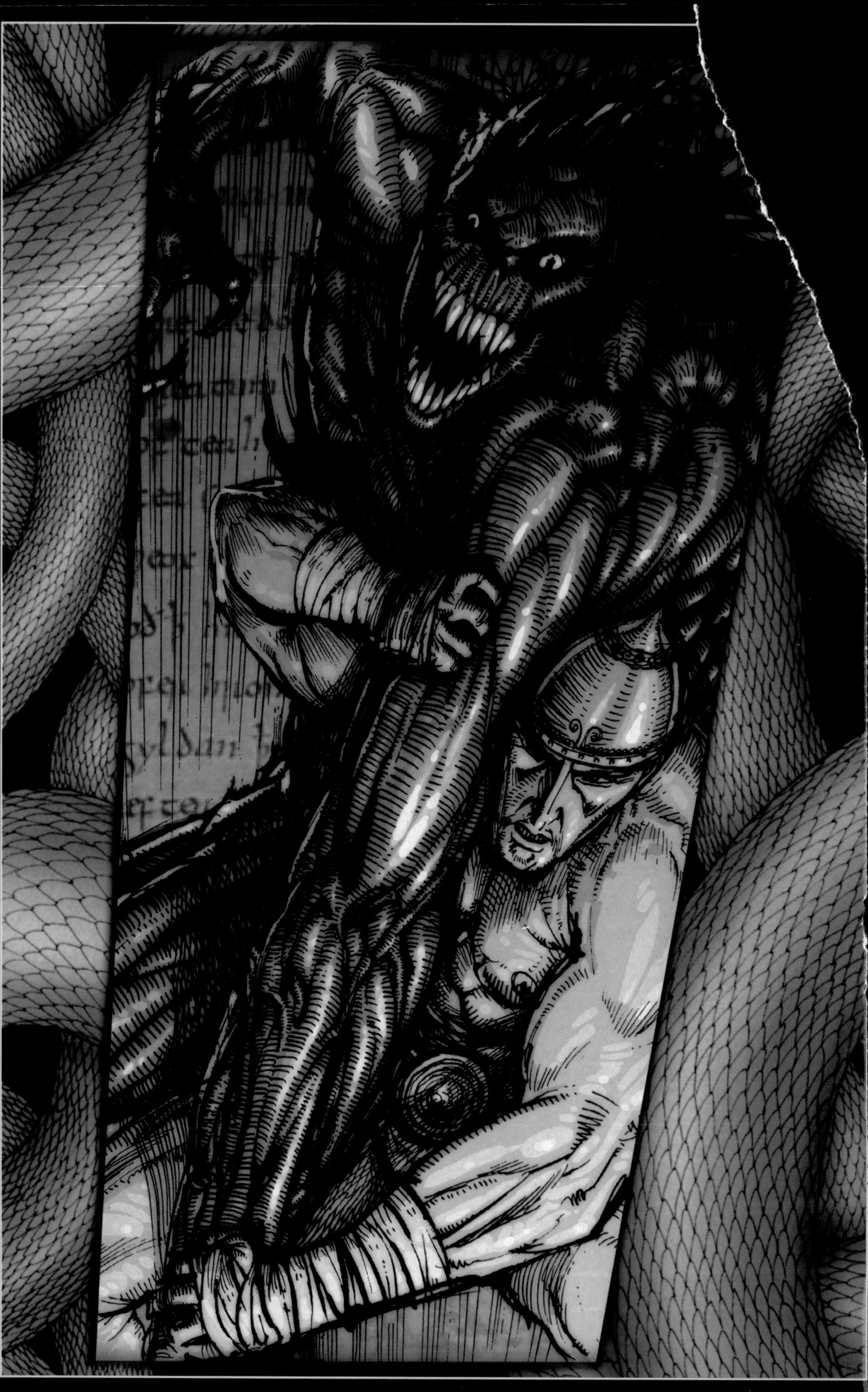

Gallery - cover Beowulf #1

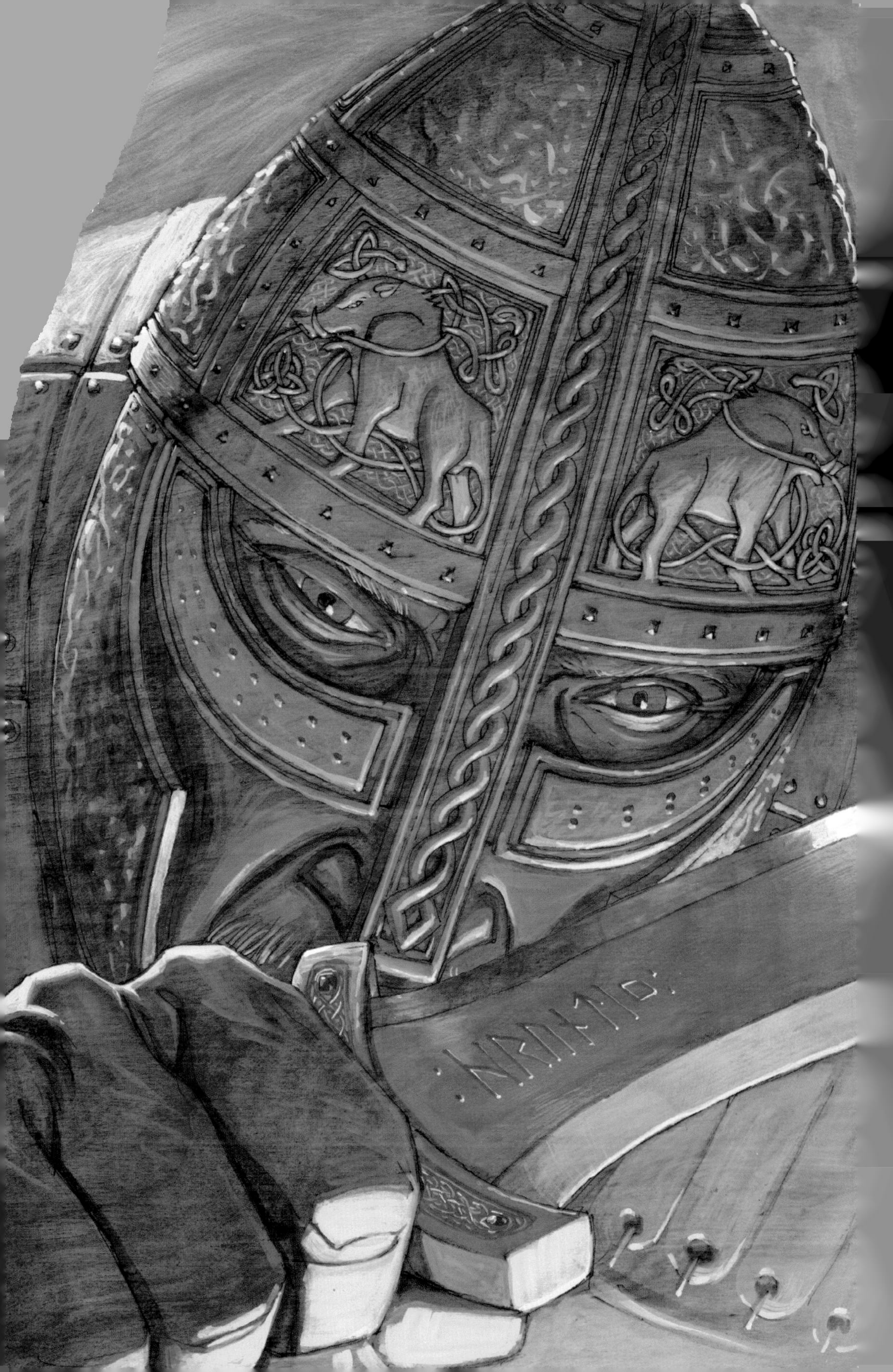

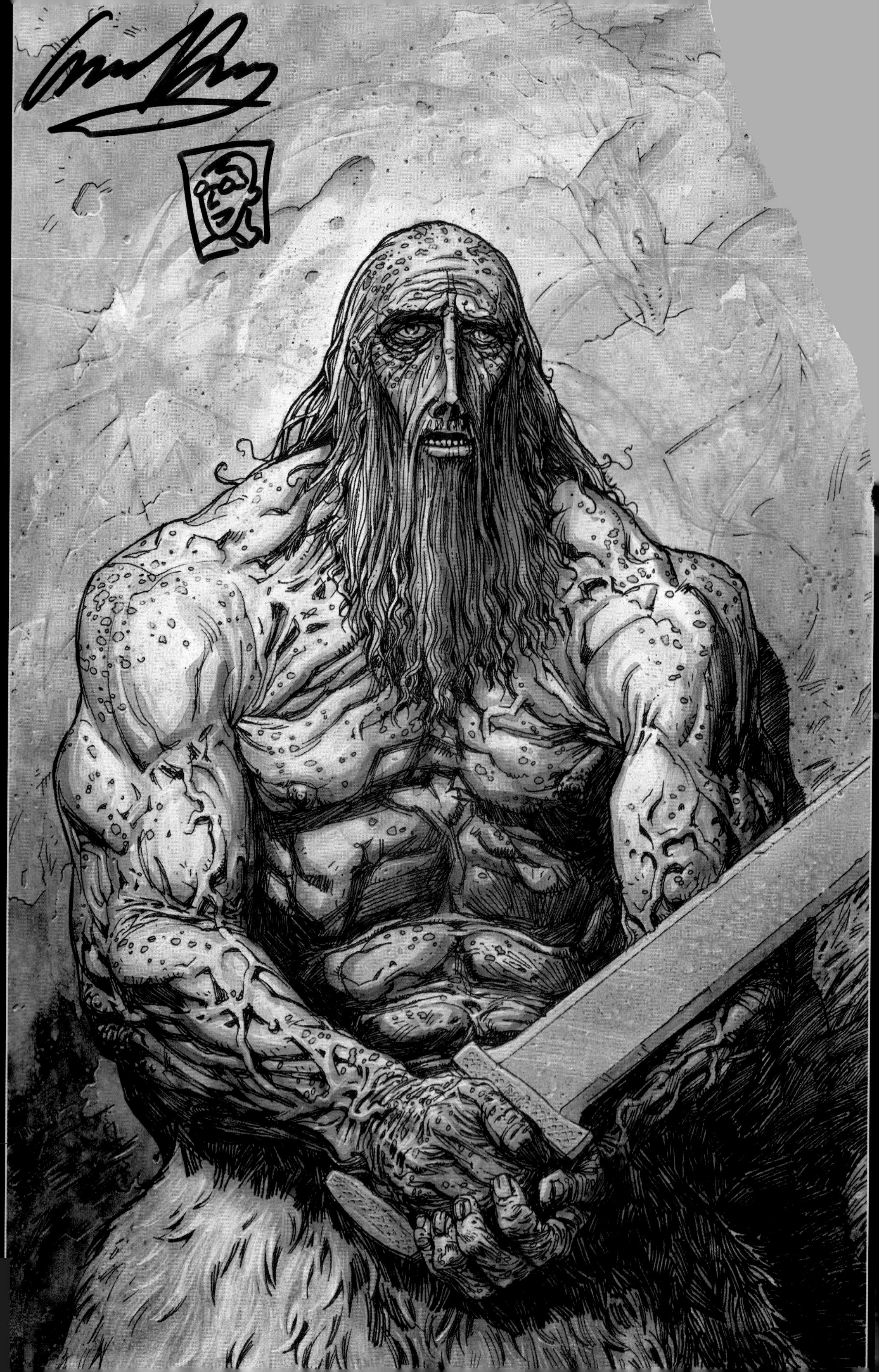